Exploring Tourism

The building Blocks of a Global Industry

AF603782

Editors

Ms. M. L. Nivedita, Ms. Arokiya Anbazhagi. J, Ms. J. Ishwarya, Dr. K. S. Beena, Dr. M. Jansi, Dr. Cinthia Jude

Associate Editors

Dr. Archana Soman, Dr. B. Jishamol, Dr. F. Roselin Mary

Cover Illustration

Ms. Maragathameena Ravisankar

Copyright © 2025

All Rights Reserved.

This book has been self-published with all reasonable efforts taken to make the material error-free by the author. No part of this book shall be used, reproduced in any manner whatsoever without written permission from the author, except in the case of brief quotations embodied in critical articles and reviews.

The Author of this book is solely responsible and liable for its content including but not limited to the views, representations, descriptions, statements, information, opinions and references. The Content of this book shall not constitute or be construed or deemed to reflect the opinion or expression of the Publisher or Editor. Neither the Publisher nor Editor endorse or approve the Content of this book or guarantee the reliability, accuracy or completeness of the Content published herein and do not make any representations or warranties of any kind, express or implied, including but not limited to the implied warranties of merchantability, fitness for a particular purpose. The Publisher and Editor shall not be liable whatsoever for any errors, omissions, whether such errors or omissions result from negligence, accident, or any other cause or claims for loss or damages of any kind, including without limitation, indirect or consequential loss or damage arising out of use, inability to use, or about the reliability, accuracy or sufficiency of the information contained in this book.

Made with ♥ on the Notion Press Platform

www.notionpress.com

Authors List

S. No	Topic	Name
1	Introduction to Tourism	Dr. I. Princes
2	Tourism Management	Dr. Gughan Babu Azhageshan Dr. Girija Gughan Babu
3	Tourism as a business	Ms. P. Sinduja
4	Tourism Product	Ms. A. Karoliya Jansirani
5	Tourism and Sustainability	Ms. Surumbayee Nagaraj
6	Tourism and Hospitality	Ms. S. Gajalakshmi
7	Tourism and Culinary Industry	Ms. Ivan Nancy A
8	Tourism and Transportation	Dr. Gayathri S
9	Tourism and Journalism	Ms. N. Balagomathy Ms. R. M. Pavithra
10	Tourism and Geography	Dr. Cinthia Jude
11	Tourism and Environment	Dr. D. Benitha Golda
12	Tourism and Marketing	Dr. P. Senkathir Selvi
13	Tourism and Staged Culture	Mr. Ashwin Prakash Ms. Lara Chamberlain
14	Tourism and Human Trafficking	Dr Marilyn Gracey Augustine
15	Tourism and Public Administration	Dr. C. Esther Buvana Mr. M L Manikandan
16	Tourism and Human Rights	Dr. Dolly Thomas
17	Tourism and Five-year plans	Dr. M. Sabeera Sulthana Bijli
18	Tourism and International Regulations	Dr. K. S. Beena
19	Tourism and Heritage destinations	Mr. K. Selvakumar
20	Tourism and Museology	Ms. K. Sharon Dr. Hemalatha
21	Tourism and technology	Dr. S. Meenakshi

Contents

Preface

The tourism industry has ascended to a position of paramount importance in the modern era, emerging as a pivotal driver of economic growth, cultural exchange, and environmental sustainability. As the world becomes increasingly interconnected, tourism has evolved into a complex, multifaceted, and dynamic phenomenon, exerting a profound influence on the lives of millions of people globally. Despite its far-reaching implications, the tourism industry remains poorly understood, with many of its underlying dynamics, nuances, and consequences often overlooked or underappreciated.

"Exploring Tourism: The Building Blocks of a Global Industry" seeks to address this knowledge gap by providing a comprehensive, interdisciplinary, and nuanced examination of the tourism industry. This book brings together a diverse range of topics, from the fundamental principles of tourism management and tourism as a business, to the critical issues of tourism sustainability, human rights, environmental impact, and cultural heritage preservation.

Through its chapters, this book offers an in-depth, detailed, and contextualized exploration of the tourism industry, highlighting its complexities, challenges, opportunities, and contradictions. The chapters are organized around key themes, including the tourism product, tourism and hospitality, tourism and culinary industry, tourism and transportation, tourism and marketing, and tourism and staged culture, among others.

This book is designed to serve as a valuable resource for students, researchers, and practitioners in the field of tourism studies, providing a foundational understanding of the tourism industry, while also exploring the cutting-edge issues, debates, and trends that are shaping its future. By adopting an interdisciplinary approach, incorporating insights from sociology, anthropology, geography, economics, and environmental studies, this book offers a holistic and integrated understanding of the tourism industry.

By exploring the building blocks of the global tourism industry, this book seeks to inspire a deeper understanding of the complex relationships between tourism, culture, environment, economy, and society. It is our hope that this book will contribute to the development of a more sustainable, equitable, responsible, and culturally sensitive tourism industry, one that benefits both local communities and global society as a whole.

ABOUT THE EDITORS

Ms. M. L. Nivedita

M.L. Nivedita is a distinguished Lecturer at Brilliant IAS Academy, renowned for her exceptional academic background and passion for teaching and research. With a proven track record of guiding numerous postgraduate thesis projects, she has nurtured the academic growth of her students and established herself as a dedicated educator. As a prolific researcher, Nivedita has authored a range of papers on history and tourism, focusing on women's studies, tourism, and history. Her research endeavours demonstrate her commitment to advancing knowledge in these fields and contributing meaningfully to the existing body of research.

Nivedita's literary expertise is evident in her authored books, including "ABCD of Karate - From Okinawa to the world through Japan" and "The Sun, The Star, The Dragon, A biography of Lara Chamberlain: The Founder of Tida Ryu Karate Association." Her latest work, "Exploring Tourism: The Building Blocks of a Global Industry," showcases her passion for history and tourism. Throughout her academic journey, Nivedita has received several prestigious awards. She was awarded the Dr. Muthulakshmi Reddy Rolling Shield for topping in Women Studies in BA History at Ethiraj College for Women, Chennai. Additionally, she received the "Global Eminent Researcher Award" from Vij Trust, Thirunindravur, in recognition of her outstanding research contributions, selected from over one lakh applications, on October 31, 2023.

Driven by her dedication to advancing research, Nivedita has ambitious plans to author several more books on history and tourism in the future, further enriching the academic landscape and inspiring scholars to explore new avenues of inquiry.

Ms. Arokiya Anbazhagi J

Ms. Arokiya Anbazhagi J is a distinguished academician and Assistant Professor in the Department of History at Women's Christian College, Chennai. With over a decade of teaching experience at esteemed institutions, she specializes in Indian history, archaeology, socio-cultural history, and tourism studies. As a dedicated researcher, Ms. Arokiya's work focuses on social history, cultural heritage, and the societal impacts of tourism. Her notable publications include insightful studies on caste and Christianity in colonial Tamil Nadu, the historicity and heritage of Arikamedu, and the tribulations faced by migrant Northeast women in major cities. She has authored numerous articles in reputable journals and edited scholarly books, cementing her reputation as a trusted voice in her field.

Ms. Arokiya has edited two books: "India@75: Achievements, Challenges & Prospects" and "Forgotten Martyrs of INA". She is a sought-after resource person, frequently addressing seminars and workshops on diverse topics such as art, architecture, and gender perspectives. As an advocate of interdisciplinary education, Ms. Arokiya guides student research and actively participates in initiatives promoting sustainability and heritage awareness. Her commitment to heritage conservation, archaeological exploration, and community-oriented projects has fostered strong connections with her students. Through her passion for history and dedication to academic excellence, Ms. Arokiya inspires students and peers alike, leaving a lasting impact on the academic community.

Ms. Ishwarya J

Ms. Ishwarya J is a diligent research scholar, presently pursuing her Ph.D. in the Department of Historical Studies at Queen Mary's College (A), Chennai, with a specialization in the realm of tourism. Her academic trajectory is marked by a robust teaching experience spanning eight years, during which she has established herself as a distinguished expert in various tourism-related disciplines, including Tourism Products, Tourism Marketing, Air Ticketing and Fare Construction, and Hotel and Front Office Management. Throughout her academic journey, Ms. Ishwarya J has exhibited an unwavering passion for research, evident in her impressive portfolio of 16 presented and published articles, journals, and book chapters. Her research endeavours have been showcased in various conferences, underscoring her commitment to advancing knowledge in the realm of tourism studies and contributing meaningfully to the existing body of research.

As an active researcher, Ms. Ishwarya J continues to explore the intricacies of tourism, driven by an insatiable curiosity to unravel the complexities of this dynamic field. Her Ph.D. pursuits are motivated by a desire to delve deeper into the nuances of tourism, ultimately enriching our understanding of this multifaceted discipline. Through her research and academic endeavours, Ms. Ishwarya J aims to inspire and educate scholars, fostering a deeper appreciation for the multifaceted nature of tourism. Her work is characterized by a commitment to academic excellence, a passion for knowledge dissemination, and a dedication to nurturing the next generation of tourism scholars.

Dr. K.S. Beena

Dr. K.S. Beena is a distinguished academician and researcher, boasting an impressive tenure of over 17 years in the education industry. Currently, she serves as Assistant Professor and Head of the Department of Travel and Tourism at SDNB Vaishnav College for Women (Autonomous) in Chennai, a testament to her exceptional leadership and academic prowess. With a robust academic foundation, comprising a Ph.D. in Management Studies and an M.Phil. in Tourism Management, Dr. Beena has established herself as a preeminent expert in tourism and hospitality management. Her research endeavours are characterized by a keen focus on niche areas, including medical tourism, sustainable tourism, and tourism marketing.

Dr. Beena's publication record is replete with numerous papers in Scopus-indexed journals and UGC Care-listed publications, underscoring her commitment to academic excellence and her contribution to the body of knowledge in tourism and hospitality management. Her work has garnered recognition for its innovative insights and rigorous scholarship. As an educator, Dr. Beena is deeply invested in mentoring and guiding students in their research pursuits, fostering a culture of academic inquiry and exploration. She has successfully supervised several research projects, encouraging students to venture into uncharted territories of tourism and hospitality management.

Dr. Beena's affiliation with the Research India Foundation as a life member is a testament to her dedication to advancing knowledge and promoting research excellence. Furthermore, her innovative spirit is exemplified by her patent for an electronic luggage tracking tag, demonstrating her ability to translate theoretical concepts into practical applications. Through her exceptional expertise, experience, and leadership, Dr. Beena has emerged as a valuable asset to the academic community, inspiring students, and contributing meaningfully to the advancement of tourism and hospitality management.

Dr. M. Jansi

Dr. M. Jansi is a distinguished Associate Professor in the Department of Historical Studies at Government Arts College, Nandanam, Chennai. With over 25 years of teaching experience and degrees in both History and Tourism, as well as a Ph.D. in History, she has established herself as a leading scholar in her field. Dr. Jansi's research publications span a wide range of topics, including Indian art, culture, and heritage, eco-tourism, women's empowerment, and sustainable development. Her work has been featured in various international conferences, journals, and proceedings, demonstrating her expertise in historical studies, tourism, and cultural heritage. Through her research, Dr. Jansi aims to promote a deeper understanding of India's rich cultural heritage and its significance in the modern world. Her publications have been widely acclaimed for their meticulous research, insightful analysis, and engaging narrative style.

As an academic, Dr. Jansi is committed to mentoring and guiding students in their research pursuits. She has supervised numerous research projects and has encouraged students to explore new areas of inquiry in historical studies and tourism. Dr.Jansi's dedication to research and academic excellence has earned her recognition as a leading scholar in her field. Her contributions to historical studies, tourism, and cultural heritage have enriched our understanding of India's complex history and its cultural significance. In addition to her academic pursuits, Dr. Jansi has also served as Associate Editor for several publications, including "Women Rights and Duties" (Ryan Publishers, Tamil Nadu, 2023, ISBN – 978-81-19587-36-0) and "Historical Reform Movements in India" (Ryan Publishers, Tamil Nadu, 2024, ISBN – 978-81-19587-21-6). These editorial roles demonstrate her commitment to promoting scholarly research and publication in her field.

Dr. Cinthia Jude

Dr. Cinthia Jude is a distinguished academician and researcher, presently serving as Assistant Professor in the Department of History at Stella Maris College, Chennai, Tamil Nadu, India. Born and raised in Chennai, Dr. Jude's educational journey began in her hometown, ultimately leading her to earn a Ph.D. in History and a Master's degree in Tourism. With a teaching career spanning over 18 years, commencing in 2004, Dr. Jude has established herself as a seasoned educator, having taught at several esteemed institutions in Chennai. Her current tenure at Stella Maris College holds special significance, as it is her Alma Mater, where she is now living her dreams. As an ardent researcher, Dr. Jude has received several prestigious awards conferred by state and national-level organizations, underscoring her commitment to academic excellence. Her research interests are diverse, and she is passionate about exploring the intricacies of history, tourism, and cuisine.

Dr. Jude's editorial expertise is showcased in her work on two recent books, one focusing on Indian cuisine and the other on global cuisine. These publications demonstrate her ability to curate and present research in an engaging and accessible manner. As an educator, Dr. Jude is dedicated to motivating and inspiring her students to pursue their passions for travel, teaching, research, and writing. Her enthusiasm and guidance have empowered numerous students to explore their interests and achieve their academic goals. Through her teaching, research, and writing, Dr. Cinthia Jude continues to make significant contributions to the academic community, solidifying her position as a leading scholar in her field.

ABOUT THE ASSOCIATE EDITORS

Dr. Archana Soman

Dr. Archana Soman is a distinguished academician and researcher, presently serving as Assistant Professor in the Department of History, Tourism, and Travel Management at Ethiraj College for Women (Autonomous) in Chennai. Her educational background, rooted in Chennai, has equipped her with a deep understanding of the region's historical and cultural nuances. With over eight years of teaching experience, Dr. Soman has established herself as a seasoned educator, having taught History and Tourism at several prestigious institutions across the region. Her expertise in these fields has been further augmented by her research endeavors, which have yielded significant contributions to various book chapters and UGC CARE-listed journals.

Dr. Soman's research interests are diverse and far-reaching, encompassing themes such as Modern India, Water Management, Social History of India, and Tourism. Her commitment to research excellence has driven her to guide numerous postgraduate project works, fostering a new generation of scholars and researchers. Notably, Dr. Soman's editorial expertise is showcased in her work on "Exploring Tourism: The Building Blocks of a Global Industry," marking her second editorial endeavour. This accomplishment underscores her dedication to promoting high-quality research and scholarship in the fields of History and Tourism. As a keen and dedicated researcher, Dr. Soman remains committed to exploring new avenues of inquiry and contributing meaningfully to the academic discourse. Her future research endeavours promise to further enrich our understanding of History and Tourism, solidifying her position as a leading scholar in her field.

Dr. B. Jishamol

Dr. B. Jishamol is a renowned academician, researcher, and educator with a strong background in history and social sciences. As an Assistant Professor in the Department of History, Tourism, and Travel Management at Ethiraj College for Women, Chennai, she brings a wealth of knowledge to her students. Dr. Jishamol holds a Ph.D. in History and has authored numerous publications in UGC Care-listed journals and international conferences. Her academic excellence has been recognized with the prestigious Loyola Research Award and the Women Achievers Award from Loyola College. With over ten years of teaching experience, Dr. Jishamol has guided undergraduate and postgraduate students in their academic pursuits. Her areas of specialization include Ancient Indian History, Socio-Cultural History, and Tourism Studies. She has presented papers on diverse topics, including labour history, trade unions, and women's empowerment, at various national and international conferences.

Dr. Jishamol has completed a project funded by ICSSR titled "Buckingham Canal: Growth and its decline by urban encroachments - impact and result on the population of Madras – A Historical Study." Currently, she is the Project Director for the ICSSR-funded project "Digital Documentation and Dissemination of Culture of Kurmba Tribes: Implications of Development." Additionally, she is the Co-Investigator for the project titled "Migration-Driven Transformation: The Feminization of Tamil Nadu's Agricultural Labour Force" funded by the National Commission for Women (NCW).Dr. Jishamol serves as the Managing Editor of the International Journal of Current Humanities and Social Science Researches, showcasing her leadership skills and commitment to promoting interdisciplinary research in the humanities and social sciences.

Dr. Roselin Mary

Dr. Roselin Mary is a distinguished scholar and educator, boasting an impressive academic pedigree in the fields of History and Education. Her academic pursuits commenced with a Bachelor of Arts degree in History from the esteemed University of Madras, followed by a Master of Arts degree in Historical Studies from the same institution. She further augmented her educational expertise by earning a Bachelor of Education degree from the prestigious St. Xavier's College in Kolkata. The culmination of her academic journey was marked by the conferral of a Doctor of Philosophy (Ph.D.) degree from Presidency College in Chennai.

Dr. Roselin Mary's teaching career, spanning over a decade, is characterized by diversity and adaptability. Her professional odyssey began as a primary teacher at Jousha Matriculation Higher Secondary School, Padi, where she honed her skills in pedagogy and classroom management. Subsequently, she assumed the role of a middle school teacher at Army Public School in Rajasthan, further refining her teaching acumen. Her tenure at Kendriya Vidyalaya in Avadi as a Secondary Grade Teacher (SGT) afforded her the opportunity to instruct students at the secondary level. Moreover, she served as an Assistant Professor at Anna Adarsh College for Women in Anna Nagar, albeit temporarily, where she taught undergraduate students and mentored them in their academic pursuits. Throughout her academic and professional trajectory, Dr. Roselin Mary has consistently demonstrated a profound passion for History, Education, and research. Her Ph.D. from Presidency College, Chennai, is a testament to her academic excellence, research prowess, and unwavering commitment to her chosen field. As a scholar and educator, Dr. Roselin Mary continues to inspire and educate students, fostering a deeper understanding and appreciation of History and its relevance in contemporary society.

INTRODUCTION TO TOURISM

Dr. I. Princes
Assistant Professor
Department of History
Loyola College
Chennai 600034

Introduction

Travel and tourism are an integral part of human culture and history, driven by humanity's innate curiosity and desire for exploration. As a multifaceted industry, tourism encompasses a broad spectrum of activities, including leisure, business, education, health, and religious travel, which are facilitated by interconnected sectors such as transportation, accommodation, and attractions. This dynamic industry plays a vital role in modern life, fostering global connectivity, cultural exchange, and economic development.

Tourism has a profound impact on global economies, societies, and cultures, driving economic growth, promoting cultural understanding, and preserving cultural heritage and natural wonders. By generating employment, stimulating investments in infrastructure, and supporting local businesses, tourism contributes significantly to global GDP and sustains local economies, particularly in developing regions. Furthermore, tourism facilitates cross-cultural exchange, tolerance, and appreciation, transforming perceptions, inspiring creativity, and strengthening global unity, while ensuring the preservation of our collective cultural and natural heritage for future generations.

Cultural tourism showcases the richness of art, architecture, festivals, and customs, helping travellers connect with the essence of a destination. Technology has revolutionized the travel and tourism sector, making it more accessible, efficient, and enjoyable. From online booking platforms and mobile apps to artificial intelligence and virtual reality, innovations have transformed how people plan and experience travel. Social media, too, plays a pivotal role, in inspiring wanderlust and influencing travel choices through shared stories and images.

Advances in technology, including online booking systems and virtual tours, have made travel more accessible and personalized, revolutionizing how people plan and experience journeys. However, travel and tourism face challenges, including over-tourism, environmental degradation, and the impact of global crises such as pandemics. The strain on popular destinations can lead to loss of biodiversity, pollution, and cultural erosion. Sustainable tourism has emerged as a solution to these issues, emphasizing practices that minimize environmental harm and maximize benefits for local communities. Initiatives such as eco-friendly accommodations, responsible wildlife tourism, and community-based programs aim to balance tourism growth and environmental conservation. Travel and tourism are not merely about reaching a destination but about the journey of discovery, connection, and enrichment. While the industry continues to evolve and adapt to changing global dynamics, its fundamental purpose remains unchanged: to inspire individuals, connect cultures, and create memorable experiences that last a lifetime. As a global force for good, travel and tourism continue to inspire, educate, and unite individuals, while shaping the world's future meaningfully. As the world becomes more interconnected, the importance of sustainable and responsible travel practices will be key to ensuring that tourism remains a force for good, benefiting both travellers and the destinations they visit.

Historical Background

The history of tourism dates to ancient civilizations, when travel was primarily undertaken for necessity, trade, conquest, or religion. In ancient Egypt, people traveled to witness the grandeur of pyramids and temples, marking some of the earliest forms of leisure tourism. Similarly, in ancient Greece, citizens journeyed to attend the Olympic Games or visit oracles such as the one at Delphi. The Roman Empire further advanced tourism with its extensive network of roads and inns, enabling affluent Romans to explore countryside villas, coastal resorts, and cultural hubs like Athens. During the Middle Ages, tourism largely shifted to religious pilgrimages, with notable examples including the Hajj to Mecca, the Camino de Santiago in Spain, and pilgrimages to Jerusalem. While these journeys were often arduous, they became pivotal in maintaining travel traditions during this period.

The Renaissance and Age of Exploration in the 15th and 16th centuries reignited curiosity about the world. Wealthy Europeans began embarking on the "Grand Tour," a cultural pilgrimage across France, Italy, and Greece to study art, architecture, and classical heritage. This form of tourism was considered a rite of passage for aristocratic young men, fostering the appreciation of foreign cultures and ideas. By the 17th and 18th centuries, advances in transportation, such as improved roads and stagecoaches, made travel more accessible to the upper middle class.

The Industrial Revolution of the 19th century marked a turning point in tourism history, introducing innovations like steamships, railways, and later, automobiles. These technologies democratized travel, enabling the burgeoning middle class to explore destinations once reserved for the elite. Entrepreneurs like Thomas Cook pioneered organized tourism by offering package tours, making leisure travel more affordable and efficient. Resorts, spas, and seaside towns flourished during this era, with destinations like Brighton and the French Riviera becoming popular among vacationers. In the 20th century, air travel revolutionized tourism, allowing people to reach distant locations quickly and affordably. Post-World War II economic growth, coupled with advancements in aviation and the rise of international travel agencies, led to the era of mass tourism.

Destinations like Hawaii, Switzerland, and the Caribbean became global hotspots. Governments and private sectors invested heavily in infrastructure, building airports, hotels, and attractions to accommodate the growing influx of tourists. Cultural tourism, adventure travel, and eco-tourism emerged, diversifying the reasons for travel beyond traditional leisure. The 21st century ushered in a new era of tourism driven by globalization and technology. Online platforms, budget airlines, and social media have made travel more accessible than ever, enabling people to explore even remote corners of the world. However, this growth has also brought challenges, such as over-tourism, environmental degradation, and cultural homogenization.

Definitions of Tourism

Tourism definitions offer insights into the various dimensions of tourism, from its economic importance to its cultural, environmental, and social implications. One of the most basic and widely accepted definitions of tourism comes from the Oxford English Dictionary, which describes tourism as "the commercial organization and operation of vacations and visits to places of interest".

Burkart and Medlik (1974) describe tourism as "a composite phenomenon involving the interaction of tourists, businesses, and government agencies in the process of attracting, transporting, hosting, and managing travellers". This definition highlights tourism as a system that includes various stakeholders, such as businesses and government entities, which play key roles in making the tourism process function smoothly.

Gilbert (1990) defines tourism as "a form of human behavior involving leisure travel, motivated by the desire for relaxation, discovery, and social interaction". This definition emphasizes the personal and social dimensions of tourism, where individuals or groups travel for relaxation, exploration, and to connect with others. Middleton and Clarke (2001) focus on the operational side of tourism, defining it as "the marketing and provision of goods and services to meet the leisure and travel needs of tourists". This definition frames tourism within the context of the service industry, highlighting its commercial and operational aspects.

Smith (1988) defines tourism as "an interchange system that admits persons to understanding other cultures and environments". This definition frames tourism as an experience that fosters cultural exchange and dialogue, emphasizing the importance of understanding and respect between tourists and host communities. It suggests that tourism has the potential to promote cultural awareness, broaden perspectives, and reduce prejudices by allowing people from different backgrounds to interact and learn from one another.

Williams and Shaw (1991) offer a definition that sees tourism as "a temporary geographical movement of people that is socially and economically organized and that affects and is affected by the environment". This definition situates tourism as a dynamic force that is both shaped by and shapes social, economic, and environmental contexts. It recognizes that tourism has social implications for both the tourists and the host communities, influencing their behaviors, interactions, and expectations.

Butler (1993) defining as "tourism that is developed and maintained in such a manner that it remains feasible over an unspecified period and does not degrade or alter the environment, culture and social structure of the destination". This definition brings attention to the growing need for tourism to be developed responsibly, with minimal negative impacts on the environment, local cultures, and communities. Tourism is increasingly becoming a global activity, and the role of digital technology in facilitating tourism has been central in the last few decades. Kotler et al. (2002) define tourism marketing as "the process of creating, promoting, and delivering products and services that satisfy tourists' needs and wants, while also achieving the business objectives of the destination". This definition underscores the importance of effective marketing in attracting tourists and ensuring that destinations meet the desires of the tourists. Tourism is often viewed as a significant sector of the economy, contributing to national income, employment, and social development. The definitions of tourism reflect its complexity, diversity, and the variety of lenses through which it can be understood. From the economic perspective of tourism as a business activity to the social and cultural dimensions that emphasize cultural exchange and mutual understanding, each definition offers a unique insight into the nature of tourism.

Elements of Tourism Product

The elements of tourism are essential for creating a vibrant tourism industry that not only meets the needs of travellers but also ensures the sustainability and growth of the destination. The core elements of tourism can be broken down into several distinct categories:

the tourist, the destination, attractions, accommodation, transportation, activities, services, and sustainability.

The Tourist

The heart of the tourism industry is the tourist — the individual or group who engages in travel for various reasons, whether for leisure, business, cultural exploration, or even medical treatment. The tourist's behavior, preferences, and motivations directly influence the demand for tourism services. It is essential to understand the diverse motivations of tourists for the development of tourism products and services. The profile of the tourist, including factors such as age, income, nationality, and interests, determines the type of experiences they seek and the destinations they are likely to choose.

The Destination

A destination is the place or region that attracts tourists due to its unique characteristics, be they cultural, natural, or man-made. The concept of a destination is multi-dimensional, encompassing the physical location as well as the experiences it offers. Several factors contribute to the appeal of a destination, such as its cultural heritage, historical significance, natural beauty, infrastructure, and accessibility. In addition, the destination's branding and marketing efforts play a crucial role in attracting tourists.

Attractions

Attractions are the primary motivators for tourists, drawing them to a particular destination. Attractions can be grouped into three broad classifications like natural, cultural, and man-made. Natural attractions include landscapes such as beaches, mountains, lakes, and wildlife reserves, while cultural attractions encompass historical monuments, museums, art galleries, festivals, and religious sites. Man-made attractions often include theme parks, shopping centers, entertainment venues, and resorts. The combination of these different types of attractions within a destination creates a diverse and appealing offering for various types of tourists. Attractions often play a pivotal role in the destination's tourism development, requiring effective marketing and preservation efforts to maintain their appeal.

Transportation

Transportation is one of the most serious constituents of tourism, as it admits tourists to travel to and within destinations. It includes a wide range of options, such as air travel, railways, buses, private vehicles, cruise ships, and bicycles, among others. The rise of low-cost airlines and budget travel options has made international travel more affordable, significantly expanding the reach of tourism to broader demographics. Additionally, local transportation within the destination is equally important for ensuring that tourists can move around easily, visit multiple attractions, and access services. Public transport, taxis and rental cars have become integral parts of the tourism infrastructure, providing convenient solutions for visitors.

Accommodation

Accommodation is a fundamental component of the tourism experience, as it provides comfort and rest for travellers. Accommodation options are vast and varied, ranging from luxury hotels, resorts, and boutique properties to more budget-friendly options such as motels, hostels, homestays, and even camping sites. The type of accommodation a tourist chooses is often influenced by factors such as budget, destination, purpose of the trip, and personal preferences. Furthermore, the quality and range of accommodation available at a destination are essential for attracting tourists.

Activities

Activities form a significant part of the tourism experience, providing tourists with opportunities to engage with the destination in meaningful ways. Common activities include sightseeing tours, hiking, water sports, cultural performances, shopping, gastronomy experiences, and wildlife safaris. The availability of activities determines how well tourists can experience the essence of a destination. For example, a coastal destination might offer water-based activities such as snorkeling, diving, or surfing, while a cultural destination may provide walking tours of historical sites, visits to museums, or participation in local festivals.

Services

Services encompass all the support systems that enhance the tourist experience. These include restaurants, cafes, shopping facilities, entertainment venues, healthcare, and financial services, among others. Customer service is a vital aspect of the tourism industry, as the interaction between tourists and service providers can significantly impact the perception of a destination. The quality of service, friendliness of staff, and efficiency of operations can influence whether tourists have a positive or negative experience. These services provide essential support to tourists before, during, and after their trips, ensuring a smooth and enjoyable travel experience.

Sustainability

Sustainability has become an increasingly important element of modern tourism. As the global tourism industry continues to grow, there is rising concern about its environmental and social impact. The principles of sustainable tourism emphasize minimizing negative effects on the environment, preserving cultural heritage, and ensuring that tourism benefits local communities. Eco-friendly practices, such as reducing carbon emissions, conserving water, and supporting local businesses, are gaining traction in the tourism sector. Sustainable tourism also includes initiatives like responsible wildlife tourism, where efforts are made to protect animals and their habitats while offering tourists opportunities to learn about wildlife conservation. Similarly, destinations are adopting green certifications and eco-labels to promote sustainable practices in accommodations, transportation, and attractions. The elements of tourism are interconnected and interdependent, creating a dynamic ecosystem that contributes to the success and sustainability of the industry.

Types and Forms of Tourism

The types and forms of tourism can be categorized based on the purpose of travel, the activities involved, and the type of destination. In this discussion, we will examine some of the most prominent types and forms of tourism.

Mass Tourism

Mass tourism refers to the large-scale movement of people to popular tourist destinations. It typically involves standardized travel packages that include transportation, accommodation, and guided tours, making it highly affordable and accessible to a broad audience. Mass tourism is often associated with popular cities, beach resorts, and natural wonders that attract large numbers of visitors. The downsides of mass tourism include overcrowding, environmental degradation, and the potential loss of cultural authenticity.

Adventure Tourism

Adventure tourism is a subset of niche tourism that focuses on physical and challenging activities in outdoor environments. It is aimed at thrill-seekers and those who want to engage in activities that test their limits and involve some degree of risk. Common activities within adventure tourism include hiking, trekking, mountain climbing, bungee jumping, skydiving, white-water rafting, and paragliding. Adventure tourism is popular among younger, more adventurous travellers who seek adrenaline-filled experiences in remote or rugged landscapes. This type of tourism not only offers excitement but also provides opportunities for personal growth and connection with nature.

Cultural Tourism

Cultural tourism allows travellers to explore a destination's historical, artistic, and cultural heritage. It involves immersing oneself in the traditions, customs, arts, music, and history of a place. Cultural tourists may visit museums, historical landmarks, architectural marvels, and attend performances or festivals that reflect the destination's cultural identity. Cultural tourism provides an opportunity to foster greater understanding and appreciation of diverse cultures, while also contributing to the preservation of cultural heritage through tourism revenue and awareness.

Ecotourism

Ecotourism is a growing segment within sustainable tourism, emphasizing responsible travel to natural areas that help conserve the environment and improve the well-being of local communities. It aims to provide travellers with an opportunity to experience wildlife and nature, while also promoting conservation, education, and sustainability. Ecotourism destinations often include national parks, rainforests, wildlife reserves, and coastal areas that are protected due to their ecological significance. Ecotourism is also an important tool for environmental education, encouraging travellers to adopt sustainable practices and raise awareness about the fragility of the natural world.

Medical Tourism

Medical tourism involves traveling to another country for medical treatment, often due to the affordability and availability of specialized services. Many travellers seek out medical tourism opportunities for procedures such as dental work, cosmetic surgery, fertility treatments, or even life-saving medical care unavailable or too expensive at home. Popular medical tourism destinations include India, Thailand, Singapore, and Mexico, which offer state-of-the-art medical facilities and experienced doctors at lower costs compared to Western countries. Medical tourists often combine treatment with leisure, recovering in comfortable resort-style accommodations after procedures.

Business Tourism

Business tourism refers to travel for professional purposes. It includes attending business conferences, seminars, workshops, corporate meetings, and incentive travel for employees. Business tourism contributes significantly to the economy of host destinations, as business travellers often spend more than leisure tourists. The growing trend of virtual and hybrid events has further expanded the scope of business tourism.

Rural Tourism

Rural tourism focuses on travel to rural areas, offering visitors an opportunity to experience life away from urban centers. This type of tourism typically involves activities such as farm stays, agritourism, village tours, and participation in traditional crafts or farming activities. Rural tourism helps preserve local cultures and economies by providing rural communities with an alternative source of income. It allows travellers to experience authentic local lifestyles and peacefully connect with nature. The world of tourism is broad and diverse, with numerous types catering to different interests and demographics. Whether it's mass tourism, which focuses on popular destinations, or niche tourism which offers unique, tailored experiences, the industry provides something for everyone. Each form of tourism brings with it its own set of challenges and opportunities, particularly when considering environmental impact, sustainability, and the long-term benefits for local communities.

Travel Agencies

Travel agencies are essential to the promotion and growth of the tourism industry across its various forms. They serve as facilitators, educators, and curators, helping to connect travellers with destinations, services, and experiences that align with their interests and needs. One of their primary functions is trip planning and itinerary creation, where they assist clients in organizing every aspect of their travel, from selecting destinations and accommodations to arranging transportation and activities. They provide expert advice, ensuring that travellers make informed decisions based on their preferences and budget. Travel agencies also handle bookings for flights, hotels, car rentals, cruises, and other essential services, often leveraging their partnerships with airlines, hotels, and tour operators to secure competitive rates and exclusive offers. In addition to general travel services, they specialize in creating customized travel packages, catering to niche markets such as adventure tourism, cultural tourism, luxury travel, and ecotourism. They design personalized itineraries that align with the interests of the traveler, offering unique experiences that go beyond conventional travel. Travel agencies are also responsible for managing group tours, coordinating logistics such as transportation, accommodation, and activities for large groups, ensuring that these trips run smoothly. They assist in arranging visas and travel documentation, helping clients navigate the complexities of entry requirements for various countries, which is especially important for international travellers.

Travel agencies also offer travel insurance, protecting unexpected events such as trip cancellations, medical emergencies, or lost luggage. Additionally, they play a vital role in promoting tourism products and destinations through marketing campaigns, travel fairs, and digital platforms, thereby helping destinations attract more visitors. Moreover, travel agencies offer post-travel services, such as soliciting feedback, addressing any issues that arise during the trip, and assisting clients with changes to their plans if necessary. Through their multifaceted role, travel agencies help enhance the travel experience, making it easier, more enjoyable, and more accessible for millions of tourists worldwide.

Tour Operator

Tour operators play an essential role in the tourism industry by designing, organizing, and selling travel packages that cater to various traveler needs. Their primary function is to create pre-arranged or customized holiday packages that include a combination of transportation, accommodations, meals, sightseeing, and activities, offering travellers a convenient and organized way to experience a destination. Tour operators typically work with hotels, airlines, transport companies, and local service providers to assemble these packages, ensuring that each component aligns with the interests and preferences of the target market. They play a significant role in coordinating logistics for travellers, from booking flights and arranging transfers to managing guided tours and excursions, ensuring a seamless travel experience from start to finish.

In addition to offering set packages, many tour operators also provide tailor-made services for specialized tourism, such as adventure tours, luxury vacations, cultural trips, or eco-friendly travel options.

They curate these specialized itineraries, considering the unique requirements of their clients, and work closely with local operators to deliver exceptional experiences. Tour operators are also responsible for pricing these packages competitively, factoring in costs, margins, and market demand, while also promoting and marketing their offerings to reach a wide audience. They often collaborate with travel agents, who sell the packages to individual travellers, and handle all customer inquiries, offering expert advice on the best destinations, activities, and travel routes.

Tour operators ensure that customers are informed about travel documentation, visas, health and safety precautions, and insurance requirements, which are all critical to the success of a trip. Another important function is risk management, where tour operators are responsible for ensuring the safety and security of their clients, addressing any issues that arise during the trip, and helping in case of emergencies, such as flight cancellations or health concerns. Additionally, tour operators are actively involved in promoting destinations, supporting local economies, and driving tourism demand through innovative and creative marketing strategies, including advertising campaigns, digital media, and direct outreach to travel agents and consumers. As intermediaries between suppliers and travellers, they play a central role in shaping the tourism industry, offering valuable services to clients while driving growth and sustainability within the global travel sector. Through their multifaceted responsibilities, tour operators make travel planning easier for tourists, offering convenient, cost-effective, and enjoyable vacation experiences while ensuring that all aspects of the journey are well-organized, safe, and memorable.

Travel Documents

Travel documents are essential for ensuring smooth and legal travel across borders, serving as proof of identity, nationality, and authorization to enter or stay in a country. The most fundamental of these is the passport, which is issued by a national government and certifies a person's identity and citizenship, allowing for international travel. A passport typically includes the traveler’s name, photo, date of birth, nationality, and passport number, and often features biometric data for enhanced security, such as fingerprints or facial recognition. For international travel, it is essential that a passport is valid for at least six months beyond the planned departure date. Alongside a passport, many travellers also require a visa, which is an official document that grants permission to enter, transit through, or stay in a country for a specified period. Visas may be single-entry or multiple entry, depending on the conditions of the traveler's trip, and are typically applied for at the embassy or consulate of the destination country. Some countries also offer e-visas, which can be applied for and obtained online, simplifying the process. Another key travel document is the national identity card, which serves as an official proof of identity for citizens of certain countries.

Additionally, travel insurance documents are increasingly important, especially for international trips, providing coverage for unforeseen events such as medical emergencies, cancellations, or lost luggage. These documents are essential for mitigating the financial risks associated with travel and ensuring a smoother journey. Health and vaccination records also play a critical role in international travel. Travellers may be required to present vaccination certificates, particularly when traveling to regions with specific health concerns. A travel itinerary is another important document, detailing the traveler's plans such as flight details, hotel bookings, and scheduled activities. This document is especially useful when applying for visas or if travellers need to provide evidence of their travel plans to border control authorities. Proof of financial means is also necessary in some countries, particularly when applying for a visa. This proof can include bank statements, employment letters, or credit card statements to demonstrate that the traveler can support themselves during their stay. The travellers should carry emergency contact information, including details of family members, friends, or colleagues who can be reached in case of an emergency during the trip. This document is particularly important when traveling abroad, where travellers may face medical or legal issues. Customs declarations and import/export permits are required when carrying goods that may be subject to customs duties or restrictions, such as electronics, currency, or plants. Travellers need to fill out customs forms to declare such items upon entering or leaving a country to comply with national laws and regulations. Finally, a return ticket or proof of onward travel may be required by some countries to ensure that travellers do not overstay their visas and have a confirmed exit plan. These documents help border authorities verify the traveler's intentions and compliance with the country's immigration policies.

Tourism in the present Scenario

The global travel landscape has witnessed significant shifts in recent years, with technology playing a central role in transforming the way people plan, book, and experience travel. The rise of digital platforms, online booking systems, and travel apps has made it easier for travellers to access a wide array of information and services, streamlining the process of organizing trips. Social media and influencers have further fueled the growth of tourism by showcasing unique destinations and experiences, influencing travel decisions across various demographics. Tourism in the present scenario is characterized by a focus on sustainability, technology-driven innovation, and a shift in traveler preferences toward more meaningful and responsible experiences. As the industry continues to recover and adapt, the role of responsible travel practices, health and safety measures, and environmental consciousness will remain central to shaping the future of tourism. The ability of the industry to innovate and align with these changing demands will determine its long-term resilience and success in a post-pandemic world.

Conclusion

Tourism is a dynamic and integral part of the global economy, contributing significantly to cultural exchange, economic growth, and the development of various sectors, including hospitality, transportation, and entertainment. The essence of tourism lies in the movement of people, driven by the desire for new experiences, relaxation, and the exploration of different cultures and landscapes. In today's interconnected world, tourism has become more accessible and diverse, with advancements in technology and transportation enabling people to travel across borders with relative ease. However, it also presents challenges such as environmental sustainability, the preservation of cultural heritage, and the balance between tourism growth and the well-being of local communities. Tourism plays a vital role in connecting people, expanding horizons, and promoting mutual understanding, making it a key force in shaping our globalized world.

TOURISM MANAGEMENT

Author
Dr. Gughan Babu Azhageshan
Assistant Professor
Department of History,
Madras Christian College,
Chennai - 600 059.

Co-Author
Dr. Girija Gughan Babu
Guest Faculty
Department of History,
Pondicherry University,
Pondicherry.

Introduction

Tourism has become one of the world's largest and fastest-growing industries, contributing significantly to global economic development, job creation, and cultural exchange. The established destinations continue to attract millions of visitors annually, emerging destinations are increasingly gaining attention as new and unique tourism hotspots. These emerging destinations, often located in developing regions, offer untapped potential for growth and exploration.[1] The industry also faces unique challenges and opportunities that require careful management to ensure sustainable development and the long-term success of the tourism industry. Tourism management in emerging destinations is particularly a leisure development due to the delicate balance between maximizing economic benefits and minimizing negative social, cultural, and environmental impacts. As these destinations attract more tourists, they must confront infrastructure limitations, environmental degradation, overcrowding, and the preservation of local cultures and traditions. At the same time, these regions have the opportunity to position themselves as key players in the global tourism market by implementing innovative strategies and sustainable practices that appeal to modern traveller's values.

The challenges and opportunities faced by tourism managers in emerging destinations. The emerging destinations can leverage their unique assets while addressing the challenges of rapid growth. From sustainable tourism practices to community engagement and technology adoption, the management strategies in these destinations can set a precedent for future development in tourism. As tourism continues to expand, stakeholders including government agencies, local communities, businesses, and tourists themselves must work together to create an environment where tourism can thrive without compromising the authenticity or long-term viability of the destination.

Tourism management

Tourism management refers to the process of overseeing and regulating tourism activities to ensure that destinations are developed in a sustainable, profitable, and responsible manner. This involves balancing economic growth with environmental and cultural preservation, as well as ensuring that the needs of tourists, local communities, and other stakeholders are met. As global tourism continues to expand, emerging destinations typically areas that are not yet established as major tourist hubs are gaining increasing attention. These regions, often in developing countries, have unique characteristics, rich cultural heritage, and natural beauty that make them attractive to travellers seeking novel experiences. Spring-up destinations, unlike well-known tourist hotspots, often face distinct challenges when it comes to tourism management. These challenges include inadequate infrastructure, limited access to resources, environmental degradation, and the risk of over-tourism.

Tourism can bring significant economic benefits, but it can also strain local resources, cause damage to fragile ecosystems, and lead to cultural dilution or loss. Emanate destinations often lack the expertise or capacity to implement sustainable tourism practices and manage rapid visitor growth effectively. These challenges are coupled with substantial opportunities. This industry has the advantage of being able to learn from the mistakes of established destinations, allowing them to implement best practices in tourism development from the outset. By focusing on sustainability, community involvement, and local culture preservation, these destinations can offer unique and authentic travel experiences that appeal to conscious, modern travellers. The adoption of new technologies and innovative marketing strategies can help attract tourists while managing the volume and impact of their visits. The management of tourism involves a delicate balancing act. Successful tourism management strategies in these areas can lead to economic development, job creation, and cultural exchange while minimizing negative impacts. This requires effective planning, the engagement of local communities, government support, and collaboration between the public and private sectors. With the specific challenges and capitalizing on opportunities, arise destinations can carve out a sustainable path for tourism that benefits all stakeholders.

Historical Development

The notion of tourism management has evolved significantly over the past century, influenced by changes in global travel trends, economic priorities, and cultural perceptions. In the early stages, tourism management was primarily focused on established destinations in Europe and North America, where tourism infrastructure had been developed for decades. As international travel became more accessible, particularly after World War II, the tourism industry began to expand beyond these traditional hubs to include less-developed regions, giving rise to the concept of "emerging destinations." The post-World War II era saw significant increases in global travel, driven by improvements in transportation, such as commercial aviation and the rise of mass tourism. As tourism became more widespread, governments and private sector actors began to recognize the economic potential of tourism in less-developed areas, particularly in the Global South. In the 1970s and 1980s, countries in Southeast Asia, Latin America, and Africa started promoting their unique attractions to international tourists, often relying on the natural environment, cultural heritage, and low-cost travel experiences to attract visitors. This marked the early stage of tourism development in emerging targets.

Tourism grew in these regions, and the adverse impacts of mass tourism became evident. The quick influx of tourists often leads to environmental degradation, overcrowding, and cultural erosion, especially in regions with limited infrastructure or management expertise. During the 1990s and early 2000s, the tourism industry began to focus more on sustainability and responsible tourism practices, in response to these challenges. International organizations such as the World Tourism Organization (UNWTO) and the Global Sustainable Tourism Council (GSTC) played a key role in advocating for sustainable tourism policies, which emphasized the importance of preserving local cultures, protecting the environment, and ensuring that tourism benefits were equitably distributed. In recent years, the growth of emerging destinations has been influenced by several global trends, including the rise of niche markets such as ecotourism, adventure tourism, and cultural tourism.[6] The advent of digital technologies, including social media and online travel platforms, has allowed emerging destinations to reach a global audience more easily, but it has also raised concerns about over-tourism and its associated impacts. Tourism in emerging destinations is at a crossroads. While these industries offer vast economic opportunities, they navigate the complexities of growth, sustainability, and community engagement. The historical development of tourism in these areas highlights both the potential and the challenges, emphasizing the need for innovative management strategies that balance development with preservation.

Sustainable Tourism Management

The core principle in tourism management is sustainability. This concept intensifies the need to balance economic, social, and environmental factors in tourism development. Sustainable tourism aims to reduce the negative impacts of tourism, such as environmental degradation, resource depletion, and cultural disruption, while enhancing positive outcomes, including economic growth, local empowerment, and the preservation of heritage. The triple bottom line framework, which focuses on environmental, social, and economic sustainability, is commonly applied to tourism planning in emerging ambition. Sustainable tourism is one of the most prominent forms of tourism management, it involves creating tourism experiences that meet the needs of tourists and the local population while preserving the environment, culture, and resources for future generations. Environmental sustainability refers to strategies to minimize the negative environmental impact of tourism, such as promoting eco-friendly infrastructure, waste reduction, energy efficiency, and wildlife conservation. Cultural sustainability ensures that tourism development respects local traditions, customs, and heritage, preventing cultural erosion. Economic sustainability fosters long-term economic benefits from tourism by ensuring that the profits are distributed equitably among local communities and that tourism does not overshadow other local industries.

Community-Based Tourism (CBT)

The CBT highlights the involvement of local communities in tourism planning and decision-making. This idea promotes the recommendation that communities should have control over the development of tourism in their areas, ensuring that tourism benefits are distributed equitably. CBT helps preserve cultural heritage, supports local economies, and fosters a sense of ownership and pride among residents. This approach helps mitigate the risks of exploitation and ensures that the local population directly benefits from tourism. Community-based tourism is a form of tourism management that emphasizes the active participation of local communities in the planning, development, and operation of tourism activities. This approach empowers Indigenous people and allows them to directly benefit from tourism while preserving cultural and environmental integrity. Important components of CBT include community members being involved in decision-making processes related to tourism development, and ensuring that tourism practices align with local needs and priorities. By promoting local traditions, folklore, and customs, CBT helps preserve cultural identity while providing authentic experiences for visitors. The profits from tourism are reinvested into the community, supporting local businesses, infrastructure, and social services. CBT is a powerful tool for creating tourism products that are both economically beneficial and culturally sensitive, fostering a sense of ownership and responsibility among local populations.

Ecotourism Management

Ecotourism is a niche form of tourism that focuses on the responsible exploration of natural environments, with an emphasis on conservation, education, and sustainability. With rich natural resources, ecotourism management is crucial. Ecotourism can help fund conservation projects that protect biodiversity, such as national parks, wildlife sanctuaries, and marine reserves. Ecotourism aims to minimize the ecological footprint of tourism activities, emphasizing low-impact transportation, waste management, and eco-friendly accommodations. Tourists are educated about the local ecosystem, wildlife, and conservation challenges, fostering a deeper appreciation for nature.[12] Ecotourism offers a sustainable alternative to mass tourism by drawing attention to the region's natural beauty while generating economic benefits for local communities and conservation efforts.

Cultural and Heritage Tourism Management

Tourism is centred around cultural, historical, or indigenous heritage. Cultural and heritage tourism management focuses on the preservation and promotion of cultural sites, festivals, traditions, and art forms. Efforts are made to protect and maintain tangible and intangible cultural assets, including monuments, artifacts, traditions, and rituals. Tourism is used as a tool to showcase local music, dance, art, and cuisine, providing visitors with authentic experiences. Ensuring that tourism does not lead to the commercialization or loss of cultural identity is a key challenge in managing cultural tourism with rich cultural and historical assets, this form of tourism management offers an opportunity to diversify the economy while safeguarding local heritage.

Adventure and Niche Tourism Management

Adventure tourism is another form of tourism management that pivots on attracting visitors seeking unique, thrilling experiences. These can include activities such as trekking, scuba diving, wildlife safaris, and mountain climbing. Targeting specific tourist segments by focusing on niche markets like adventure tourism, wellness tourism, or agro-tourism, emerging destinations can carve out unique identities in the global tourism market. Minimizing overcrowding niche tourism typically involves smaller groups of tourists, which helps to avoid overcrowding in the destination, ensuring a more sustainable flow of visitors. Economic diversification niche tourism can provide high-value, low-volume tourism that benefits specific local sectors, such as outdoor guiding, hospitality, and local artisans. Managing niche tourism requires tailored marketing strategies and the development of specialized services and infrastructure that cater to the interests of specific types of tourists.

Digital and Smart Tourism Management

The rise of digital technologies has transformed how tourism is managed and experienced. Smart tourism involves using technology to enhance the efficiency and quality of the tourist experience while managing resources effectively. Online booking and marketing digital platforms such as travel websites, social media, and review platforms help attract global tourists to lesser-known destinations, expanding their reach. Smart infrastructure technologies such as free Wi-Fi, mobile apps, and digital kiosks can improve the visitor experience and help manage tourist flows more efficiently. Data-driven decision-making big data and analytics can help tourism managers monitor trends, predict tourist behavior, and optimize resource allocation, ensuring more sustainable management of the destination. Embracing digital and smart tourism can increase global visibility and enhance visitor satisfaction, while also improving operational efficiency.

Crisis and Risk Management

The emerging industry is often vulnerable to external shocks, such as natural disasters, political instability, health crises, and the COVID-19 pandemic. Crisis and risk management in tourism involves developing strategies to mitigate risks and recover from disruptions. Emergency preparedness plans having clear protocols for evacuations, disaster relief, and health crises can help minimize the impact of crises on tourists and local communities. Crisis and effective communication with tourists and stakeholders are critical during emergencies, ensuring that visitors are informed and supported. Tourism management strategies should aim to build the resilience of destinations, ensuring that they can quickly recover and adapt to unforeseen challenges. Risk management is essential to maintaining long-term stability in the face of unpredictable global events.

Destination Lifecycle

The idea, introduced by Butler (1980), is the stages that a tourism destination typically goes through, from exploration to development, consolidation, stagnation, and potential rejuvenation or decline. Tourism destinations often find themselves in the early stages of this lifecycle, where growth is quick and unregulated. Understanding this idea helps tourism managers anticipate future challenges, plan for sustainable development, and prepare for the inevitable shifts in tourist interest and market dynamics.

Carrying Capacity

The destination has a maximum capacity to host tourists without causing detrimental impacts on its environment, culture, or infrastructure. Managing the tourism carrying capacity whether in terms of physical infrastructure, social tolerance, or environmental health is crucial. Over-tourism, often driven by unregulated growth, can overwhelm local communities and ecosystems, making carrying capacity an important concept in balancing growth with sustainability.

Tourism Impact

The positive and negative impacts of tourism on a destination. The tourism impact is often amplified due to the lack of established management practices. Key impacts include economic, social, environmental, and cultural effects, which need to be carefully monitored and managed. The challenge for destinations is to harness the positive impacts of job creation, infrastructure development, and cultural exchange while mitigating the negative impacts of pollution, displacement, and cultural commodification.

Competitive Advantage

In an increasingly globalized tourism market, must find their unique competitive advantages. Porter's Competitive Advantage theory emphasizes the need for destinations to leverage unique resources whether natural, cultural, or historical to differentiate themselves from other destinations. the idea is the importance of identifying and promoting unique offerings that appeal to specific niches such as ecotourism, adventure tourism, or cultural tourism.

Tourist Experience

The tourist experience focuses on how visitors perceive and engage with a destination, from pre-arrival expectations to post-visit reflections. capitalize on offering authentic, immersive, and personalized experiences that attract conscious travellers. The importance of managing not just the physical aspects of a destination but also the emotional and psychological connections that tourists form during their visit. The specific challenges and opportunities these regions face. Effective tourism management can take several forms, depending on the nature of the destination, its resources, and the priorities of local stakeholders.

Benefits of Tourism Management

- One of the primary benefits of tourism management is its potential to drive economic growth, often relying on tourism as a source of income, creating jobs in sectors such as hospitality, transportation, retail, and local services. This intrusion of tourist spending can support small businesses, encourage infrastructure development, and contribute to the broader economy. Tourism can stimulate investment in areas like airports, roads, and public services, further boosting economic development.

- Tourism management can help protect and promote local culture and heritage. By emphasizing cultural tourism or community-based tourism, emerging destinations can showcase their unique traditions, crafts, and customs. Well-managed tourism encourages the preservation of historical sites and cultural landmarks, which, in turn, becomes a source of pride for local communities. Revenue generated from cultural tourism can be reinvested into conservation and heritage protection efforts.

- Environmental Tourism, especially ecotourism and nature-based tourism, can be a powerful tool for environmental conservation. Entrance fees to national parks, wildlife reserves, or eco-lodges can generate revenue for conservation projects. Rich biodiversity or pristine ecosystems, tourism management focused on sustainability can help fund preservation initiatives and raise awareness about the importance of protecting natural resources.

- Effective tourism management helps gain visibility on the global stage. Through marketing strategies and partnerships with international travel platforms, lesser-known destinations can attract visitors, diversifying the tourism market and reducing dependency on a single or a few regions.

Impacts of Tourism Management

- One of the major challenges faced is the risk of over-tourism, which can lead to environmental degradation, resource depletion, and loss of local character. Poorly managed tourism can strain local infrastructure, contribute to waste and pollution, and damage fragile ecosystems.

- Tourism can sometimes lead to the commercialization and dilution of local cultures may face the challenge of balancing the influx of tourists with the preservation of their cultural identity. Over-commercialization can turn local customs, traditions, and festivals into "tourist attractions," detracting from their authenticity and significance.

- Tourism can generate income, but it can also exacerbate social inequality if the benefits are not distributed equitably. In some cases, tourism development may lead to the displacement of local populations or increase the cost of living for residents, making it difficult for them to benefit from the influx of visitors.

- Rapid tourism growth can place significant pressure on infrastructure and public resources. The demand for water, energy, and waste management services can outstrip the capacity to manage these needs. This can result in inadequate facilities, overcrowding, and a diminished experience for both tourists and residents.

- The benefits of tourism management are clear economic growth, cultural preservation, environmental conservation, and global visibility. These benefits come with challenges, including environmental degradation, cultural erosion, and the pressure on local infrastructure. Balancing these opportunities and challenges requires careful planning, sustainable practices, and stakeholder collaboration to ensure that tourism remains a positive force for both the destination and its people.

Challenges and Opportunities

Tourism offers significant opportunities for economic growth, cultural exchange, and environmental conservation. These destinations face numerous challenges and constraints that require careful planning and sustainable practices.

- **Inadequate Infrastructure**

One of the most pressing challenges is the lack of adequate infrastructure. Roads, airports, public transport systems, and communication networks may be underdeveloped or outdated. This can hinder access to the destination, limit visitor experiences, and strain local resources. Without proper infrastructure, managing large numbers of tourists becomes difficult, leading to overcrowding and poor service delivery.

- **Environmental Degradation**

The unique natural landscapes, ecosystems, and biodiversity make them attractive to tourists. Tourism is not carefully managed, it can lead to environmental degradation, such as deforestation, soil erosion, pollution, and loss of biodiversity. Uncontrolled tourism can also strain water resources, damage coral reefs, or contribute to the depletion of natural resources, leaving the destination vulnerable to long-term environmental damage.

- **Over-Tourism and Crowding**

Over-tourism is a significant challenge due to the lack of effective visitor management strategies. With proper regulations, tourism growth can become unsustainable, leading to overcrowding in popular areas. This not only reduces the quality of the tourist experience but can also negatively affect residents, who may face increased living costs, displacement, and social tensions. Managing the volume and distribution of tourists is key to ensuring that destinations do not suffer from the adverse effects of over-tourism.

- **Cultural Erosion**

The authenticity of local culture may be at risk. The commercialization of cultural practices, traditions, and festivals to cater to tourist expectations can lead to cultural erosion. The traditional crafts, ceremonies, or food may be adapted to fit tourist tastes, undermining their cultural significance. The influx of foreign tourists can also lead to the adoption of outside cultural norms, diminishing the value of local traditions.

- **Economic Inequality**

Tourism can drive economic growth, but it may also aggravate economic inequality. The benefits of tourism may not be equitably distributed among local communities. Large multinational companies or external investors may dominate the tourism sector, leading to a concentration of profits in the hands of a few. Local workers may face low wages and poor working conditions, while the cost of living in tourist areas can rise, making it difficult for locals to afford basic necessities.

- **Lack of Skilled Workforce**

The lack of a well-trained workforce to support the tourism industry. This includes a shortage of skilled workers in hospitality, tour guiding, and management, as well as expertise in areas such as marketing, sustainable practices, and crisis management. This skills gap can undermine the quality of service provided to tourists and hinder the destination's ability to manage growth effectively.

- **Political Instability and Governance Issues**

Political instability or weak governance structures can also present challenges for tourism management in emerging destinations. Corruption, poor policy implementation, and lack of coordination among stakeholders can lead to mismanagement, ineffective regulations, and missed opportunities for sustainable tourism development. The political instability may deter tourists from visiting or disrupt tourism operations altogether.

- **Health and Safety Concerns**

Significant challenges in maintaining health and safety standards. Poor sanitation, inadequate healthcare facilities, and the lack of emergency services can pose risks to both tourists and residents. Health crises, such as outbreaks of diseases can severely impact tourism in these regions, making it essential for destinations to develop robust health and safety protocols.

- **Dependency on Tourism**

Reliant on tourism as a primary economic driver, which can create vulnerability to fluctuations in tourist arrivals due to external factors such as economic recessions, natural disasters, or global pandemics. This dependence on tourism for economic stability can create a fragile economy that is difficult to diversify or adjust when tourism demand decreases.

Opportunities of Technology and Innovation in Tourism Management

- Smart tourism leverages digital technologies, such as IoT (Internet of Things), big data, and mobile apps, to enhance the visitor experience and improve destination management. Smart technologies can optimize tourist flow, reduce overcrowding, and distribute visitors more evenly across different sites. Real-time data on visitor numbers, weather conditions, and popular attractions can help authorities make informed decisions on crowd management and resource allocation. Smart transportation systems using GPS tracking and mobile apps can improve the efficiency of public transport and reduce congestion.

- Tourism often struggles with visibility in the global tourism market. Digital marketing tools, including social media, online advertising, and influencer partnerships, can increase global awareness and attract new tourists. Platforms like Instagram and YouTube are particularly influential, allowing destinations to showcase their unique cultural, natural, and heritage attractions to a worldwide audience. These digital tools also help destinations create targeted campaigns for niche markets, such as adventure tourism or wellness tourism, thereby diversifying their tourism offerings.

- Technological innovations can help emerging destinations pursue more sustainable tourism practices. Energy-efficient hotels, solar-powered infrastructure, and waste-reducing technologies can lower the environmental impact of tourism. Blockchain technology can also be used to track the carbon footprint of tourism activities, ensuring greater transparency and accountability. Eco friendly apps that promote sustainable activities like cycling tours, eco-lodges, or responsible wildlife experiences can guide tourists towards more responsible choices.

- Mobile apps, virtual reality (VR), and augmented reality (AR) are transforming how tourists engage with destinations. Virtual tours, VR simulations of historical sites, and AR-guided city tours enhance the visitor experience by providing immersive, interactive ways to explore attractions. These technologies can also help preserve fragile sites by allowing virtual visits to destinations that are at risk of over-tourism or environmental damage.

Challenges of Technology and Innovation in Tourism Management

- In many tourist areas technological infrastructure is underdeveloped, making it difficult to implement advanced digital solutions. Inadequate internet access, poor mobile networks, and lack of investment in technology can hinder the adoption of smart tourism systems. Overcoming these infrastructure challenges requires significant investment in digital and technological infrastructure.

- While technology offers great opportunities, there is a risk of excluding certain groups, especially in less-developed regions. Low-income communities or rural areas may not have the access or skills to benefit from digital platforms. Ensuring digital inclusivity is crucial to avoid deepening inequalities and ensuring that all stakeholders, including local businesses and communities, can participate in and benefit from tourism-driven innovation.

- The increased use of digital platforms for booking, payments, and navigation raises concerns about data privacy and cybersecurity. Must implement robust data protection policies to protect tourists' personal and financial information. Without proper security measures, destinations risk damaging their reputation and losing the trust of potential visitors.

- The technology can enhance tourism management, but there is a risk of becoming overly dependent on it. Need to strike a balance between technological solutions and human interaction. Over-relying on automated systems may alienate tourists seeking authentic experiences or personalized services. Tourism managers must ensure that technology complements, rather than replaces, the local cultural elements that make a destination unique.

- Technology and innovation hold significant promise for tourism management in emerging destinations. By harnessing smart tourism, digital marketing, sustainable innovations, and enhanced customer experiences, these destinations can improve their competitiveness and sustainability. Challenges such as infrastructure gaps, digital exclusion, and cybersecurity risks must be carefully addressed. A balanced approach that integrates technology with local cultural values, community involvement, and sustainable practices will ensure that emerging destinations can fully capitalize on the opportunities presented by innovation.

Opportunities of Policy and Regulatory Frameworks

- A well-designed regulatory framework can support **sustainable tourism** by implementing policies that protect the environment and ensure responsible tourism practices. Regulations can limit visitor numbers to fragile ecosystems, introduce eco-certifications for accommodations and tour operators, and require tourism businesses to adhere to sustainability standards. In places like North East India, where sustainability is a core principle, introducing environmental certifications and regulations has contributed to protecting natural resources while fostering long-term tourism growth.

- Policies encouraging community-based tourism (CBT) can empower local populations by involving them in decision-making and ensuring they benefit from tourism-related activities. Implement regulations that mandate local ownership of businesses, encourage partnerships with local communities, and provide training programs for skill development. In the Himalayas, community-based trekking programs have successfully empowered local communities in rural areas, where tourism revenue directly supports community development projects such as education and healthcare.

- Tourism regulations can help preserve the cultural integrity and heritage of a destination by setting clear boundaries for tourism development. Policies can regulate the commercialization of cultural practices, prevent over-tourism in heritage sites, and encourage the protection of traditional practices. Gingee and Devagiri, have introduced visitor caps and ticketing systems to prevent over-tourism and preserve its cultural and archaeological significance.

Challenges of Policy and Regulatory Frameworks

- Emerging destinations often face challenges with weak governance structures and insufficient enforcement of regulations. Corruption, inadequate resources, and lack of institutional capacity can undermine policy implementation, leading to poor management of tourism resources. In regions where local authorities lack the means to enforce policies effectively, regulations may not be adhered to, resulting in environmental degradation, illegal tourism practices, and uneven economic benefits.

- Tourism can be an essential economic driver, but over tourism remains a significant challenge in emerging destinations that lack adequate regulatory frameworks. Balancing the economic benefits of tourism with the need for conservation and community welfare is a complex task. Regulatory frameworks need to evolve to address these challenges, which may involve implementing new measures like dynamic pricing, visitor quotas, and zoning to limit tourism pressure in sensitive areas.

- The tourism industry often involves multiple stakeholders, including national and local governments, private businesses, and communities. Fragmented policies and lack of coordination between these stakeholders can lead to inconsistent regulations, misaligned goals, and missed opportunities for integrated tourism management. Effective tourism management requires harmonizing policies across different sectors environmental protection, infrastructure development, and cultural heritage to create a cohesive approach.

- The industry may face pressure from external stakeholders, such as multinational tourism corporations or international organizations, which may prioritize growth over cultural preservation. Creating policies that balance the needs of global tourism players with the preservation of local culture and traditions is a delicate challenge. Andaman and Nicobar Islands faced challenges from both local communities and large-scale tourism operators over issues like resource allocation and cultural authenticity.

Future Directions and Prospects

As tourism continues to evolve globally, it faces both challenges and opportunities in shaping the future of its tourism sectors. The evolving landscape presents new ways to manage tourism sustainably while maximizing its economic, social, and environmental benefits. Future tourism management in these regions will likely focus on innovation, sustainability, and resilience, but also confront persistent issues like over-tourism and resource depletion.

- **Sustainable and Resilient Tourism Models**

The demand for sustainable tourism is expected to grow, with tourists becoming increasingly aware of their environmental impact. Will need to prioritize eco-friendly infrastructure, waste management, and conservation to mitigate tourism's ecological footprint. Circular economy models, where tourism businesses recycle resources, reuse materials, and minimize waste, are likely to gain traction. In addition, resilience planning will be a key focus, with destinations developing strategies to adapt to the impacts of climate change, natural disasters, and economic volatility. Opportunity can capitalize on the growing eco-tourism trend by developing more nature-based tourism experiences that focus on conservation and community benefits. This could include promoting biodiversity preservation, marine conservation, and agro-tourism. The growing popularity of sustainable resorts and eco-lodges provides an opportunity to attract high-value tourists who prioritize environmental consciousness.

➢ **Digital Transformation and Smart Tourism**

Technology will continue to shape the future of tourism management. Smart tourism powered by IoT, AI, and data analytics will enable real-time monitoring and management of visitor numbers, ensuring that destinations can mitigate issues like over-tourism and resource strain. Virtual reality (VR) and augmented reality (AR) will enhance the visitor experience by offering immersive and educational tours. Blockchain could revolutionize booking systems, ensuring transparency and trust, particularly in destinations with complex regulatory environments. Opportunities can harness these technological innovations to improve visitor experiences, streamline operations, and ensure efficient resource management. Digital platforms will also open up new markets, making it easier for destinations to reach niche tourism sectors like wellness, adventure, or cultural tourism. By investing in digital infrastructure, emerging destinations can position themselves as forward-thinking and attractive to tech-savvy tourists.

➢ **Community Empowerment and Inclusive Tourism**

Future tourism management will emphasize inclusive and community-based tourism. Policies and practices will aim to distribute the benefits of tourism more equitably across local populations, ensuring that marginalized communities have a stake in tourism development. Local ownership and the active participation of communities in tourism decision-making will be central to creating a more sustainable and socially responsible tourism model. Opportunists can invest in capacity-building programs to train local communities in hospitality, guiding, and entrepreneurship, thus enabling them to create their tourism-related businesses. The growth of community-based tourism will empower local populations and ensure that tourism benefits are shared fairly, especially in rural or off-the-beaten-path areas.

- **Integration of Cultural and Heritage Preservation**

As tourism grows, the preservation of local cultures and heritage will be even more critical. Industry will increasingly need to integrate cultural conservation into their tourism strategies, balancing the needs of tourists with the preservation of cultural identity. New models of cultural tourism, where heritage is shared responsibly, will allow local traditions to thrive without exploitation or commodification. Opportunity can use tourism as a tool for cultural revitalization. By promoting indigenous crafts, traditional performances, and heritage sites, destinations can create immersive experiences that highlight their unique cultural narratives. This approach can also help to preserve intangible cultural heritage while generating economic benefits for local communities.

- **Managing Over Tourism through Policy Innovation**

Over-tourism remains a persistent challenge, particularly in high-demand destinations will need to adopt more dynamic and flexible regulatory policies that address peak-season pressures and overcrowding. Visitor caps, staggered entry times, dispersal strategies, and sustainable transport solutions will become essential tools for managing visitor flows effectively. Innovative policy solutions that balance growth and conservation could position emerging destinations as models for responsible tourism. Implementing tourist quotas or charging entry fees to high-demand areas could help manage visitor numbers while generating revenue for conservation. This could also encourage a shift towards year-round tourism rather than peak-season congestion, benefiting both the tourism industry and local communities. The future of tourism management in embracing sustainability, technological innovation, community empowerment, and cultural preservation. By prioritizing these factors, emerging destinations can overcome current challenges and unlock opportunities for long-term, resilient growth. The key to success will be developing integrated, flexible strategies that address both local needs and global trends, ensuring that tourism benefits all stakeholders and minimizes its negative impacts on the environment and society.

Conclusion

Tourism management in emerging destinations is both an exciting and complex endeavour. As these regions develop their tourism industries, they face a unique set of challenges that require thoughtful strategies and innovative solutions. Balancing economic growth, environmental sustainability, social equity, and cultural preservation is critical to ensuring that tourism benefits both visitors and host communities in the long term. The opportunities are abundant, with tourism acting as a significant economic driver that can create jobs, generate revenue, and spur infrastructure development. Industry can leverage their unique natural, cultural, and historical assets to attract tourists while preserving these resources for future generations.

Sustainable tourism practices, such as eco-tourism and community-based tourism, offer promising avenues for growth without sacrificing environmental integrity or cultural authenticity. By investing in smart tourism technologies, destinations can enhance the visitor experience, improve resource management, and reduce overcrowding, while ensuring that the benefits of tourism are more widely distributed. The challenges are substantial over-tourism, environmental degradation, and social inequality are among the most pressing concerns. Many emerging destinations lack the necessary infrastructure, regulatory frameworks, and governance structures to effectively manage the pressures of increasing tourist numbers. The risk of cultural erosion and economic dependency on tourism further complicates the task. Weak enforcement of policies, limited local involvement in decision-making, and insufficient investment in capacity building often undermine the positive potential of tourism. To address these challenges, emerging destinations must adopt integrated, sustainable tourism management strategies that involve all stakeholders' governments, local communities, the private sector, and tourists themselves. The key lies in striking a balance between growth and sustainability, ensuring that tourism supports long-term development without compromising the destination's cultural, environmental, and social values. By learning from best practices, embracing technological innovations, and fostering inclusivity, emerging destinations can unlock the full potential of tourism while safeguarding their unique assets for future generations. Tourism management is a dynamic field with vast potential, but it requires careful planning, robust policies, and a shared commitment to sustainability to ensure that the opportunities outweigh the challenges.

TOURISM AS A BUSINESS

Mrs. Sinduja Palaniappan
Assistant Manager
8 ball contractors, Chennai

Introduction

Tourism, often called the world's largest industry, has an immense global presence. It impacts almost every country, supports millions of jobs, and plays a central role in local and national economies. The industry includes everything from the transportation of travellers, accommodation, food services, entertainment, and cultural experiences. As a business, tourism is uniquely complex, as it involves several sectors and is influenced by a broad range of factors like economic conditions, technology, customer preferences, and government policies. This chapter explores tourism as a business, delving into its economic impact, key business models, market segments, marketing strategies, challenges, and opportunities.

Tourism is deeply integrated into nearly every industry, creating a broad and interconnected economic ecosystem. Its impact stretches beyond traditional sectors like travel and hospitality, influencing industries such as transportation, retail, food and beverage, entertainment, healthcare, and technology. Airlines, car rentals, and rail services thrive on tourism demand, while local retailers, restaurants, and attractions benefit from the influx of visitors. Even sectors like construction and real estate are influenced by tourism, as the need for hotels, resorts, and vacation homes grows.

Furthermore, tourism drives advancements in technology through the development of booking platforms, mobile apps, and digital marketing tools. The widespread influence of tourism fosters growth and innovation across diverse industries, highlighting its role as a major economic driver in the global marketplace. Tourism as a business has evolved significantly over the centuries, with its roots traceable to ancient civilizations. In ancient Greece and Rome, travel for leisure, religious pilgrimages, and trade were common, though the infrastructure to support tourism as we know it today was not yet in place.

The concept of tourism began to take a more recognizable form during the Grand Tour of the 17th and 18th centuries, when young Europeans, particularly from the upper classes, travelled across Europe to explore cultural landmarks and refine their education. This early form of tourism was largely a privilege of the wealthy and was supported by emerging travel services like inns and coaches.

In the 19th century, with the advent of the Industrial Revolution and the rise of steamships and railways, travel became more accessible to the general population. The establishment of rail networks, such as the British Great Western Railway, opened up new tourist destinations and made travel faster and more affordable. In the mid-20th century, the mass production of automobiles and the growth of air travel transformed tourism into a global industry. International travel became increasingly popular, and major companies like Thomas Cook and TUI began organizing package tours, making travel more affordable and convenient for a broader audience.

By the late 20th and early 21st centuries, the digital age further revolutionized tourism, with online booking platforms, digital marketing, and social media playing key roles in expanding the tourism business globally. Today, tourism is a multibillion-dollar global industry, integral to economies worldwide and deeply embedded in virtually every sector. Its historical development highlights a gradual transformation from exclusive travel to a widespread, accessible, and essential part of modern life.

The Economic Significance of Tourism

Tourism has long been recognized as a major contributor to global economic development. According to the World Travel & Tourism Council (WTTC), tourism accounts for a significant portion of global GDP, supporting millions of jobs in various sectors like transport, hospitality, and entertainment. Understanding the economic significance of tourism involves evaluating its direct, indirect, and induced impacts.

1. **Direct Economic Impact**

The direct impact of tourism refers to the revenue generated by businesses directly serving tourists, such as hotels, airlines, tour operators, and restaurants. Every time a tourist spends money on travel-related services, it contributes directly to the economy of the destination.

2. **Indirect Economic Impact**

Indirect impacts arise when the money spent by tourists filters through the local economy. For example, a hotel's purchases of food, beverages, and cleaning services support local suppliers, contributing to the broader economic activity.

3. **Induced Economic Impact**

Induced impact occurs when employees within the tourism sector spend their earnings on local goods and services. This creates further economic activity and contributes to the general economic wellbeing of the region.

4. **Global Impact**

Globally, tourism drives infrastructure development, increases global trade and investment, and enhances a country's image on the international stage. As one of the largest foreign exchange earners, tourism is also crucial in stabilizing national economies.

Business Models in the Tourism Industry

The tourism industry is composed of a variety of business models, each serving a different segment of the market. Understanding these models helps tourism entrepreneurs and stakeholders navigate the complexities of this vast sector.

1 Tour Operators

Tour operators bundle services such as transportation, accommodation, and activities into packages and sell them to tourists. They often work with hotels, airlines, and service providers to negotiate bulk rates, making it easier for travellers to book vacations.

2 Accommodation Providers

Accommodation businesses are integral to the tourism sector, including hotels, resorts, hostels, vacation rentals, and bed-and-breakfast establishments. These businesses must cater to various consumer preferences and price points while ensuring a high level of customer service.

Hospitality and tourism are inherently linked, with hospitality acting as the foundation of the traveller's experience. The hospitality industry includes services such as accommodation, food and beverage, transportation, and leisure activities, all of which are essential to the tourism sector. Whether it's a hotel providing a restful stay, a restaurant offering local cuisine, or a tour company organizing excursions, the quality of hospitality directly influences the success of a destination in attracting and retaining tourists. Tourism generates demand for these services, and in return, the hospitality sector contributes to a positive travel experience, creating lasting impressions. Together, hospitality and tourism form a symbiotic relationship that not only enhances the traveller's journey but also drives significant economic benefits, supporting local businesses and communities worldwide.

3 Transportation Providers

Airlines, trains, cruise ships, and bus companies are responsible for moving tourists from one place to another. The transportation sector is highly competitive, and businesses must focus on operational efficiency, customer service, and pricing strategies to succeed.

Transportation and tourism are closely linked, with transportation serving as the critical means for travellers to reach and explore destinations. Whether through air, rail, road, or sea, transportation makes it possible for tourists to move from one location to another, enabling the flow of visitors to diverse regions. The development of efficient, affordable, and accessible transport systems plays a vital role in shaping travel patterns, influencing both domestic and international tourism. Airlines, trains, buses, and car rentals are just a few examples of how transportation supports the tourism industry. In turn, the demand generated by tourism encourages continuous innovation in transportation, improving service quality and increasing connectivity. This relationship creates a mutually beneficial cycle where enhanced transportation options make travel more convenient, and higher demand for travel services drives further improvements in transportation infrastructure.

4 Online Travel Agencies (OTAs)

OTAs like Expedia, Booking.com, and Airbnb have transformed the tourism industry by offering platforms where travellers can easily compare prices, read reviews, and book services like flights, accommodations, and excursions. These businesses use cutting-edge technology to provide convenience and attract a global customer base.

Local travel agencies play a crucial role in the tourism industry by offering personalized services that cater to the unique needs and preferences of travellers. Unlike larger global agencies, local travel agencies have a deep understanding of their region's culture, attractions, and hidden gems, allowing them to provide customized itineraries that enhance the travel experience. They offer expert advice on local accommodations, transportation, and activities, ensuring that travellers make the most of their visit. Additionally, local agencies can offer more flexible and intimate travel experiences, which are often tailored to specific interests such as adventure tourism, cultural exploration, or culinary experiences. By supporting local businesses and promoting regional tourism, these agencies also contribute to the local economy. Furthermore, their ability to offer personalized, hands-on customer service creates stronger relationships with travellers, fostering loyalty and positive word-of-mouth that benefits both the agency and the destination.

5 Destination Management Companies (DMCs)

DMCs focus on providing in-destination services, such as guided tours, event planning, and transportation. They collaborate with local service providers to enhance the travel experience and often work closely with other tourism businesses, like hotels and tour operators, to deliver seamless services.

6 Attraction and Entertainment Providers

This segment includes theme parks, museums, galleries, sports events, and concerts. These businesses are essential for diversifying the tourist experience and creating memorable moments for travellers. Successful attractions invest in unique offerings and high-quality customer experiences to attract repeat visitors.

Market Segmentation in Tourism

Understanding market segmentation is crucial for tourism businesses that aim to tailor their services to specific customer groups. Different tourists have distinct motivations, needs, and behaviors, and businesses must adapt to these segments to remain competitive.

1 Leisure Tourism

Leisure tourism involves travel for relaxation, recreation, or cultural experiences. Family holidays, honeymoon packages, and beach vacations fall under this category. To succeed in this segment, businesses must focus on comfort, value for money, and personalized experiences that meet the needs of leisure travellers.

2 Business Tourism

Business tourism is focused on corporate travel for meetings, conferences, and trade shows. Business tourists prioritize convenience, efficiency, and technology, making it crucial for hotels, airlines, and transport companies to offer flexible services like early check-ins, fast internet, and conference facilities.

3 Medical and Wellness Tourism

Travellers in this segment seek medical procedures, wellness treatments, or spa experiences. With increasing demand for healthcare tourism, businesses in this space must maintain high standards of safety, professionalism, and quality while ensuring the privacy and comfort of their clients.

4 Adventure Tourism

Adventure tourism includes activities such as hiking, mountain climbing, scuba diving, and safaris. Tour operators and local guides specializing in this niche must ensure safety, provide expert guidance, and create thrilling experiences that align with the target audience's adventurous spirit.

5 Cultural and Heritage Tourism

Cultural tourism attracts visitors who want to explore a destination's heritage, history, art, and traditions. Museums, historic landmarks, and cultural festivals are key attractions in this segment. Tourism businesses must collaborate with local communities to preserve and promote cultural assets.

6 Eco-Tourism

Eco-tourism appeals to travellers who seek to experience nature while minimizing their environmental footprint. It includes activities like wildlife watching, nature hikes, and visiting eco-friendly accommodations. Sustainability practices are paramount in this segment, as tourists are increasingly aware of environmental concerns.

Marketing Strategies for Tourism Businesses

In the competitive world of tourism, businesses need effective marketing strategies to stand out and capture the attention of travellers. Marketing in tourism requires a deep understanding of the customer journey, branding, and the use of digital tools.

1. Digital Marketing and Online Presence

Digital marketing is the cornerstone of tourism business strategies. With a significant portion of travellers researching and booking online, having a well-optimized website, active social media presence, and engaging content is essential. Search Engine Optimization (SEO) and content marketing help businesses rank high in search results, attracting more traffic.

2. Branding

Branding in tourism involves creating a distinct identity for a destination or service provider. The branding process includes developing a unique value proposition, maintaining consistency across platforms, and fostering emotional connections with travellers. A strong brand identity is especially important for destinations aiming to become iconic.

3. Partnerships and Collaborations

Collaborations between tourism businesses, local governments, and international organizations can enhance visibility and extend market reach. For instance, destination marketing organizations (DMOs) work with travel agencies, airlines, and hotels to create joint promotional campaigns.

4. Customer Relationship Management (CRM)

Tourism businesses can use CRM systems to track customer preferences, purchasing behavior, and interactions with the company. This information can be leveraged to provide personalized experiences, build customer loyalty, and increase repeat business.

5. Influencer and Social Media Marketing

Social media influencers play a significant role in shaping travel decisions. Tourism businesses often collaborate with influencers to reach a broader audience and increase brand awareness. Additionally, user-generated content, such as reviews and travel blog, also influences decisions and builds credibility.

Challenges Facing the Tourism Industry

While tourism presents immense opportunities, it also comes with various challenges that businesses must navigate to stay profitable.

1) Seasonality

Tourism is often seasonal, with peak seasons during holidays or specific times of the year, and off-seasons when demand drops. Managing staffing, inventory, and pricing during off-peak periods requires strategic planning to maintain profitability.

2) Environmental Impact and Sustainability

As awareness of climate change and environmental degradation grows, there is increasing pressure on the tourism sector to adopt sustainable practices. This includes reducing waste, minimizing energy consumption, and preserving natural resources.

3) Competition

With the growth of online platforms and global travel networks, competition within the tourism industry is fierce. Businesses must continually innovate, improve customer service, and offer unique experiences to differentiate themselves from their competitors.

4) Economic and Political Instability

The tourism industry is highly sensitive to global events such as economic downturns, political instability, and natural disasters. Events like the COVID-19 pandemic have shown how quickly tourism demand can drop due to unforeseen global crises.

5) Cultural Sensitivity and Ethical Issues

Businesses in tourism must be culturally sensitive and ethically responsible. This means respecting local customs, supporting fair wages for workers, and promoting inclusivity and diversity in their services.

Global travel software companies are crucial players in the tourism and travel industries, providing innovative solutions that streamline operations, enhance customer experiences, and drive efficiencies in travel management, booking, and logistics. These companies leverage advanced technologies like artificial intelligence, machine learning, and big data to offer personalized travel experiences, dynamic pricing, and real-time analytics.

Here's an overview of some leading global travel software companies and their worth:

1. Amadeus IT Group

Overview: Amadeus is one of the largest global travel technology companies, offering solutions for airlines, hotels, travel agencies, and other segments of the travel industry. It provides tools for booking management, revenue management, inventory management, and more.

Worth: As of 2024, Amadeus has an estimated market capitalization of around **€20 billion** (approximately **$21.5 billion**). The company has a strong presence in over 190 countries, with a dominant share in the airline reservation systems market.

2. Sabre Corporation

Overview: Sabre is a leading provider of software and technology solutions to the global travel industry. Its products include reservations, distribution systems, and travel data management tools used by airlines, hotels, and travel agencies.

Worth: Sabre Corporation's market capitalization is around **$5 billion** (as of 2024). It provides services to a vast network of customers in more than 160 countries, making it a major player in the global travel technology sector.

3. Travelport

Overview: Travelport offers global distribution systems (GDS), which connect travel agents with services from airlines, hotels, car rentals, and other travel providers. The company also provides digital platforms for the management of bookings, payments, and travel content.

Worth: Travelport's market value fluctuates around **$2 billion** (as of 2024). The company continues to innovate with new digital and mobile solutions, and is focused on improving the travel ecosystem through its partnerships and technology.

4. Expedia Group

Overview: While primarily known as a major online travel agency, Expedia Group also owns a wide range of travel technology solutions, including tools for booking flights, hotels, car rentals, and vacation packages. They operate platforms such as Hotels.com, Trivago, and Orbitz, alongside their core Expedia service.

Worth: Expedia Group's market capitalization is approximately **$17 billion** (as of 2024). The company is a major force in online travel distribution and continues to expand its software services for both consumers and travel professionals.

5. Booking Holdings (formerly Priceline Group)

Overview: Booking Holdings owns a range of travel-related brands, including Booking.com, Kayak, and Agoda, and provides comprehensive travel solutions, including hotel bookings, car rentals, and flight reservations. The company offers advanced software for both consumers and travel industry professionals.

Worth: As of 2024, Booking Holdings has a market value of approximately **$85 billion**. It is one of the largest online travel companies globally, providing a significant share of the travel tech ecosystem with a focus on both business and leisure markets.

6. Airbnb

Overview: While primarily a platform for short-term rentals, Airbnb has evolved to offer an extensive suite of travel-related software tools, including dynamic pricing for hosts, integrated payment systems, and experience booking. The company has revolutionized the accommodation sector with a peer-to-peer model.

Worth: Airbnb's market capitalization is approximately **$78 billion** (as of 2024). Its innovative approach to booking and customer engagement continues to disrupt the global travel and hospitality industries.

7. Hotelogix

Overview: Hotelogix provides cloud-based property management software for hotels, motels, and resorts. The platform includes tools for reservations, front desk management, guest management, and reporting. Hotelogix aims to simplify operations for small and mid-sized hotels.

Worth: While specific market capitalization figures are not publicly available for private companies like Hotelogix, estimates suggest its valuation is in the range of **$50-$100 million**. The company has a growing customer base in over 100 countries.

8. Tramada Systems

Overview: Tramada Systems provides integrated travel management software solutions, including booking, reporting, and data analytics tools. The company primarily serves travel agencies, corporations, and other travel service providers, with a focus on automating the travel process.

Worth: Tramada's market valuation is not publicly disclosed, but as a niche provider, it is estimated to be valued at around **$20 million** to **$50 million**. Its software serves a wide range of corporate clients.

9. GetYourGuide

Overview: GetYourGuide is an online platform for booking travel experiences, including tours, activities, and attractions. Their software provides services for customers to book and manage their travel experiences directly, as well as offer booking management for operators.

Worth: GetYourGuide has been valued at approximately **$2 billion** in recent funding rounds (2024). The platform has grown rapidly and is now one of the leading players in the travel experiences and tours market.

10. FareHarbor

Overview: FareHarbor is a booking and management software solution for tour operators and activity providers. The platform allows businesses to manage bookings, payments, and customer communications, making it easier for operators to handle bookings at scale.

Worth: FareHarbor was acquired by **Booking Holdings** in 2018, but its value at the time was estimated to be around **$250 million**. It continues to operate under Booking Holdings' umbrella and contributes to its growing experience-based platform.

Conclusion

The global travel software industry is a dynamic and highly competitive market with significant players offering a range of products to streamline operations across the travel value chain. From flight and hotel bookings to tour management and customer service platforms, these companies provide innovative solutions that help improve efficiencies and enhance customer experiences. Companies like Amadeus, Sabre, Expedia, and Booking Holdings lead the market, but a diverse array of smaller players also contributes to the evolving landscape, particularly in niche sectors like travel experiences and property management. With the ongoing growth in global travel and technological advancements, these companies are expected to continue to thrive and expand their influence in the years to come.

Tourism is a dynamic and multifaceted industry that offers vast business opportunities across a variety of sectors. From accommodation and transport to niche experiences like eco-tourism and adventure travel, businesses must understand market demands, develop effective marketing strategies, and address key challenges such as seasonality and sustainability. As the industry continues to evolve, tourism businesses that prioritize innovation, customer experience, and environmental responsibility.

TOURISM PRODUCT

Ms. A. Karoliya Jansirani
Assistant Professor
Department of History
Loyola College
Chennai-34

Introduction

A tourism product refers to any offering that meets the needs of tourists. In a broader context, a product can encompass an object, location, activity, event, organisation, or individual that fulfils the desires of a person. It can be viewed as a composite entity, representing the collective array of a nation's tourist attractions, transportation options, accommodations, and entertainment, all contributing to the overall satisfaction of tourists. Travel can be motivated by numerous factors such as pleasure and recreation, health considerations, educational objectives, business purposes, religious activities, special interests, and visiting friends and family. Therefore, a tourism product is an amalgamation of several components and services. These may include festivals, wildlife attractions, beach outings, yoga practices, spa experiences, adventure sports, conventions and conferences, shopping venues, and the purchase of souvenirs.

A tourism product is defined as one that meets the psychological and physiological needs of tourists during their entire journey away from their usual residence. The requirements of individuals can vary significantly, as can the motivators that influence their decision to embark on a holiday. Different travel motivators give rise to a variety of tourism products, including those focused on natural beauty, infrastructure, and cultural attractions.

Definitions

According to the definition provided by the UNWTO, a tourism product consists of a blend of tangible and intangible factors, which encompass natural, cultural, and constructed resources, along with attractions, facilities, services, and activities that revolve around a specific focal point of interest. This combination forms the foundation of the destination marketing mix and contributes to the overall experience of visitors, encompassing emotional dimensions for prospective customers. Moreover, a tourism product is priced and distributed through various channels and is subject to a life cycle.

Suwantoro (1997) defines a tourism product encompasses the entirety of services that tourists experience and appreciate, beginning from their departure from home to their chosen destination and concluding upon their return.

According to Roger Dosewell (1997), a distinguished expert in tourism product development, "Tourism products at a destination consist of all attractions, amenities, and services that are engaged with or visited throughout a visitor's stay. Additionally, it encompasses every event and experience that visitors encounter."

Factors influencing the Tourism Products

The various factors play a significant role in determining tourism products. In a competitive setting, operators are obligated to develop a diverse range of offerings that reflect consumer needs. These factors can be classified as either external influences on the tourism industry or internal dynamics.

External factors

External factors impacting the tourism industry encompass the environmental, economic, and societal contexts in which it functions. Variations in cultural and environmental aspects, demographic shifts, and the forces of globalization significantly shape tourist preferences. Consequently, service providers adapt to these changes by developing new offerings. Additionally, advancements in technology, fluctuations in the economic landscape, political developments, and regulatory changes exert a profound influence on the industry. Therefore, these external elements play a crucial role in determining the quality of tourism products and services, prompting the creation of innovative offerings that enhance tourist satisfaction and help sustain market share.

Internal factors

In recent years, there has been a significant transformation in tourists' perceptions and motivations. The traditional appeal of modern cities, luxury hotels, amusement parks, and well-known beach resorts is undergoing a notable shift. Tourists are no longer confined to stereotypes; instead, they seek opportunities to bask in the sun, explore less polluted environments, engage in adventure sports, connect with local communities, and practice yoga and meditation. An increasing awareness of health, environmental issues, and contemporary tourism has fostered the development of natural and picturesque destinations that support conservation efforts.

The focus of tourism has transitioned from built heritage to nature-based experiences. Planners are now prioritising community involvement and equitable distribution of investments and benefits to enhance the economic impact of tourism.

Additionally, rising concerns regarding safety due to terrorism and natural disasters have heightened the need for secure travel experiences. The advancement of the Internet, along with new technologies and the influence of multinational corporations, continues to play a crucial role in shaping the diverse tourism offerings of the future.

Table.1 Factors Influencing Tourism Products

External Factors	Internal Factors
Socio-cultural and environmental change	Change in taste and preferences
Demographic change	Sustainability approach
Globalization	Ethical issues
Transportation	Technological Change
Change in technology and economic environment	Health, Safety and security issues
Change in political scenario	Quality issues
Change in Government regulation	Competition in the market

Unique Characteristics of Tourism Products

The tourism industry operates by offering products for sale. However, it is important to note that the products created within this sector possess unique qualities and attributes that set them apart from those in other industries. Although the tourism industry generates products that hold economic significance, its operations diverge from those of traditional industries for several reasons. These distinctions arise from specific characteristics inherent to the tourism sector. This discussion will explore these characteristics, supported by relevant examples. The unique characteristics of Tourism Products are as follows:

1. Intangibility

The primary characteristic of tourism products is their intangible nature, as they cannot be physically touched or held. These products are meant to be experienced rather than interacted with in a physical sense. When planning a trip, individuals often envision the experiences that await them at their destination. It is only upon arrival that they can truly gauge their satisfaction and the value of their expenditure. For example, a tourist in Darjeeling can appreciate the region's stunning natural beauty and the inviting atmosphere of their accommodations, both of which are intangible experiences.

Tourism products often encompass both tangible and intangible elements. For example, upon checking into a hotel at a particular destination, the hotel room represents a tangible aspect, as it can be physically seen and touched, along with the amenities provided. Conversely, the services associated with the room, such as laundry, food and beverage, and front office assistance, are intangible, as they cannot be physically perceived. Additionally, souvenirs purchased by tourists exemplify tourism products that possess a tangible form.

2. Heterogeneity

Tourism products exhibit heterogeneity due to the nature of the service industry, where human interaction is fundamental. In this field, services are provided by people to people, making it challenging to achieve uniformity in service delivery. Therefore, purchasing a tourism product does not assure a uniform experience or benefit, as the same offering can evoke different responses from various individuals in distinct situations. The perception of quality in tourism products varies among individuals; for example, a waiter may exhibit different behaviors and levels of service on different occasions, highlighting the significant role of the human factor in tourism-related services.

3. Perishability

One of the most significant attributes of a tourism product is its perishability. Unlike other consumer goods, tourism products cannot be stored for extended periods, making them highly perishable commodities. If not consumed within a specific timeframe, a tourism product effectively ceases to exist. For example, an unsold airline ticket or a vacant hotel room cannot be preserved for future sale. If an airline ticket remains unsold before the aircraft departs, the opportunity for revenue is lost. The tourism industry is heavily influenced by seasonal variations, and as a result of this perishability, both the accommodation and transportation sectors often offer significant discounts during these off-peak periods.

4. Inseparability

In the field of tourism, products cannot be stored for future use or moved to different locations for consumption, as their production and consumption occur simultaneously. For instance, when one purchases a television, they typically go to a store, buy the item, and take it home. In the modern era, such products can be ordered online and delivered, which creates a separation from their sellers. However, tourism products require individuals to be physically present at the destination to experience them, rendering them inseparable from their providers. The production and consumption of tourism services can only take place when the tourist is situated at a specific location and time. Furthermore, tourism is heavily influenced by seasonal trends, resulting in significant discounts in the accommodation and transportation sectors during off-peak seasons due to their perishable characteristics.

5. Ownership

In the context of tourism products, the transfer of ownership does not occur as it does with other consumer goods. For example, when a person buys a car, the ownership title is automatically assigned to them. However, in the case of tourism products and services, individuals pay for the opportunity to use these offerings without ever becoming their owners. For instance, while one pays for accommodation at a hotel, they do not gain ownership of the establishment. Similarly, purchasing a ticket for air travel allows access to a seat, but does not result in ownership of that seat. Therefore, the non-transfer of ownership in these services only grants the right to use them for a limited time.

6. Fluctuation in demand

The tourism sector is significantly influenced by seasonal variations, leading to fluctuations in the demand for tourism-related products. For example, hotels in Rajasthan, India experience peak demand during the winter months, specifically from September to February, while the summer months, from April to July, are generally avoided by tourists due to the extreme heat. Additionally, the demand for tourism products is susceptible to various external factors, including global economic conditions and the political climate within the country. A notable instance of this occurred during the global economic crisis of 2008-09, when the tourism industry in India faced substantial challenges, resulting in a marked decline in tourist activity.

7. Composite in nature

The concept of a tourism product encompasses a variety of components that are combined to deliver a comprehensive experience for visitors. Unlike standard products, which are entirely produced by a manufacturer for consumer use, the tourism industry presents a product that consists of several interrelated services provided over a specific timeframe. For instance, in a holiday package, transportation is offered by airlines, accommodation is provided by hotels, various attractions and entertainment services are included, insurance companies supply travel insurance, and restaurants cater to the dining needs of tourists. In addition to these elements, tourists also engage with the infrastructure, security, and other amenities available at the destination, all of which together create a complete tourism product. Thus, the tourism product can be understood as a fusion of various interrelated offerings that are consumed in unison as a cohesive experience.

8. Dominant role of intermediaries

Intermediaries, such as travel agents and tour operators, are pivotal in the tourism industry. The tourism product comprises various interconnected elements, which can make it a daunting task for tourists to assemble their travel arrangements. Consequently, intermediaries like travel agents, tour operators, and reservation agents play a significant role in the provision of tourism products. Their importance in the tourism value chain is twofold: they provide essential information and serve as a bridge between the primary service providers and the tourists.

9. Complexity in marketing

As the tourism product is articulated through words and figures, it demands substantial effort to convince potential buyers, rendering the demonstration of such products a complex task.

Types of Tourism Products

Tourism products serve as crucial attractions for any tourist destination. The variety of these products draws a significant number of visitors to the location. Establishing a detailed inventory of tourism products is a critical step in ensuring they are marketed to the right tourists. Let us discuss about the various types of tourism products.

- Natural Tourism Products
- Man-made Tourism Products
- Symbiotic Tourism Products

- Site based Tourism Products
- Event based tourism Products

Natural Tourism Products

The term "natural tourism products" encompasses those experiences and attractions that are derived from nature's resources. These products are fundamentally connected to the natural environment and typically feature attractions that serve as significant motivators for visitors to travel to specific locations. The beauty of these natural landscapes has historically attracted humanity. Iconic examples include the towering Himalayas in the North, the serene beaches of the South, and the expansive deserts of Rajasthan, all of which have consistently enchanted tourists from various parts of the world.

Scenic attractions, Mountains, Land forms, Glaciers, Climate, Caves, Deserts, beaches, Rivers, Lakes, Waterfalls, Springs, Islands, Wildlife, Forests, Flora and fauna

Table.2 India is endowed with immense natural resources with examples

Natural Tourism Products	Examples
Scenic attractions	Natural Scenery- Manali
Mountains	Ooty, Kodaikanal, Wayanad, Darjeeling, Shillong
Deserts	Desert Triangle of India- Jodhpur, Jaisalmer- Bikaner
Beaches	Marina Beach- Chennai, Kovalam Beach-Thiruvananthapuram, Cherai Beach- Kochi, Calangute Beach-Goa
Lakes	Pulicat, Dal, Hussain Sagar, Sambhar salt
Waterfalls	Dudhsagar fall -Goa, Hogenakkal Water Falls
Islands	Andaman & Nicobar and Lakshadweep Islands

Flora and fauna	Kaziranga National Park- Assam
Wildlife	Gorumara Wildlife Sanctuary- West Bengal
Forests	Tropical evergreen rain forests- Andaman

Man-made Tourism Products

Manmade tourism offerings are designed and developed by humans to cater to the leisure, enjoyment, or business demands of tourists. These offerings can take the form of museums, casinos, and theme parks. It is important to note that some manmade attractions, such as forts, palaces, and temples, were not specifically created to draw tourists. The customs and traditions inherent to a destination also constitute manmade attractions, including folk and classical dances, music, handicrafts, and numerous fairs and festivals. Furthermore, conventions and conferences are illustrative of manmade products that fulfil the professional needs of tourists.

Monuments, Museums, Gardens, Zoos, Fair and Festivals, Music, Dance, Handicrafts, Paintings, and Theme Parks.

Table.3 Man-Made Tourism Products with examples

Man-Made Tourism Products	**Examples**
Monuments	Great Bath, Mound, Granary, Taj Mahal, Red Fort, Humayun's Tomb, Sanchi Stupa, Khajuraho temples, Ajanta Caves, Konark Sun Temple, Brihadeshwara Temple, Meenakshi Temple, Bascilica of Bom Jesus, Char Minar, Mysore Palace
Museums	National Museum in Delhi, Chhatrapati Shivaji Maharaj Vastu Sangrahalaya Museum, Mumbai Rail Museum, Madras Museum, Calico Museum of Textiles in Ahmedabad, Nizam Museum in Hyderabad, Albert Hall Museum in Jaipur.

Gardens	Mughal gardens, botanical gardens, Brindavan Gardens, Pinjore Garden, Rock Garden
Zoos	Alipore Zoological Gardens, Amirthi Zoological Park, Vandalur Zoo, Assam State Zoo
Fairs and Festivals	Dusshera of Mysore, Jallikattu Bull Festival, Rajasthan Pushkar Fair, Holi of Barsana.
Music	Carnatic Music, Hindustani Music,
Dance	Bharatanatyam, Kathakali & Mohiniattam of Kerala, Kathak, Odissi, Kuchipudi, Folk Dances-Karakattam , Oyilattam, Garba, Gidda, Lavani, Teratali, Goti Pua
Paintings	Miniature, Kalamkari, Madhubani, Tanjore and Ajanta paintings

Symbiotic Tourism Products

These tourism offerings represent a remarkable integration of both natural and manmade resources. The natural environment supplies the essential resources, which are then transformed into tourism products through human management. Consequently, these offerings are referred to as the result of a symbiotic relationship between nature and humanity. In the development of these symbiotic tourism products, it is crucial to ensure that natural resources are not overexploited and are utilized within sustainable limits. Humans plays a vital role in preserving the natural beauty to the greatest extent possible.

Table 4 Symbiotic Tourism Products with examples

Symbiotic Tourism Products	**Examples**
National Parks	Jim Corbett National Park, Kaziranga National Park, Ranthambhor National Park, Kanha National Park, Gir National

	Park, Periyar National Park, Mukurthi National Park
Marine Parks	Gulf of Kutch Marine National Park, Mahatma Gandhi Marine National Park, Malvan Marine Sanctuary, Gahirmatha Marine Sanctuary, Gulf of Mannar Marine National Park, Rani Jhansi Marine National Park.
Wild life Sanctuaries	Anaimalai Wildlife Sanctuary, Chinnar Wildlife Sanctuary, Chilika Lake Bird Sanctuary

Site Based Tourism Products

A site or location that serves as an attraction is categorized as a site-based tourism product. It is clear that these sites are fundamentally permanent and cannot be wholly replaced; however, they can be modified to cater to the needs of tourists. To enhance visitor interest, new attributes are sometimes added to these tourism products like Taj Mahal, Tea Gardens in Assam, Munnar, Darjeeling, Snow Capped Himalayan Mountains and Sand Dunes, Jaisalmer.

Table 5 Site Based Tourism Products with examples

Site Based Tourism Products	Examples
Memorials	Taj Mahal, Victoria Memeorial
Tea Gardens	Assam, Munnar, Darjeeling
Sunsets	Kanyakumari, Jaisalmer, Himalayas

Event Based Tourism Products

When an event is recognized as an attraction, it invites tourists to attend either as spectators, participants, or occasionally in both roles. These events may be categorized as traditional, occasional, or promotional. An event is essentially a significant occurrence, typically planned as a public or social gathering. In the realm of event-based tourism, such attractions appeal to visitors who may choose to either observe or participate. The Kite Flying Festival in Ahmedabad exemplifies this, drawing tourists who engage in both watching and flying kites. Tourists are able to participate as spectators in major sporting events, including the Olympics, the Football World Cup, and Formula One races. Moreover, cultural festivities such as the Carnival in Rio de Janeiro and Mardi Gras in New Orleans exemplify important components of event-based tourism like Cultural/Religious Events, Sports Events, Tourism Events and Business Events.

Table.6 Event Based Tourism Products with examples

Event Based Tourism Products	Examples
Cultural/Religious Events	Holi, Barsana Dusshera, Mysore Rath Yatra, Puri Kumbha Mela, Goa Carnival, Makar Sankranti, Onam, Eid al-Fitr, Christmas, Pushkar Camel Festival.
Sports Events	Formula One Race, Indian Premier League, Kabadi Premier League
Tourism Event	Desert Festival, International Flower Festival, Taj Mahotsav, Kite Festival, Khajuraho Dance Festival, Hornbill Festival.
Business Events	International Trade Fair, New Delhi

Conclusion

A tourist destination provides a variety of tourism products, which can be categorized based on their shared characteristics. This classification aids the destination in effectively marketing its offerings to the appropriate audience. The tourism products serve as significant attractions for the destination, making it essential to preserve and safeguard these assets.

TOURISM AND SUSTAINABILITY

Ms. Surumbayee Nagaraj
Independent Researcher,
Trichy

Introduction

The 21st century has witnessed a growing focus on the importance of tourist places and their sustainability, with governments worldwide prioritizing the development and preservation of ancient, medieval, and modern monuments and sites. These tourist destinations not only contribute significantly to state economies but also provide a means for governments to reduce unemployment and fund social welfare activities. The United Nations Educational, Scientific and Cultural Organisation (UNESCO) plays a crucial role in recognizing and protecting world heritage sites, while private actors are increasingly creating new tourist attractions, promoting competition and innovation. This chapter aims to explore the concept of tourism and sustainability, examining the various types of tourist places, values of sustainability, and relevant national and international laws, with a focus on the role of sustainable development goals in tourism.

Conceptualization of Sustainability:

Sustainability is a multifaceted concept that encompasses economic, social, and environmental considerations, aiming to fulfil present needs without compromising future generations' ability to meet their own. It involves balancing economic growth, social justice, and environmental conservation, with a focus on environmental sustainability, social sustainability, and economic sustainability. The concept of sustainability is closely linked to the idea of the "triple bottom line" and resilience, and has been applied in various contexts, including business, government, and civil society. Achieving sustainability requires a deep understanding of complex relationships and interdependencies within and between systems, as well as a commitment to promoting social justice, human rights, and environmental conservation.

Typologies of Tourist Places with Various Values:

Tourism sustainability involves managing destinations to maintain ecological, cultural, historical, and social integrity. Various typologies of tourist places offer diverse values, including: Nature Places (e.g., national parks, eco-tourism sites) emphasizing ecological preservation; Historical Places (e.g., heritage monuments, archaeological sites) connecting visitors to the past; Educational Places (e.g., museums, universities) promoting learning and intellectual growth; and Cultural Places (e.g., festivals, ethnic villages, religious sites) celebrating living traditions and local lifestyles. Each typology contributes uniquely to tourism sustainability, ensuring responsible enjoyment for current and future generations.

Existing legislations and other means of strengthening sustainability in Tourism

National Legislations Related to Tourism Sustainability:

India has a robust legislative framework governing the tourism industry with a focus on sustainability. Key legislations include the Environment (Protection) Act of 1986, Wildlife (Protection) Act of 1972, and Forest (Conservation) Act of 1980, which regulate tourism activities, protect the environment, and conserve natural resources. Additionally, initiatives like the Sustainable Tourism Criteria of India (STCI) and the National Strategy for Sustainable Tourism promote sustainable tourism practices. Various states, such as Kerala, Rajasthan, and Goa, have also enacted laws and regulations to promote sustainable tourism. India's five-year plans have emphasized sustainable tourism development, with the Ministry of Tourism working towards making tourism growth sustainable.

International Legislations Related to Tourism Sustainability:

The rapid growth of the tourism industry has led to significant environmental, social, and economic impacts, highlighting the need for international legislations promoting sustainable tourism practices.

Key legislations include the United Nations World Tourism Organization (UNWTO) Global Code of Ethics for Tourism, Convention on International Trade in Endangered Species of Wild Fauna and Flora (CITES), International Union for Conservation of Nature (IUCN) guidelines for sustainable tourism, the World Heritage Convention, and International Civil Aviation Organization (ICAO) guidelines for sustainable aviation practices. These frameworks emphasize responsible tourism development, environmental protection, cultural heritage preservation, and support for local communities, with regional and national initiatives also emerging to promote sustainable tourism practices.

Measures to be taken to sustain Tourism values:

Tourism, a burgeoning economic sector, presents a paradoxical scenario, offering immense potential for economic growth, cultural exchange, and environmental protection, while also posing significant threats to the environment, cultural heritage, and local communities. To mitigate these negative impacts, it is imperative to adopt sustainable tourism practices that harmonize economic benefits with environmental conservation and cultural preservation, aligning with global development goals, such as the Millennium Development Goals and Sustainable Development Goals. By embracing strategies like eco-tourism, safeguarding cultural heritage, supporting local economies, and leveraging technology, tourism can evolve into a more responsible and sustainable industry, yielding benefits for both travellers and host destinations, while preserving the integrity of natural and cultural resources for future generations.

Tourism and Global Development Framework

Millennium Development Goals (MDGs) (United Nations, 2000) and Tourism:

The Millennium Development Goals (MDGs) (United Nations, 2000), established in 2000, aimed to address some of the world's most pressing challenges, including eradicating poverty, promoting universal education, and ensuring environmental sustainability by 2015. Although tourism was not directly highlighted in the MDG framework, its indirect contributions to poverty alleviation and economic empowerment, particularly in developing countries, were undeniable. Tourism created employment opportunities, stimulated local economies, and enhanced infrastructure in underserved regions. Additionally, the MDG period saw the emergence of eco-tourism and sustainable practices as a response to environmental degradation caused by unchecked tourism activities. These initiatives sought to balance economic growth with environmental preservation and social equity.

Sustainable Development Goals (SDGs) (United Nations, 2015) and Tourism:

The United Nations' Sustainable Development Goals (SDGs), adopted in 2015, acknowledge tourism's transformative potential, highlighting its importance in three key goals: Goal 8 (promoting sustained and inclusive economic growth), Goal 12 (adopting sustainable consumption and production patterns), and Goal 14 (conserving marine resources). Tourism is recognized as a crucial sector for driving economic progress while preserving cultural heritage and natural ecosystems, emphasizing the need for a balanced approach that integrates economic, social, and environmental priorities.

Barriers To Sustaining Tourism Values

Despite its vast potential, the tourism industry is confronted with numerous challenges that imperil its sustainability. A paramount concern is overtourism, which inundates fragile ecosystems and urban centres, precipitating severe environmental degradation. Popular destinations frequently succumb to deforestation, water pollution, and wildlife displacement due to excessive tourist activity. Another pressing issue is the commercial exploitation of cultural heritage, whereby traditions, festivals, and historical sites are commodified to satiate tourist demands, leading to the erosion of cultural authenticity and the disempowerment of local communities. Unplanned tourism development also perpetuates negative social impacts, including the displacement of indigenous populations, disruption of traditional livelihoods, and exacerbation of social inequality. Furthermore, climate change poses an existential threat to natural and cultural landmarks, with rising sea levels, extreme weather events, and desertification imperilling numerous tourist attractions worldwide.

Strategies to Sustain Tourism Values

Environmental Protection

Sustaining tourism begins with environmental preservation. Encouraging eco-tourism—which focuses on minimizing environmental impacts while benefiting local communities—is a crucial strategy. Implementing effective waste management systems in tourist hotspots ensures that waste is recycled or disposed of responsibly. Additionally, adopting renewable energy sources in tourism infrastructure, such as solar-powered hotels and electric transportation, can reduce the sector's carbon footprint. Governments must also enforce strict regulations in ecologically sensitive areas, limiting activities that could harm biodiversity.

Cultural Conservation

Preserving cultural heritage is vital for maintaining tourism values. Community-based tourism, which directly involves local populations in decision-making and revenue generation, can help safeguard traditions and foster a sense of ownership. Protecting traditional art forms, cuisines, and festivals ensures that these elements remain authentic and valued. Educating tourists on respecting local customs and practices can prevent cultural misunderstandings and foster harmonious interactions between visitors and host communities.

Economic Inclusion

Economic equity is central to sustainable tourism. Efforts should be made to ensure that local populations benefit directly through fair employment opportunities and equitable revenue sharing.

Supporting small and locally-owned businesses in the tourism sector can empower communities and reduce dependency on multinational corporations. Collaborations between public and private stakeholders can enhance tourism infrastructure, ensuring long-term benefits for both investors and local communities.

Policy Implementation and Oversight

Comprehensive policies aligned with the SDGs are essential to guide tourism development. Governments and organizations should introduce certifications for businesses that adhere to sustainability standards, encouraging the adoption of best practices. Strengthening legal frameworks to protect cultural and environmental resources can deter harmful practices and ensure compliance. Regular monitoring and evaluation of tourism policies can also help identify gaps and improve implementation.

Awareness and Capacity Building

Creating awareness about sustainable tourism is key to changing attitudes and behaviors. Awareness campaigns targeting tourists, industry stakeholders, and local communities can promote responsible tourism practices. Including topics related to sustainability in training programs and educational curricula can equip future professionals with the knowledge and skills to drive change. Additionally, leveraging digital platforms and social media can help spread awareness about ethical tourism on a global scale.

Technological Advancements Supporting Sustainability

Technology plays a pivotal role in propelling sustainable tourism, leveraging data analytics, artificial intelligence, and eco-friendly innovations to mitigate environmental pressures, manage overcrowding, and reduce ecological footprints. The tourism industry can harness virtual reality and augmented reality to offer immersive experiences, diminishing the need for physical travel and associated carbon emissions.

To unlock tourism's potential as a driver of sustainable development, concerted efforts are necessary to address environmental, social, and economic challenges. By embracing eco-friendly practices, safeguarding cultural heritage, ensuring equitable economic benefits, and harnessing technology, tourism can evolve into a transformative force for good, aligning with the Sustainable Development Goals to preserve the planet's natural and cultural treasures for future generations, and necessitating collective efforts from governments, private sectors, local communities, and travellers to ensure a harmonious coexistence of economic benefits, cultural preservation, and environmental protection.

Achievements of Sustainable Tourism

Environmental conservation:

Sustainable tourism has gone a long way in conserving natural resources through the promotion of responsible use of environmental assets. This type of tourism has contributed to the conservation of biodiversity, protection of ecosystems, and preservation of vital ecological processes. Investments and energy efficiency have reduced carbon-di-oxide emissions by 52%, water consumption by 18%, and energy use by 44% in green economy scenarios.

Economic integration and local development:

Sustainable tourism has integrated local economies by emphasizing community involvement. It is observed that local householding countries like Panama capture 56% of the income generated from tourism showing the potential of tourism to benefit local communities.

Cultural heritage preservation:

Cultural heritage is a large part of sustainable tourism. Investments, restoration and promotion of cultural and traditional assets have helped in preserving them. It has also made them profitable tourism resources. Strategies of sustainable tourism have included building tangible monuments, historical sites, and intangible traditions, languages, and cultural assets.

Standardization and awareness:

It is the global sustainable tourism criteria that are inclusively implemented to measure, implement and monitor sustainability goals. The milestone has motivated the industry to adopt energy efficiency, proper waste handling and incorporation of local culture into tourism policies.

Benefits of Sustainable Tourism:

Economic contributions:

Tourism contributes 5% to the global GDP and accounts for 8% of global employment. Sustainable tourism enhances these contributions by supporting local hirings, sourcing local products and fostering tourism activities centred around culture and nature.

Job creation:

Travel and tourism are labour-intensive industries. Sustainable tourism encourages local employment for opportunities and ecotourism, cultural tourism, and green tourism infrastructure. It also encourages interactive job creation in elite sectors such as agriculture, handicrafts, and transportation.

Cost reductions for businesses:

Sustainable practices, including energy-efficient systems and waste-reduction strategies, have reduced the operational cost of tourism businesses. In addition, these practices enhance the attractiveness of destinations, ensuring long-term profitability.

Tourist satisfaction and awareness:

Sustainable tourism provides meaningful experiences to visitors, encouraging cultural understanding and environmental awareness. Surveys have found that over a third of tourists pay for environmentally friendly travel options and are willing to pay a premium for them.

Poverty alleviation:

Sustainable tourism has been seen to be instrumental in reducing poverty by increasing local community participation in the tourism value chain. For example, rural tourism creates economic opportunities in underdeveloped areas through ecotourism and cultural tourism.

Effects of Sustainable Tourism:

Sustainable tourism has a multifaceted impact, yielding both positive and negative consequences. On the positive side, it mitigates environmental degradation through efficient resource use, reduced greenhouse gas emissions, and improved waste management, thereby conserving ecosystems and biodiversity. Additionally, sustainable tourism preserves the socio-cultural authenticity of host communities, promoting intercultural understanding and tolerance. Economically, it generates investments in infrastructure and services that benefit both tourists and local populations, such as renewable energy, public transportation systems, and local businesses. However, if not effectively managed, tourism can lead to environmental degradation, cultural disruption, and economic inequality, highlighting the need for responsible and sustainable tourism practices.

Challenges addressed:

Sustainable tourism addresses major global challenges such as climate change, overconsumption of resources, and biodiversity loss. For example, tourism's contribution to global greenhouse gas emissions, estimated at 5%, has been systematically reduced through the adoption of green practices. Sustainable tourism is the paradigm shift for mass tourism, which incorporates economic, social, and environmental goals. It serves a mind with global efforts and sustainability by promoting green investment, reducing environmental degradation, and empowering local communities.

All of the above, achievements, benefits, and impacts demonstrate that sustainable tourism is a driver toward equitable and responsible development. The case for continued investment in green tourism practices is robust, offering long-term environmental and socio-economic benefits.

Conclusion

Tourism has emerged as a pivotal driver of economic growth, cultural exchange, and environmental conservation, necessitating a profound emphasis on sustainability to preserve the natural, cultural, and historical resources that underpin this industry. Sustainable tourism strives to strike a delicate balance between economic benefits and the imperative to protect ecosystems, cultural heritage, and local communities. Legislative frameworks, such as India's Environment (Protection) Act and international agreements like the UNESCO World Heritage Convention, have made significant strides in promoting sustainable tourism practices. These efforts not only safeguard biodiversity and cultural assets but also foster responsible tourism that benefits local economies and mitigates environmental degradation.

The trajectory of sustainable tourism is contingent upon innovation, collaboration, and the adoption of holistic approaches that integrate economic, social, and environmental priorities. Strategies like eco-tourism, community-based tourism, and technological advancements in data-driven monitoring and virtual tourism offer pragmatic solutions to pressing challenges. By engaging local communities, creating employment opportunities, and promoting traditional knowledge, tourism can serve as a potent tool for empowerment and resilience. Ultimately, the sustainability of tourism hinges on collective efforts from governments, private enterprises, and tourists to preserve the integrity of tourist destinations and foster equitable benefits, ensuring that tourism continues to contribute positively to global development.

TOURISM AND HOSPITALITY

Ms. S. Gajalakshmi., M.A., M.Phil.,
Assistant Professor
Department of History and Tourism
SDNB Vaishnav College for Women,
Chromepet, Chennai - 44

Introduction

The biggest thriving tertiary business in India nowadays is tourism, which is worth billions of dollars. Tourism, which was formerly known primarily for its historical and cultural aspects, is now being highlighted for its vast financial prospects. The potential and performance of India's tourism business must be evaluated in terms of its socio-economic magnitudes due to its lucrative connections with the transportation, hotel, and other industries. One of the world's most promising travel markets is India. It has grown quickly in recent years, supported by government assistance, rising incomes, and several international sporting events. In the upcoming years, the Indian tourist sector will continue to expand at the fastest rate. This paper seeks to explain the importance and benefits of Tourism and hospitality.

Definition of Tourism

Tourism is a dynamic, evolving, consumer-driven force and is the world's largest industry, or collection of industries when all its interrelated components are placed under one umbrella: tourism, travel, assembly, destination, and event management and recreation. (John Walker, 2009).

Tourism is a social, cultural, and economic phenomenon in which people go to nations or locations outside their typical surroundings for personal, business/professional reasons.

Definition of Hospitality

The term "hospitality" comes from the Latin word "hospes," which means host, visitor, or stranger. It refers to welcoming visitors or providing a home away from home. The hospitality industry is part of a larger enterprise known as the travel and tourism industry. The travel and tourism industry is vast group of businesses with one goal in common: providing necessary or desired products and services to travellers. Hospitality can be termed as a deliberate, planned and sustained effort to establish and maintain mutual understanding between an organization and the public i.e., the business of making and keeping friends, and promoting an atmosphere of better understanding.

According to Oxford Dictionary, Hospitality is defined as Reception and entertainment of guest, visitors or strangers with liberality and goodwill. The word hospitality is derived from the Latin word *Hospitalitias*. The hospitality industry consists of broad category of fields within the service industry that includes lodging, restaurants, event planning, theme parks, transportation, cruise line, and additional fields within the tourism industry. The hospitality industry is a several billion–dollar industry that mostly depends on the availability of leisure time and disposable income.

A hospitality unit such as a restaurant, hotel or even an amusement park consists of multiple groups such as facility maintenance, direct operations (servers, housekeepers, porters, kitchen workers, bartenders, etc.), management, marketing and human resources. A wide number of businesses providing lodging and food service are included in the hospitality sector. Based on the skill sets needed for the work involved, the industry is separated into sectors. Accommodations, food and drink, events and meetings, gaming, entertainment and leisure, tourism services, and visitor information are some of the sectors. Travel for business, pleasure, or recreation is referred to as tourism. Tourists are defined by the World Tourism Organization as individuals who travel to and remain in locations outside of their normal surroundings for leisure, business, or other reasons for a maximum of one year in a row. Since tourism and hotels are two sides of the same coin, it is crucial for anyone wishing to study either of these fields to be knowledgeable about both. The tourism industry is a collection of companies that advertise travel and vacations and include travel and transportation suppliers for air, rail, cruise, and motor coach travel.

Hotels and tourism are two sides of the same coin, so it's critical for anyone interested in studying either to be knowledgeable about both. The hotel and tourism industry are introduced to you in this block. The travel and transportation sector, which includes companies that sell air, rail, cruise, and motor coach travel, is known as the tourism industry. There are five primary components to the travel and tourism industry, and each of these components has numerous subcomponents. The hospitality sector includes lodging and food and beverage businesses, as well as institutional food and beverage services that do not serve tourists. Many lodging properties provide food and beverage service, recreational activities and more.

Hotels may be classed in a variety of ways based on their size, location, customer, duration of stay, and other features. There are several reasons for categorizing the hotels. When reserving a hotel, it's important to understand its location, pricing, and facilities. A hotel may fall into one or more of the categories listed below. Hotels can be classed in the following ways.

1. Star Classification
2. Classification based on hotel location.
3. Classification according to clientele
4. Classification based on the length of the visitor stay.
5. Classification based on size
6. Classification based on plan
7. Classification according to ownership and association.
8. Other sorts of hotels.

Types of Accommodation in the Tourism and Hospitality Industry

Hotels can be categorized according to their size, location, clientele, length of stay, and other characteristics. They are categorized for a number of reasons. It's critical to comprehend a hotel's location, cost, and amenities before making a reservation. One or more of the following categories may apply to a hotel.

Accommodation

One of the fundamental requirements of travellers at the destination is lodging. This kind of residential facility offers boarding and accommodation to travellers who are away from home for longer than a day and require a place to sleep, rest, eat, stay safe, shelter from the cold or rain, store their luggage, and access basic household amenities. A variety of accommodations that fall into the **primary** and **secondary** categories Primary Accommodation

Hotel

A commercial establishment providing lodging, meals, and other guest services, is termed as hotel. Thus, a hotel is a place where a Bonafide traveller can get food and accommodation where he is in a position to pay for it and is in a fit condition to be received. Today, hotels not only provide accommodation and meals but also offer a variety of other services as per the needs of the guest. For example, many hotels offer a health club, crèche, etc.

Types of hotels

Hotels can be broadly categorized into the following types based on the amenities they provide to tourists. International hotels are contemporary, western-style lodging establishments that are mostly found in big cities and popular tourist spots. These hotels are categorized using a globally recognized star rating system that goes from one to five stars. The hotel receives a grade based on the amenities and services it offers. The five-star establishments offer a variety of amenities, including a travel desk, conference centre, information desk, banquet halls, multi-cuisine restaurants, room service, a swimming pool, a gym, health clubs, shopping arcades, beauty salons, and cultural or entertainment events.

Floating Hotels

These types of hotels are located on the surface of water such as the sea, river, or lake. These hotels have facilities which are similar to a regular hotel. For example: Houseboats of Kashmir and Kerala or old cruise liners which have been converted into a hotel.

Commercial Hotels

These hotels cater mostly to middle-class and business travellers as well as their loyal clientele, and they are typically found close to commercial or business districts. The majority of these hotels have restaurants, parking, and amenities for business travellers, like conference rooms and convention centres.

Heritage Hotels

These are the old properties like castles, forts, palaces, and havelis belonging to royalty which have been renovated and converted into hotels. Here, tourists enjoy the majestic grandeur and splendour of the olden days. Some examples of heritage hotels are Umaid Bhavan Palace in Jodhpur, Rambagh Palace in Jaipur, Shalini Palace in Kolhapur, Lalitha Mahal in Mysuru and Sheesh Mahal in Orchha.

Every economy in the world now has a respectable amount of gross revenue from tourism, which is sometimes considered to as the most outstanding economic activity. In the past, travel was viewed as a luxury phenomenon and a service that only a select few could afford and access. However, the rise in popularity and the emergence of numerous tourism markets, goods, and information sources about these goods and services made travel accessible to a wide range of tourists from varied socioeconomic backgrounds. In India, the Ministry of Tourism is the nodal agency responsible for coordinating the activities of various agencies related to tourism and they have an important role to play in framing and maintaining policies related to tourism and allied activities in the country.

The government recently made the decision to provide up to 50% of its budget for marketing travel in the nation to private tourism industry participants, such as qualified hotels, travel agents, internet portals, and airline firms. The multiplier effect of tourism and its contribution to employment creation in the nation were also taken into consideration by the government. At the moment, only 0.63% of all international visitors arrive in the nation. The government should be required to make investments in infrastructure, marketing, and branding of the nation's tourism-related goods and services in order to raise this numbers.

Terms used in Tourism and Hospitality Industry

Tourist
Any person coming to country for legitimate reason and who stays atleast 24 hours and at most 6 months during the same

Traveler
Any person on a trip between two or more localities

Excursionist
A traveller spending less than 24 hours in a country One who goes on an excursion, or pleasure trip

Backpackers
A hiker who wears a backpack A traveller whose luggage consists of a backpack; especially, such a traveller who uses hostels, public transport, and other inexpensive services

Guest
A person who is the recipient of hospitality in the form of entertainment: At someone's home, as a visiting participant in a program, or as a customer

Visitor
Any person travelling to place other than their usual environment for less than 12 consecutive months

Travel and Tourism

India has been successful in attracting both local and foreign travellers, making it one of Asia's most popular travel destinations. India's culture and secularism have captivated many travellers from around the world. India is a popular travel destination for people from all over the world because of its beautiful terrain, hill stations, historical sites, architecture, monuments, beaches, enchanted backwaters, and locations of religious significance.

India's tourism sector has enormous potential to grow into a lucrative one. Both domestic and international tourism have increased as a result of enhanced communication and transportation links, better hospitality services, higher living standards, and better value for foreign visitors. One of the most significant and rapidly expanding sectors in the modern world is tourism, which generates a large number of work possibilities. It contributes to the nation's economy and makes a significant amount of money. In addition to creating employment and income, it enables individuals from other nations and cultures to travel and interact with others in social settings for both work and pleasure. The only way for people to get to know one another on a social, cultural, and religious level is through tourism. It fosters positive relationships between speakers of various languages and cultural backgrounds. It also paves the way to understand and explore the rich heritage and ancient history of an unknown place. It is an export that is not visible and earns valuable foreign exchange without any substantial or actual loss of internal resources.

Tourism is a unique type of highly labor-intensive industry. It provides different services that are needed as well as expected by the incoming tourists. Tourism is one of the largest industries in terms of money spent by tourists in the countries they visit. The amount received from the Tourism industry sometimes exceeds the Gross National Product of many countries.

India is one of the most preferred tourist destinations in Asia because of its beautiful landscape, rich cultural heritage, myriad attractions and valuable ancient history. India serves as the hub of different cultures and languages within it and has always attracted domestic and international tourists. In 2019 it attracted 10.93 million international tourists and this contributed to almost 4.7% of India's GDP. India has also attracted international tourists because of the liberty it gives to different religions. The peaceful existence of people of 22 languages and 9 religions is a source of attraction for all international tourists. India has a mosaic of enchanting hill stations, magnificent architecture and monuments, picturesque beaches, and enchanting backwaters. India has always been famous for its hospitality services. Our guests are considered as God and the tourists feel quite safe in India. A lot of solo travellers prefer certain parts of India over any other place in the world. Indian Tourism gives proper value to tourists from foreign countries.

Benefits of Tourism in India

People can find a variety of jobs in the tourism business. In addition to giving people work, it has reduced poverty and promoted long-term human growth. Small, regional handicrafts and cultural endeavours have benefited from and been encouraged by tourism. It has been crucial in advancing both worldwide understanding and national integrity. The primary advantage of tourism is that it allows people to unwind and feel relieved when they are worn out from their busy schedules and the bustle of the city. It is a welcoming entryway for people.

Other industries including aviation, transportation, agriculture, and handicrafts have also profited from the tourism sector. Tourism has greatly helped the hotel sector, which offers a large number of jobs and aids in generating foreign cash. This sector now accounts for a significant portion of the nation's GDP. By enhancing the nation's infrastructure and transportation, it has made a substantial contribution to India's economic growth. The revival of India's art and culture has been greatly aided by tourism. Foreign visitors' intense curiosity in India's rich history and legacy raises the spirits of tiny craftspeople and contributes to their uniqueness.

Promotion and Development of Tourism

The Indian government is actively marketing several tourist segments, including adventure, eco-tourism, spiritual tourism, spa tourism, and rural tourism, in order to promote greater growth. Medical tourism has grown to be a significant source of income for the healthcare industry in recent years. For reasonably priced, top-notch healthcare services and treatment, many individuals from our neighbouring countries as well as Western nations are looking to India.

Over the years, Indian tourism has expanded considerably. The main output of the tourism sector is the services provided to international visitors to India. Because they produce a lot of revenue without ever leaving Indian territory, these goods, such as various forms of hospitality services for visitors, become invisible exports. The Indian Ministry of Tourism has been instrumental in the growth of the sector. The tourism department established the India Tourism Development Corporation (ITDC), which has implemented several significant initiatives to promote travel to India. The ITDC hotels offer cozy and reasonably priced boarding and accommodation, and they are located in the best areas of India's major tourist attractions.

Promoting India as a comprehensive travel destination in both local and foreign markets is made possible by the Government of India's introduction of the "Incredible India" campaign. Under the banner of "Incredible India," several specialized worldwide media campaigns have been started, and even our nation's superstars have been enlisted to help make this campaign a huge success abroad. The Indian government's "Clean India" initiative guarantees complete cleanliness, which is now a must at all tourist locations.

The Government has also conducted regular studies to analyze the market to identify the key factors, income figures, holiday habits, and psychology of people. This helps them to identify the key drivers in the Tourism industry and tackle the issues that deter the scope of Tourism.

Importance of Tourism

Tourism is important for many reasons. It helps the economy by creating jobs and bringing in money. It supports businesses like hotels, restaurants, and transport services, which helps local economies. Tourism also helps keep cultural sites and historical landmarks in good shape, as many of these are funded by money from tourists. Tourism also helps people from different places learn about each other. It builds connections between people from different cultures and promotes understanding and acceptance of different ways of life.

Tourism is important because it brings many benefits to both economies and cultures. It generates income and creates jobs in areas like hotels, restaurants, and transportation. Many places depend on tourism to support their local businesses and improve their infrastructure. Traveling also has personal benefits. It allows people to experience new cultures and lifestyles, which can expand their views and understanding of the world. This exposure helps people appreciate global diversity and fosters greater cultural understanding.

Furthermore, tourism helps to maintain historical sites and cultural heritage. The money from tourists often goes towards preserving these landmarks so that future generations can enjoy them. However, it is important to manage tourism responsibly to avoid problems like environmental damage and overcrowding. By focusing on sustainable practices, tourism can continue to be a positive influence on economies and cultures around the world.

Indian tourism Millions of tourists visit India every year because of its diverse landscapes, fascinating history, and lively culture, making it an important element of the country's economy and culture. From the majestic Himalayas in the north to the serene beaches in the south, India's natural beauty provides visitors with a wide variety of experiences. Famous sites like the Red Fort, Qutb Minar, and Taj Mahal are essential to India's allure as a travel destination. A testament to architectural genius and unending love, the Taj Mahal is one of the

Seven Wonders of the World. Similar to this, India's historical and architectural accomplishments are revealed through the Red Fort and Qutb Minar.

India's cultural diversity is another significant attraction. The country is home to numerous festivals such as Diwali, Holi, and Durga Puja, which are celebrated with great enthusiasm and colour. These festivals offer visitors an immersive experience of India's vibrant cultural traditions. Additionally, the diverse Indian cuisine, ranging from spicy North Indian dishes to flavorful South Indian specialties, adds to the country's allure. Tourists can enjoy a variety of regional foods and culinary traditions; making their visit even more memorable.

India's economy depends heavily on the tourist sector. It promotes a number of industries, such as local crafts, transportation, and hospitality. The creation of jobs in lodging, dining, and travel agencies creates job possibilities and boosts the local and national economies. Both visitors and locals gain from the infrastructure and services that are developed thanks in part to tourism revenue.

Additionally, tourism aids in the promotion and preservation of India's historical and cultural legacy. In order to preserve significant locations and monuments for future generations, tourism-related funds are utilized for their upkeep and restoration. This funding is essential to preserving India's cultural legacy and ensuring that visitors can enjoy it.

However, tourism in India faces several challenges. The high number of visitors can lead to environmental issues such as pollution and damage to natural areas. Overcrowding at popular tourist sites can strain local infrastructure and disrupt the lives of residents. Additionally, the demand for resources such as water and waste management can put pressure on local systems.

To solve these problems, sustainable tourism practices are essential. Reducing adverse environmental impacts, limiting the number of tourists, and ensuring that tourism benefits the community are all crucial steps. Adopting measures like reducing plastic usage, improving waste management, and conserving water can help mitigate the negative effects of tourism. Teaching tourists to respect local cultures and ecosystems is another important aspect of conserving India's natural and cultural heritage.

The tourism sector in India is flourishing and has a lot of room to grow both economically and culturally. Addressing its problems and putting an emphasis on sustainable practices would help India keep its standing as one of the world's most popular tourism destinations.

Conclusion

The Tourism industry is the largest service industry in India and has the potential to stimulate the economic growth of the country. It becomes important for all citizens to develop the Tourism infrastructure and maintain tourist destinations, railway stations, airports, rest houses, and hotels.

TOURISM AND CULINARY INDUSTRY

Ms. Ivan Nancy
Assistant Professor
Department of History
Stella Maris College (Autonomous)
Chennai- 86

Introduction

Tourism and the culinary industry share an inseparable bond, creating a multidimensional cultural and economic phenomenon that attracts millions worldwide. Tourism, fundamentally, is driven by the human desire to explore, experience, and connect with diverse cultures, histories, and lifestyles. The culinary aspect enhances this experience by providing a sensory journey through taste, smell, and visual presentation, making gastronomy a cornerstone of the tourism experience. Food plays a pivotal role in shaping tourist experiences. It is not merely sustenance but a gateway to understanding a region's culture, traditions, and identity.

Culinary tourism, also known as gastronomy tourism, focuses on the exploration of local cuisines as the primary motivation for travel. This form of tourism allows visitors to immerse themselves in the lifestyle of a destination, connecting deeply with its people and heritage through the preparation and consumption of food.

The culinary experience offers more than just dining; it includes activities like participating in food festivals, taking cooking classes, visiting food markets, and engaging with local chefs and producers. For example, destinations like France, Italy, and India have leveraged their rich culinary traditions to become hubs for food tourism. The famed wine and cheese tours of France or the diverse street food of India exemplify how cuisine can be a powerful draw for tourists.

Culinary Tourism as a Motivator for Travel

Culinary tourism has evolved into a dynamic segment of the tourism industry, attracting a wide array of travellers, from those seeking luxury wine tours in Napa Valley to adventurers savouring street food in Bangkok. The increasing desire for authentic and memorable experiences has made food an essential part of travel planning. In fact, food is often cited as one of the primary motivators for selecting travel destinations, alongside climate and cultural landmarks. This trend is further supported by the rise of food festivals and events worldwide, such as the Wild Food Festival in New Zealand, the Onion Market in Switzerland, and the Dumpling Festival in Hong Kong. These events showcase local flavours and foster community pride while attracting global attention, boosting both tourism and local economies.

Cuisines Cultural Connection

Cuisine serves as a cultural artifact, narrating the story of a region's history, geography, and social structure. For example, India's culinary landscape reflects its vast diversity, with dishes varying significantly across regions, from the rich Mughlai cuisine of the north to the spicy seafood delights of the south. Similarly, the pasta and pizza of Italy or the baguettes and croissants of France offer glimpses into these countries' agricultural practices and culinary innovations over centuries. Food is a universal language, and its preparation and sharing foster connections among people, bridging cultural gaps. This universality makes culinary tourism not only an economic driver but also a means of promoting global understanding and appreciation.

The culinary industry significantly boosts tourism economies by creating jobs, encouraging entrepreneurship, and promoting sustainable practices. Restaurants, food markets, and culinary tours generate revenue while preserving traditional cooking techniques and local food production. In rural areas, agritourism—where visitors engage with farming activities—further enhances the economic potential of gastronomy tourism. For instance, the rise of Ludlow in the United Kingdom as a food tourism destination demonstrates how a small town can transform into a vibrant economic hub by focusing on its culinary offerings. From Michelin-starred restaurants to farmers' markets, Ludlow has used food tourism to create a sustainable economic model.

Culinary Industry

The culinary industry, a cornerstone of global culture and economy, encompasses the art and science of food preparation, service, and management. It spans a wide range of activities, from cooking and catering to food innovation and hospitality. This sector not only caters to the essential need for sustenance but also fosters creativity, cultural exchange, and economic growth. With its multifaceted nature, the culinary industry includes professional kitchens, restaurants, food manufacturing, and event catering services, as well as research in gastronomy and nutrition. Technology is playing an increasing role in reshaping the culinary industry. Innovations like automated kitchen equipment, mobile ordering apps, and data analytics enhance efficiency and customer satisfaction. Moreover, the industry is deeply influenced by trends such as farm-to-table dining, sustainable sourcing, and plant-based diets, which cater to evolving consumer preferences for ethical and health-conscious dining options. Training and education are vital components, with culinary schools and certifications ensuring a steady stream of skilled professionals equipped to meet the demands of this dynamic field. Overall, the culinary industry thrives on its ability to blend tradition with innovation, sustaining a significant impact on society and the global economy.

Restaurants

Restaurants play a pivotal role in the tourism industry, serving as essential components of the hospitality sector. They provide travellers with opportunities to experience local cuisine, culture, and hospitality, significantly enhancing the overall travel experience. The diversity within the restaurant industry caters to various tourist preferences and budgets. Fine dining establishments offer high-end services with quality food and sophisticated presentation, appealing to tourists seeking luxury experiences. Casual dining venues provide a more relaxed atmosphere, attracting travellers looking for affordable yet authentic local flavours. Additionally, fast-food outlets and cafés offer quick and convenient options for tourists on the go.

Beyond dining, restaurants contribute to the local economy by creating employment opportunities and supporting local suppliers and producers. They also play a role in preserving and promoting regional culinary traditions, which can be a significant draw for cultural tourism. The ambiance and service quality of restaurants can influence tourists' perceptions of a destination, potentially affecting their satisfaction and likelihood of return visits. In summary, restaurants are integral to the tourism experience, offering diverse dining options that reflect the local culture and hospitality. Their contribution extends beyond mere food service, impacting economic development, cultural preservation, and the overall attractiveness of tourist destinations.

Types of Culinary Industry

The culinary industry can be broadly categorized into several types based on the nature of services and offerings:

- Fine Dining: This segment is characterized by high-quality food, exceptional service, and luxurious ambiance. Fine dining establishments often feature elaborate menus crafted by renowned chefs.
- Casual Dining: Casual restaurants offer a more relaxed environment with moderately priced menus, blending quality and affordability.
- Fast Food: Known for speed and convenience, fast-food outlets focus on standardized menus and quick service. This segment caters to a broad demographic.

- Catering Services: Catering businesses provide food and beverage services for events like weddings, corporate meetings, and parties. They emphasize customization and logistics.
- Food Trucks: Mobile culinary establishments serve diverse cuisines, often experimenting with innovative concepts and reaching varied audiences.
- Specialty and Ethnic Cuisine: This segment focuses on specific cuisines or dietary needs, such as vegan, gluten-free, or international foods, emphasizing authenticity and niche markets.
- Institutional Food Services: These cater to specific institutions like schools, hospitals, and corporate offices, balancing nutrition, budget, and scalability.

By diversifying offerings and adapting to consumer preferences, these segments collectively contribute to the culinary industry's growth and vibrancy.

Types of Culinary Travellers

Culinary tourism, also known as food tourism, appeals to a wide range of travellers, each motivated by unique culinary experiences:

- Food Connoisseurs: These travellers seek gourmet experiences, often visiting Michelin-starred restaurants or regions renowned for their culinary excellence, such as Tuscany or Bordeaux.
- Cultural Enthusiasts: For these individuals, food serves as a gateway to understanding a region's heritage. They explore local markets, street food, and traditional cooking methods.
- Adventure Seekers: Driven by curiosity, these travellers pursue unconventional or exotic food experiences, including rare ingredients or unique preparation styles like foraging or farm stays.

- Health-Conscious Travellers: Focused on wellness, these tourists explore destinations known for organic, vegan, or therapeutic cuisines, aligning their travels with health goals.
- Budget Explorers: This group seeks affordable yet authentic culinary experiences, often gravitating towards street food, local diners, or regional specialties.
- Sustainability Advocates: These travellers prioritize eco-friendly dining options, emphasizing sustainable sourcing, zero-waste practices, and ethical food production.
- Food Festival Enthusiasts: Drawn by gastronomic events, these travellers plan trips around food festivals, wine tastings, and culinary workshops.

By catering to these varied motivations, the culinary tourism sector enhances the travel experience while promoting cultural exchange and economic development in host regions.

Challenges and Opportunities

While culinary tourism offers immense opportunities, it also faces challenges such as the need for quality control, sustainability, and infrastructure development. Emerging destinations often struggle with inadequate marketing and logistical support, which can limit their ability to attract international tourists. Additionally, ensuring that tourism benefits local communities without causing cultural dilution or environmental degradation remains a critical concern. Technological advancements and digital marketing have provided new avenues for promoting culinary tourism. Social media platforms, online travel agencies, and virtual food tours have made it easier for travellers to discover and plan food-centric trips, broadening the appeal of gastronomy tourism.

Wine tourism

Wine tourism, also known as ecotourism or vino tourism, is a growing segment of the global tourism industry that combines agriculture, gastronomy, and cultural heritage. This specialized branch of tourism offers immersive experiences in wine-producing regions, contributing to rural economies, cultural preservation, and sustainable tourism practices. Wine tourists range from casual enthusiasts seeking relaxation and cultural enrichment to connoisseurs interested in winemaking. The concept has evolved from simple vineyard visits to comprehensive cultural experiences, with countries like France, Italy, Spain, and Australia integrating their winemaking traditions with tourism to create globally recognized destinations. Wine tourism has become a key driver of economic growth in rural areas, supporting local businesses and creating employment opportunities. It also helps preserve cultural heritage by promoting traditional winemaking techniques and regional customs. Wine tourism offers a diverse range of activities beyond wine tasting, including vineyard tours, winery visits, wine festivals, culinary pairings, workshops, and courses. These offerings reflect the multifaceted nature of wine tourism, integrating elements of education, entertainment, and cultural exchange.

Food festivals

Food festivals are a significant part of tourism, combining culinary traditions with cultural expressions to showcase local flavours and heritage. These events, held annually, attract food enthusiasts from around the world, showcasing regional ingredients, cooking techniques, and dining customs. They not only showcase a destination's gastronomic identity but also promote its cultural, economic, and tourism potential. Food festivals are important for cultural exchange and celebration, allowing visitors to delve deeply into a region's culinary heritage. They cater to diverse palates, featuring traditional recipes, fusion cuisines, and contemporary innovations. This also promotes a sense of community, gratification, and cultural preservation among locals.

For tourists, these festivals offer immersive experiences, allowing them to witness live cooking demonstrations, participate in food workshops, and savour dishes prepared by renowned chefs. These engagements connect people to the roots of a cuisine, often motivating repeat visits and word-of-mouth promotions. Some of the most famous food festivals worldwide include the Wild Food Festival in New Zealand, Switzerland's Onion Market in Bern, the Bacon Festival in California, the Dumpling Festival in Hong Kong, Italy's Pizza Fest in Naples, and Thailand's Vegetarian Festival. These festivals not only showcase a destination's culinary heritage but also promote its cultural, economic, and tourism potential.

Cultural, Economic, and Environmental Impact of Food Festivals

Food festivals significantly enhance a destination's appeal by showcasing its culinary expertise and cultural heritage. They attract domestic and international tourists, boosting local economies through increased spending on accommodation, transport, and dining. For example, food festivals in France, India, and Mexico have gained global recognition, often becoming synonymous with the destinations themselves. Events such as France’s wine and cheese fairs, India’s street food fests, and Mexico’s Day of the Dead culinary offerings contribute to the countries' reputations as top food tourism destinations. Culturally, these festivals act as custodians of heritage by preserving traditional recipes, cooking methods, and local ingredients. They encourage intergenerational learning, where older community members pass down culinary knowledge to younger participants.

Socially, food festivals foster connections among people, bridging cultural and linguistic divides. Economically, these festivals stimulate local businesses by attracting tourists and providing opportunities for small-scale producers and artisans. Environmentally, many festivals emphasize sustainability by promoting local, organic produce and eco-friendly practices, as seen in the Wild Food Festival. However, organizing food festivals is not without challenges. Issues such as overcrowding, maintaining food safety standards, and managing waste require strategic planning. Despite these challenges, food festivals remain essential cultural and economic events, playing a pivotal role in global tourism while celebrating the diversity and artistry of cuisines.

Food trails

Food trails, encompassing self-guided or guided tours centred on local culinary experiences, play a significant role in promoting food tourism. They offer tourists immersive opportunities to explore regional specialties, thereby enhancing the appeal of destinations. The key contributions of food trails to tourism are as follows:

- Promotion and Preservation of Local Food Culture: By spotlighting local delicacies, food trails help sustain culinary heritage and traditions, ensuring their transmission to future generations.
- Attraction of Tourists: These trails draw both domestic and international visitors eager to experience authentic local cuisines, thereby boosting tourist numbers and engagement.
- Economic Benefits: Food trails can stimulate local economies by increasing demand for regional food products and services, benefiting local producers and businesses.
- Enhanced Tourist Experiences: They provide meaningful and memorable experiences, allowing tourists to connect deeply with the local culture through its culinary offerings.

To conclude, food trails serve as vital components in food tourism strategies, offering cultural, economic, and experiential advantages to destinations that develop and promote them.

Conclusion

Tourism and the culinary industry are interconnected, enhancing economic and cultural value. Food exploration in tourism provides a deeper understanding of a destination's identity and culture. As demand for genuine and sustainable travel experiences develops, the culinary industry will continue to define the future of tourism. Gastronomy tourism not only boosts local economies by creating jobs and supporting small-scale businesses but also preserves regional cuisines and practices. Food festivals, wine tourism, and food trails showcase community pride and global attention to destinations. As the culinary industry evolves with sustainability and technology-driven solutions, its role in tourism becomes even more crucial. By blending tradition with innovation, the sector meets the growing demand for authentic, health-conscious, and immersive travel experiences. The partnership between tourism and the culinary industry goes beyond economic advantages, fostering cultural connections and sustainable practices.

TOURISM AND TRANSPORTATION

Dr Gayathri S
Assistant Professor
Department of History
Stella Maris College
Chennai-600086

Introduction

Tourism and Transportation, are two giants interdependent for their survival. The nexus between the two is very strong and is a must as transportation is considered as one of the vital components of tourism. According to UNWTO "Tourism is a social, cultural and economic phenomenon which entails the movement of people to countries or places outside their usual environment for personal or business/professional purposes. These people are called visitors (which may be either tourists or excursionists; residents or non-residents) and tourism has to do with their activities, some of which involve tourism expenditure."

A very important feature of tourism activity is the movement of people from one place to another. This movement is facilitated by transportation. It is a very important component of tourism since it allows tourists to visit the places they want to see and take in a variety of experiences and sights. Among the various types of transportation that are there to tourists, includes air, rail, road travel, water travel, horse-drawn carriages, choppers, car and motor vehicles and coaches.

Factors influencing the development of Transport Systems

Trasport systems across the world has seen an evolution over several centuries. There are several factors which have influenced the same.

Before we look in the history of transportation, we will look into the factors which have influenced it.

1. Environmental factors- like hydrographical and geomorphological features at the local level, climate and distance at the national level oceanic masses and choke points at the global level can influence transportation.
2. Historical factors – Settlement patterns, colonialism, imperialism, and globalization are some of the factors that have played an influential role.
3. Technological factors- Air transport and telecommunications have helped in the development of transportation globally. At the regional level mobility and corridors play an important role in transportational growth.
   Political factors- Both at the provincial and nationwide levels, political factors impacted taxation and regulations like safety and operating conditions. By connecting nearby economic entities, trade agreements have a noteworthy global impact and have impacted the evolution of transportation by trying to coordinate commerce and physical networks. By promoting particular international connectedness, multilateral agreements especially those pertaining to trade have influenced the evolution of transportation systems.
4. Economic factors- As the main function of transportation is to enable economic activity and its linkages, economic processes influence its evolution. Transport networks are more intense and efficient in economies that are well developed. Employment and distribution are important factors at the local level. Markets are served by competing modes of transportation, a process that mostly occurs at the state level. More and more people believe that markets are world level, requiring coordinated supply methods. significant cargo and the conveyance networks that help them are influenced by competition between significant economic entities on a global scale.

History of Transportation

The earliest journeys undertaken by man was by road and sea voyages. The former was used for visiting pilgrimages and sometimes to explore new places while the latter promoted trade and exploration. During the Stone Age Road animals like horses and oxen were used to transport goods. They did not have constructed roads initially and used mountain passes and swamps but later the paths were cleared and widened to enable more movement. The very first vehicle was probably the travois which resembled a frame used to drag weight. Later sledges were developed and finally ridgeways to avoid crossing rivers.

Wheeled transport is said to have developed during 5000BC in ancient Mesopotamia probably for making pottery but they were later attached to sledges and travois to assist in movement. Two wheeled chariots developed at around 2800 BC, and by 2500 BC four wheeled wagons were developed to carry heavy weight. As a result of invention of wheels better roads were required for transport which was evident in places like Ur in Mesopotamia, Indus Valley Civilization and England. During the Islamic Middle Ages, the Arab Empire saw the construction of numerous highways. In the eighth century, tar was used to pave the most advanced roads in Baghdad, Iraq. Tar was produced via the chemical technique of destructive distillation from petroleum that was obtained from the area's oil fields.

In Germany, rails were in place as early as 1550. The earliest examples of contemporary rail transportation were these 'wagonways', which were made of wooden rails that made it simpler for horse-drawn wagons or carts to go on muddy roads. These wagonways advanced into "tramways" and became popular across Europe in the late 1700s, iron rails and wheels took the place of wooden ones. Until the invention of the steam engine locomotive in the first half of 1800s, horses were used to supply the "horsepower" for goods.

At the beginning of the 19th century, the first steam locomotives were invented in Great Britain. The steam engines which initially pulled coals soon started accommodating passengers. In the United States railroads took off because cars and planes has not yet been invented yet. During what is known as "The Golden Age" of railroads, which spanned the 1880s through the 1920s, trains were the primary means of transportation. Beginning in the early 1900s, electric and diesel-powered locomotives progressively supplanted steam-powered locomotives. By the 1980s, the majority of steam-powered locomotives had been removed from regular service routes, however some remain in use as historical or tourist lines.

Water transport, often known as maritime transport, is the usage of vessels to convey individuals or products over water, whether it is a sea, ocean, lake, river, canal, or any other waterbody. It has a lengthy history and is currently widely utilised for recreational, military, and commercial uses. The earliest known use of waterways is from Netherlands around 8200 to 7600 BC. The Egyptians used wooden boats known as Feluccas for transporting coffins and grains. The Vikings were enthusiastic about boats and used them as their main mode of transportation, making them an important character in the history of water travel. Their history may be dated back to approximately 793 AD.

The Arabs who were contemporaries of Vikings were expanding their trade at the same time they were the leading economic power at that point of time. Sea trade enabled the transportation of eatables and goods to entire nations in the Arabian countries. Long sea routes in trade also implied importing raw materials for construction as well as luxury goods for the wealthy. They employed ships known as qaribs, which later inspired the Spanish caravel.

The 1400s and 1500s were described as “Age of Discovery” as it was described as Christopher Columbus' era, when ships from Europe went throughout globally looking for novel trade routes.

Other notable figures in nautical history at the same period include John Cabot, Juan Fernandez, Jacques Cartier, Richard Hakluyt, and Vasco da Gama. Around this time, the preferred style of vessel was a wooden sailing boat with 3-4 masts.

In the 1900s, one witnessed several new inventions in waterways, including hydroplanes, hovercrafts, and nuclear-powered cargo ships like the N.S. Savannah, which navigated for three and a half years without refuelling. The advent of container ships occurred in the 1900s, specifically in the 1980s. These big and powerful cargo ships enabled for the transportation of massive volumes of material in tiny boxes known as containers; at present, containers transport approximately 90% of non-bulk cargo. Cruise liners also gained popularity in the 1900s. In the year 1901, the first cruise ship was constructed, and it was from Germany. However, it wasn't until the 1990s when cruising became more popular and accessible.

The youngest or the most modern among the types of transport is airways. Aviation industry has come a long way and today stands as the most viable mode of transport when it comes to saving time. Its history began in 1700 with the invention of the hot air balloon. The Montgolfier brothers developed this innovation, and the first public demonstration took place in France on June 4, 1783. During the 20th century, the Wright brothers emerged. Orville and Wilbur Wright were aviation pioneers, aviators, and engineers. They created the world's first aeroplane, but in order for it to fly, they needed to build an external catapult.

Next, in 1906, Romanian inventor Traiana Vuia created the first self-propelled aeroplane capable of flight. The invention of propeller planes and helicopters during World War II marked the next phase in the evolution of air transportation. As a result, the actual development of aircrafts took off only in the later half the 20th century. From there, the industry was able to construct planes that travelled at the speed of sound. Indeed, the Concorde and Boeing 747 are among the most well-known inventions in this discipline.

Currently, each country has a different airport. With the tourism boom and the need for new experiences, this industry discovered a niche in which to expand. In fact, it is one of the most popular modes of transportation among travellers on vacations and for business engagements. However, due to its agility and speed, it is increasingly being employed to transport cargo. It has even become the favoured mode of transportation for delivering specific, expensive, or urgently needed products.

Evolution of Tourism

According to UNWTO statistics in 1950 there were 25 million international tourists globally, and by 2019 this had increased to 1.5 billion. During the 17th century, a group of young noblemen from European countries embarked on a educational trip around Europe to understand its history, art and cultural heritage, this gave birth to tourism as an activity. This became a popular culture amid the wealthier classes and by 18th century it opened up globally. During the Middle Ages religious pilgrimages originated which became very popular. An aftermath of the Industrial Revolution was an increase in the movement of people from countryside to developing cities in search of the industrial houses. This resulted in the emergence of new social classes.

A great fillip for the tourism activity was the development and growth of transportation that resulted in increase in leisure and entertainment travel. Global connections and networking became easy and improved as excellent railway networks connected parts of the world.

The growth of tourism as an industry was witnessed when Travel Agencies were started for the first time in the 19th century. A pioneer among them was Thomas Cook and Sons, who was instrumental in introducing the idea of group tours or package tours, inclusive of transport, stay, food and tickets at less price.

In the first half of the 20th century there was a boom in the tourism industry due to an increase in manufacture of buses and cars.

Post World War II period saw the Mediterranean coast changing in to a holiday destination as coastal tourism gained prominence. In addition, improvements in air transportation, advancements in workers regulations, and rise in social assistance all enabled an increase in tourism activity.

During 1970s the travel industry was affected due to energy crisis that ended in fall in costs and prices leading to the emergence of mass tourism providing accessibility for all to travel. In recent years, the tourism sector has emerged as a key economic driver in many economies. With low-cost carriers and the availability of alternate places of stay managed by virtual companies, tourists can now afford to tour while also designing their own itinerary and experiences.

The year 2020 saw this industry coming to a standstill as a result of COVID-19. This caused a ripple effect affecting transport and hospitality industry equally. The situation slowly changed and limped back to normalcy after 2021. The tourism industry bounced back more strongly as an impact of lockdown and work from home where people felt they were confined to their homes and their movements restricted. They were waiting to just get out and enjoy the world as it was during the pre-pandemic period. The tourism industry opened up new opportunities to make up for the loss and it was well utilised by the people.

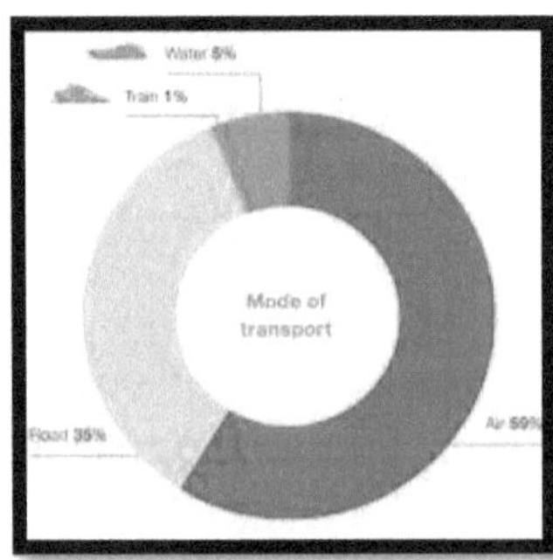

Figure 1: Source UNWTO 2021

Nexus between Tourism and Transport

Transportation is the reason behind the basis and consequence of tourism's expansion. First, improved amenities have enhanced tourism, which has stimulated the construction of transportation infrastructure. Approachability is the main function driving the fundamentals of tourism conveyance. Tourists have a number of transportation options for getting to popular attractions, which are frequently used in sequence. The primary means of international tourism is air transport, that involves long-haul travel. Tourism uses of all regular means of transport because travellers depend on existing tourist transport systems, which range from local to worldwide air transportation. Transport rules and national laws might influence tourist destinations.

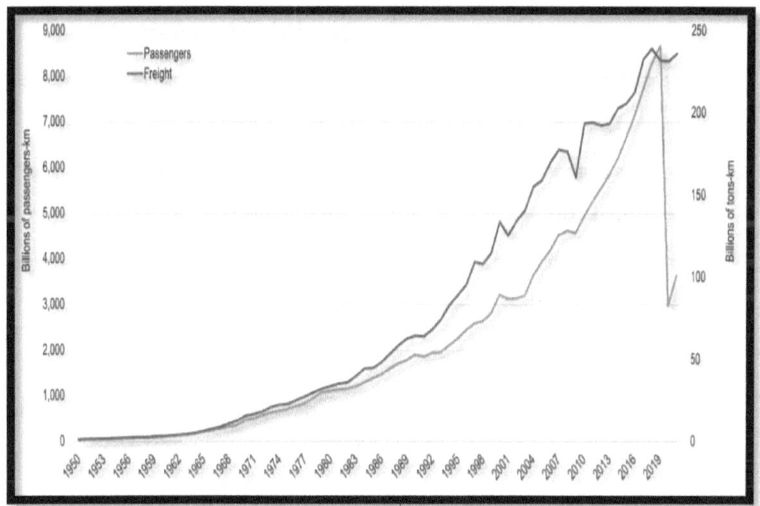

Table 1: Source: Airlines for America. IATA.

The choice of the mode of transport by the tourist is made considering the following metrics: (i) the distance of travel from the point of starting to the final destination, (ii)the time factor - It is important that the journey can be finished at the desired period and that the travelling time does not surpass certain adequate limits for the tourist in the context of the entire vacation time, (iii) the readiness and approachability of the service - from the start must have the means to carry tourists on the route or destination, (iv) security and consistency - The requirements connected to these objectives are becoming all the more rigorous for all modes of transportation, (v)the luxury of the voyage - with reference to all the mental and physical feelings felt by tourists inside the vehicle during the voyage

Tourism generally contributes sufficiently to the economy within the nation that governments are looking forward to upgrade roadways and airways, particularly in areas with few economic prospects other than tourism. Nevertheless, there are considerable disparities in spending for the mode, namely between cruises and air travel tourism. The former generates significantly less money than the latter. A big reason is that ships try to attract as much tourism expenses as possible on board their ships (food, beverages, entertainment, shopping) and have brief port stays, often less than a day. Travellers coming by flight very often stay in the same region for several days and use local amenities.

The role of transport in tourism is generally viewed as merely one of the tourism systems that is responsible for delivering tourists to the locations, a way of navigating around the site and departing it as soon as the period of the trip is over. The conveyance infrastructure of a tourist destination affects the overall tourism experience, influencing how people travel and their choice of holiday destination and mode of transportation. New transit options and affordable fares have made previously remote locations more accessible.

Access to tourism attractions varies based on site characteristics, infrastructure, and public transportation efficiency. Accessibility can determine whether a destination succeeds or fails. There are two sides to this debate: the ratio of tourists to the ratio of visitors per population. The first argument that the more the attraction the greater the number of people, which can increase weakening, reduce experience, and have an impact on the natural state of the resources. The second debate considers the ratio of visitors to the home population, as well as the impact levels and types. Finally, the issue of sustainability of tourism and transportation might be observed when connection to attractions that give destinations their tourist demand is either outside limits or constrained.

Conclusion

Tourism and transportation are inextricably linked, forming a dynamic and essential relationship that drives global travel, economic growth, and cultural exchange. As tourism continues to grow, the demand for efficient, sustainable, and accessible transportation systems becomes increasingly critical. Transportation not only enables tourists to reach their destinations but also shapes their travel experiences, influencing the development of popular destinations and creating opportunities for local economies.

The evolving nature of both industries, determined by advancements in technology, environmental apprehensions, and changing consumer beliefs, presents opportunities for innovation. From eco-friendly transportation solutions to smart technologies enhancing the travel experience, both sectors are embracing sustainability and efficiency. However, challenges such as overcrowding, infrastructure strain, and the need for greener transport options remain prevalent.

Ultimately, a collaborative approach between tourism and transportation stakeholders—governments, businesses, and communities—is essential to ensure that growth in these sectors remains balanced, sustainable, and beneficial for all. By prioritizing innovation, environmental responsibility, and accessibility, the synergy between tourism and transportation will continue to shape a more interconnected and sustainable global travel landscape.

TOURISM AND JOURNALISM

Author
Ms. N. Balagomathy
Assistant Professor
Department of History and Tourism
SDNB Vaishnav College for Women,
Chromepet, Chennai - 44

Co-Author
Ms. R. M. Pavithra
Assistant Professor
Department of History and Tourism
SDNB Vaishnav College for Women,
Chromepet, Chennai - 44

Introduction

Over the years, the role of media has exuberantly grown from just being a source of entertainment to source of information. Media is best known for vitalizing the bond between both the brands and consumers. It is through media the tourists are becoming more familiar about the tourist destinations. When travel has become an adequate need for people, media focuses on helping them collect facts about transportation, food, culture and real time data about the places.

Journalism is a way of collecting, recording and preparing of news or incidents across the globe. They distribute the collected facts through several forms of media. Different forms of media include Print media, Broadcast media, Internet media and Out-of-home media. When it comes to journalism there are several forms and travel is one such components under them.

Travel journalism is defined as a type of journalism that emphasizes on providing information about various destinations. They cover every aspect related to the destinations making it easy for the readers to plan their trips. Travel journalism not only serves as a piece of information about the destinations but also as a marketing channel for promoting tourism in different countries.

Historical context of Travel Journalism

Travel according to WTO is a person who travels from one place to other away from the place of residence. There is a certain reason to travel for everyone from one place to another. People have travelled for leisure, business and for various tourism related activities.

Christopher Columbus's voyage to India in the 15th century the purpose is to find new sea route, in the 21st century Elon musk vision's travel to space and mars is explaining us on how evolution has gradually transformed the purposes of travel.

In earlier times, the travel information was recorded by the travellers in the form of books which helped the next generations to take up their voyages. Marco polo, a remarkable merchant, traveller and voyager who has travelled across Asia and other continents, has written many books on his travel experiences. One of his famous books is *"The Description of the World,"* providing detailed explanations of Polo's global travel. *Marco polo, an Italian traveller found India during 1288-1292 AD under the reign of the Pandya kingdom.*

The publication of books made it possible to collect, store and distribute information. To promote Christianity and Islam travelling around the world happened. So many travel manuscript tales about the various travellers and their voyages helped people knowing more about the world. Through these manuscripts, we were able to get enriched information about the continents and countries. The Great British traveller David Livingstone, a national hero wrote the book *Missionary Travels and Researches in South Africa* (1857) which provided guaranteed information about the various sights on South Africa. During his expedition he lost contact with the outside world and to bring him back Compatriot Henry Morton Stanley was sent to Africa in 1871.This seemed to be the first manifestation of travel journalism. He even wrote a book on "How I Found Livingstone".

The period of the travel journalism initially originated in the 19th century when manuscripts about Italy, the Middle East, and Egypt by English, French, and German authors began to be published. In the 19th century, travel essays such as *"Journey to Valaam"* and *"Journey to Imatur"* appeared regularly in Russian magazines and newspapers. V.I. Nemirovich-Danchenko is remembered for the books he published on travel as a professional traveler. American writer John Steinbeck wrote a book entitled "Travels with Charley: In Search of America".

In India people travelled for pilgrimage, trade and conquest in the earlier sub continents. The Hindu mythological texts the *Puranas* and *Upapuranas* includes *Sthalamahatmyas*, guides travellers to sacred sites for priests and pilgrims, listing their special virtues, travel routes and topologies.

Rahul Sankrityayan who is known to be the "Father of travel literature", was a famous writer and author who documented his travels and published them as books.

British library in London has listed the travel books and ethnographical works belonging to the 17th, 18th and 19th century in their Flickr account for public reference.

In the 19th century WS Caine wrote *Picturesque Guide to India featured india's main sights. He mainly wrote this book for British tourists. Pictorial Tour Round India*, published in 1906 gives better ideas of the country's own beauty.

Going forward with digital era travel journalism has gradually evolved. One can easily find travel column in magazine, articles and journals. People prefer to get travel related information from television, social media, newspaper, travel blogs, articles, and magazines.

Key concept and theories

Travel journalism dates back to the period when Herodotus from Greece started his travel expedition. From then travel journalism took different shapes and turns in its evolution. It all started with the books the travellers like Marco Polo left behind which in turn became guides for the explorers. These travel writings remain as the earliest source of information about exploration and travel. This paved the way for the origin of the concept of travel journalism. Travel Magazines came into the limelight with the intention of providing authentic facts about destinations. All the aspects about the destinations are compiled and offered to the readers.

What is travel journalism?

Travel journalism is a profession of collecting, recording and publishing of facts about tourist destinations. A travel journalist usually travels to a wide range of destinations and records every events. They will write all the collected data about the destinations including the travel route, modes of transports, cuisine, attractions, culture, heritage and accommodation options. Usually, the travel journalists record their travel experiences and publish them in the form of travelogues. Travelogues are generally a form of writing where the travel shares his/her experiences they had throughout their trip.

On the other hand, travel journalism also promotes destinations as the trips are often sponsored by the travel companies who in turn will use the content for destination marketing. Travel journalism is a means of inspiring the readers to step out of their den to take up travel to different countries

Scope of travel writing

Travel writing is a profession that one has to take up with lot of passion and commitment. the travel writers should travel to different places and collect every piece of facts and compile them into articles. Travel literature or travel writing encompasses a wide range of works like journals, articles, travelogues, diaries and travel guides.

The essence of travel journalism writing is the ability of the writers to shift readers to different lands through their writing. Travel writers are either hired by the travel companies or they work in freelance but the prime motive its to market the destinations. To become a successful travel writer all that we need is the passion along with commitment to publish authentic data about the destinations.

Types of Travel books

In general travel journalism deals with covering adventures and tales about different places. But in specific there are different types of books dealing with different purposes. Here are the different types of travel books,

Guide books – Typically a book that contains information about destinations. Tourists use these guide books for planning their trips.

Accommodation Guides – These books are designed to help travellers find accommodation options available at the destinations. From Five-star hotels to home stays, the readers could find their suitable stays.

Coffee table books – The Coffee table books are large with eye-catching pictures. These books are of quality content and papers making it the most expensive ones. The readers can just easily flip the pages as they don't have to spend much time in reading and understanding the context.

Business travel guides – Designed and aimed at corporate travels helps the professionals plan their business trips effectively. Right from the travel cost to stay, this will help the business travellers plan accordingly.

Autobiographical novels – These books are generally based on the own life of the authors. In travel segment, these types of books focus on the author's travel expeditions and journeys in the distant lands.

Types of travel journalism

There are 9 types of travel journalist as follows:

1.Freelance travel journalist:

The traveller gives information about the tourist destination for individual clients rather than a specific company. Many freelance journalists approach the company with their project idea which is depicted in the form of articles, books, blogs and with proper approval from company the freelancer conducts research in the destination.

2.Trade Travel journalist:

Trade travel journalists create contents of the tourist destinations for tourism and travel industry. For example, a travel company may hire a travel journalist to accompany them on their trip and write about the overall experience. Many companies publish the positive reviews of trade travel journalist to attract tourist to the destination.

3.Staff travel journalist:

Staff travel journalist is more similar to trade travel journalist but they serve for only one organization. They will be allotted projects and assignments throughout the year by the management and they need to conduct research and submit the assignment in the form of articles, write-ups or a report to an organization

4. Travel Author:

Travel author is someone who gives full length write-ups like books and guide books about the tourist destinations. This type of journalists is freelancers or they might work for an organization. Since guide books require frequent update they often get work all throughout the year.

5.Travel Blogger:

Travel journalist who has the habit of giving first person information about travelling to a destination for the first time often become travel bloggers. They often have their own blogs or work for a third-party blog and post content about the destination based on their travel experiences.

6.Food Travel Blogger:

Food travel blogger is similar to travel blogger except they post content about the food in tourist destinations. A food blogger gives information about the various food cuisines from street food to multi cuisine restaurant recipes all around the destination they travel.

7.Photo Journalist:

The photo Journalist collect photograph of the destinations they travel. Each photo taken by the journalist depicts a story about the place. For example: A company may hire a photo journalist and ask them to collect cultural pictures to market a specific destination.

8. Expose Travel Journalist:

The Expose travel journalist will explore a destination and give information that no one knows about the place. They usually go for offbeat destination that is not familiar with people and in those cases, their writing will help people know about those places. Since such expose traveller may face more difficulties than a normal traveller they should have more survival skills to withstand any hindrance they face during their travel.

9.Travel Magazine Writer:

Travel magazine writer specifically write for company publication. They may work for an organization or can be a freelancer as well. They often picture their writing skills to various organization and get selected based on the skills they exhibit in their writing.

Benefits and impacts of Travel journalism

Benefits of travel journalism

Travel journalism comes with copious benefits for both the readers and journalists. The purpose of travel writing is to inspire readers to feel that traveling is more than just a dream. On the other hand, the adrenaline rush the journalist undergo during their expeditions gives them experience for their lifetime.

Job opportunities

Travel journalism open wide doors for writers to explore their writing skills along with a sense of investigation and analysis. For someone with adverse interest in writing and exploring travel journalism is a great option to discover oneself. The writers can find opportunities to work in travel magazines, travel companies and online portals. Freelance writers take up travel to different countries with the aid of the travel companies for which they have create and market the content. They do not particularly work for any companies but will take up assignments from the complete before their deadline.

Information

Travel magazines and travel journals remain as a great source of information for the readers. Readers gain knowledge about the destinations which further helps them plan their vacations effectively.

Marketing

Travel companies largely depend on travel stories or content to market their packages. Travel blogs are the best-known strategies by the companies to familiarize their packages to the customers. The travel contents are listed in their websites or social media accounts to increase their visibility among the travellers. This marketing strategy has proven to be successful for several businesses.

Real-time data

Travel writing covers a wide range of data about the destinations. It includes more practical information like the challenges, constraints, political scenario, climate and geographical data about the places. These data enhance the travellers to prepare themselves before reaching the destinations.

Impact of Travel Journalism

The impacts of travel journalism are as follows,

Creates awareness

Travelling or visiting places are still a mere dream for many. For them travelling is tedious process and often have struggle finding the potential agents. Travel writing has taken the joy of traveling to every doorstep of its readers. This makes them realize how it more practical to plan their holidays.

Motivational factor

Travel journals are indeed a great option for someone who wants to travel. These articles and blogs share every beautiful aspect they experienced during their journey which in turn motivates the readers to travel.

Navigates interest

Travel stories from writers navigates interests among the readers to take up daring trips. This not only motivates people to travel but also encourages them to become a part of the travel writer's community.

Challenges and constraints of travel journalism

1. Professional Identity

Travel journalism is an indistinct concept even though there are various travel shows, travel magazines and travel channels available. The professional identity lacks clarity among the public.

2. Socio Educational Background

Journalist as the name suggest requires basic educational and communication skill sets, news sense and attitude. The professional journalist and advertisers have been shaped by vocational schools and department of journalism and mass communication.

3. Working Condition

UNESCO World Press Freedom Day 2008 press release has mentioned journalism as a working condition which is being influenced by political, legal , professional and social environment. The journalist are also been affected all over the world by harassment, arrest detention and even life threats.

4. Highly Market Driven

Travel journalism is highly market driven which includes promotion of the destination, tourism service promotion like transportation and hotels. Travel journalism is still a niche segment since new journalism perception, Ideas, working condition are yet to be researched.

5. Logistical complications

Since travel journalist often stay on roads exploring new destinations and involving in promotion activities it's always a complication on finding a better place for stay and food.

6. Low remuneration

Travel journalists are paid low initially when they start as a freelancer and they have to work on other topics rather than tourism destination marketing and promotion to enhance their profile.

Technology and Innovation in Travel Journalism

1. Digitalisation

Travel journalist can collect various details about the destination and can present it in the form of photos videos and post their write-ups in digital media like in a blog ,website or even in news channels.

2. Artificial intelligence

Travel journalism involves incorporating artificial intelligence during their exploration by using Meta AI and Google Maps for finding the best about the location like exotic food, best tourist spots, good hotels for stay. Travellers' can also know about the destination using the reviews available in various online platforms in just one click. Voice assistance can be used by solo travel journalist on their trip to any destination.

3. Sustainable Technology

Travel journalist can use technology incorporated gadgets like a DSLR camera with a silencer just to avoid sounds during clicks in a wildlife area. Journalist can carry a drone for easily capturing the panoramic view of the destination, a solar power to avoid any fire beam during trekking.

4. Digital Payments

Contactless payments and cashless digitalization are common among the new era which makes it easy for travel journalist to carry fewer belongings. During foreign travels travellers have started using Cryptocurrencies. Bitcoins are the widely used Cryptocurrency by travellers to avoid money exchange.

5. Digital feedbacks

The feedbacks from travellers are digitally available in all travel websites and social media platforms which make the public aware of the destinations positive and negative ratings. The public can see the feedbacks and accordingly plan their future trips.

Policy and regulatory framework

For every outsider travel appears to be most enjoyable aspect but in reality, it comes with lot of challenges for travellers. Right from travel documents to seeking permissions, travel journalists have to undergo several hurdles. This segment throws light on legal and regulatory framework for the travel journalists!

Frances Quinn, an award-winning author in her book "Law of Journalists" has presented the key contexts that each journalist has to be aware of. Here is a gist about the legal proceedings advised by her,

Copyright

In every field, it is important to protect the works of the individuals. Whenever the works of a person is taken into reference, it is important for the user to acknowledge it. The travel journalists have to stick with the authenticity of the facts they publish. The copyrights of the photos and content are owned by the writers. Also, the writers are not supposed the images and contexts from others work.

Privacy

The work of the travel journalists should never affect the privacy of other individuals. Whenever the writers cover up articles about destinations or stories of the local communities, they have to refrain themselves from involving too much into their personal issues. So, it is better for the writers to take permission while taking pictures in public.

Defamation

Defamation is a process in which false information is aimed at individuals or groups which harms their reputation. There are two aspects in defamation – Libel and Slander. Defamatory statements that are published or broadcasted are termed as Libel. Whereas slander is issuing defamatory statements in transient forms. The travel writers have to extremely careful while publishing their articles. Especially in social media the hashtags used by the writers also creates a huge impact.

The law of defamation in Journalism aims to protecting the rights of citizen who in turn can file complaints against the journalists. Defamation is punishable in the eyes of law.

Ethical regulations

Travel writing is a daring job that comes with lot of responsibilities. The content they publish should be of true facts from authentic sources. The photographs from their articles should disturb the privacy of others.

Here are the few points for the travel writers to remember while taking up any assignments,

- Every country has its own culture and traditional practices. Be mindful while approaching people for your coverage or blog.
- Abide by the rules and regulations of the countries. Any apart from the rules done is considered to be illegal which will result in facing the legal procedures.
- Ask for concern. This is the biggest thing that a journalist could do before posting their writings.
- While conducting interviews with the local communities or vendors inform them about your vision. So that they could decide if they really want to be a part of it or not.
- Do not disturb or hinder the commercial activities. For eg, if you are visiting a village where the communities depend

on selling clay toys, do not disturb them during their business hours. Or take their permission and then proceed.

- Privacy of the individuals do matter. In case if you want take a group picture of the artists performing in a cultural show, approach them individually. Take a nod from and post the pictures.

Future directions and prospects

Travel journalism has its origin from the era of print media. Print media was the forerunner as it was and is the most easily available source. The looming of technology and internet saw the rise of digital/electronic media. Books, magazines and newspapers are now available in the electronic format making it accessible for all the millennials and Gen z.

Social media's entry has given enormous scope for individuals flourish in several areas. Journalism is one such field that has found its place in social media platforms. Scrolling over mobile phones have become easy rather than flipping up the papers for people. This makes it crystal clear that technology is going to be the future. Here are the ways in which the travel journalism market will flourish in the future.

- **E- books**

  As the world is progressing towards sustainability, many of them have started practicing the concept of "Go Green". Paper books and magazines are now available in non-paper format for the online users. The books will be available in electronic format making it accessible for the readers in their electronic devices. Travelogues and travel magazines in electronic formats are creating a big buzz in the market.

- **Blogs**

  Blogs are web page that are frequently updated with content on business, entertainment, sports and travel. It gives a comment section for the readers to post their reviews. Travel blogs are useful content that exclusively covers travel aspects. The writers will share their personal travel experience, information about the destinations, tips and safety precautions to be followed during the travel. These travel blogs remain great inspiration for the travellers.

- **Vlogs**

  The era of social media has given birth to the rise of influencers. Vlogs are nothing but blogs in the form of virtual representations. Travel vloggers film their travel expeditions and post them in social media. These influencers are playing a vital role in marketing products and services. Influencers travel to vast lands and cover their entire travel experiences in the form of vlogs. These vlogs help the travel companies or DMCs to market their packages to a large number of individuals. According to Google, among the other YouTube content, Travel vlogs from travel channels has the greatest number of subscribers. Hence it is clear that social media holds a significant position in travel journalism.

- **Podcasts**

  Not all individuals are good readers. Some of them love listening stories. Podcasts serve this purpose of taking content to the ears of the users. Individuals create content and share them with the listeners. Travel podcasts deal with creators sharing their travel stories universally to the readers. There will be lot of episodes which can be downloaded and listened whenever the listeners wish. Podcasts are trending these days as travel journalists use this source to market tourist destinations.

Best practices in travel journalism

Online journalism involves posting information about the destination in social platforms in the forms of blogs, vlogs, travel videos and e-content. As a profound travel journalist, the following skill sets to be included in the write-ups for better representation for their work.

- Increase the traffic of the website (Search Engine Optimization)

- Creativity
- Research concepts to be included in the article.
- In-depth analysis of the tourist spots in and around the destination.
- Technical skills including 3D and 2D images in web pages and blogs.
- Vocabulary expertise to make sure even a common man could understand.
- Critical thinking ability.
- Camera adeptness to cover the scenic view of the tourist spots in a more effective manner.

Case study

Christmas celebrations happening worldwide attracting a large number people participating the Christmas Carnival gatherings. It was Germany who initiated the concept of Christmas market which later on spread to various European countries. The European continent is known for hosting the best Christmas market and tourists flew from different countries to taste their bit of celebrations. These markets mark as a way of welcoming holidays and usually start from the mid of November. Millions of people gather to visualize the extravaganza of Christmas celebrations.

Conclusion

In conclusion, travel journalism has emerged as a vital component of the tourism industry, providing travellers with valuable insights and information about destinations around the world. From its historical roots in print media to its current digital manifestations, travel journalism has evolved to incorporate innovative technologies, social media platforms, and diverse formats such as blogs, vlogs, and podcasts. As the industry continues to grow, it is essential for travel journalists to adhere to ethical standards, respect local cultures, and provide accurate and engaging content that inspires and informs travellers. By doing so, travel journalism can promote cross-cultural understanding, support sustainable tourism practices, and enrich the travel experience for millions of people worldwide.

TOURISM AND GEOGRAPHY

Dr. Cinthia Jude
Assistant Professor
Department Of History
Stella Maris College (Autonomous),
Chennai – 86

Introduction

One of the key elements of global change in the modern era is tourism. Many people believe that tourism is the biggest industry in the world. It encourages frequent migration, resource exploitation, development processes, and unavoidable results in economic, social, and geographic areas. Geography and tourism demonstrate how local perspectives may both enrich and enlighten the tourist aspect. In order to demonstrate how tourism patterns have been established and will continue to emerge, this chapter examines the definition, scope, contents, resources, fundamentals, economic, environmental, and social impacts, and features that support the growth of domestic and international tourism.

Additionally, it offers potential remedies for the different effects and the importance of tourism and geography. Instead of referring to tourism and geography as two distinct fields, they are integrated under the umbrella term tourism geography. Both are dependent on one another and cannot exist alone. As a result, it is now referred to as tourism geography. A deeper understanding of the same will be provided by the definition of tourism geography.

Definition of Tourism Geography

The study of locations and the interactions between humans and their surroundings is known as geography. The physical characteristics of the earth's surface and the human societies that are dispersed throughout it are both investigated by geographers. Travelling from one location to another using a variety of transportation methods for various objectives is known as tourism.

According to G. Chabot, "geography and tourism are two terms that are destined to be combined because every geographer must have the characteristics of a tourist. In turn, we can say that every tourist has a hidden geographer because the astute traveller is actually a geographer who has not yet been discovered."

According to Meyer and Arendr, the work of tourism geographers can be characterised as the geography of tourism. Another definition of it is the study of geography, the cataloguing of locations and their attributes.

According to L. Merlo (1969), this science is a subfield of geography that examines the location and appearance of tourist destinations, their unique natural and cultural-historical features, the customs and attractions within the local context, the transportation system that ensures accessibility, and the connections with other tourist destinations.

Scope of Tourism Geography

A vital component of the earth system is the geography of tourism. Human life is impacted by environmental events that are influenced by atmospheric processes. The factors that determine the geography of tourism are physical geography, climatology (the study of climate), and meteorology (the study of weather). These also bring up a crucial point regarding the demand perspective in tourism and geography. Information on the destination's climate is crucial for tourism activities since it influences travellers' decisions to visit.

The geography of tourism is expanding, leading to more opportunities for employment. With the correct information and abilities, one can assess the vast potential for a prosperous career in this field. Students who receive professional tourism education are equipped with the basic understanding of many facets, instruments, and methods that enable them to gain the necessary competence and abilities needed to service clients in this field. One can access a variety of employment options in this field after completing the educational program. Jobs in cruise lines, airlines, hotels, tourist agencies, and responsibilities like that of a tour operator, travel manager, holiday adviser, event manager, and more are available.

Contents of Tourism Geography

The study of the connections between locations, people, and travel is the focus of the intriguing principle of tourism geography. Studying the management, transformation, and use of geographic places for tourism is its essence. This includes researching visitor movements, attractions, and destinations, examining how tourism affects the built and natural ecosystems, taking into account concerns about conservation, sustainability, and the environmental impact of tourism. Investigating how tourism and culture interact, including heritage tourism, cultural festivals, and how tourism affects regional customs and cultures can be observed in the working of tourism and geography. Recognising how tourism affects the economy, including how revenue is distributed, how jobs are created, and how tourist contributes to regional development, looking into how tourism affects local communities on a social and cultural level, including how lifestyle, social structures, and also how community identity evolve.

Examining the creation of tourist plans and policies as well as the planning, regulation, and promotion of tourism by institutions and governments. researching the ways that tourism is evolving, such as changes in traveller tastes, new markets, and worldwide travel trends. Investigating the reasons, inclinations, and actions of travellers, as well as the elements that affect their choice of destination and travel experiences, examining how globalisation has affected tourism, including the movement of people around the world, the function of international travel agencies, and how world events affect travel are the contents of tourism geography. Concentrating on methods that support the growth of tourism in an ethical and sustainable manner, such as eco-tourism, community-based tourism, and laws meant to reduce adverse effects are also contents of tourism and geography.

Resources for Tourism Geography

Mountains, moorlands, and coastal regions are examples of geographical resources found in the physical environment. In general, the built environment refers to the towns, cities, and historic sites that are a part of the human environment. These human and physical resources are frequently found together and are not always found apart. For instance, the physical environment of a coastal tourist resort may consist of a beach, coastline, the sea, and cliffs on either side. Besides this man-made tourism resources such as a harbour, hotels, restaurants, and bars are available.

Geographic Factors of Tourism Geography

Tourism trends and activities are greatly influenced by geographic considerations. Tourists looking for particular weather conditions, such sunny beaches, snow-capped mountains, or moderate temperatures for outdoor activities, are attracted to these regions due to the climate factor. Peak and off-peak seasons have an impact on tourist numbers, demonstrating how seasonal fluctuations also impact tourism flows. Tourists are drawn to distinctive natural characteristics including mountains, rivers, beaches, forests, and deserts. The physical geography of a place affects its scenic attractiveness and outdoor recreation options, including hiking, skiing, and water sports. Roads, airports, and ports are examples of well-developed transportation networks that increase a destination's accessibility and appeal to travellers. Another factor is proximity to important cities and transit hubs.

Cultural and heritage visitors are drawn to places with a strong cultural legacy, historical sites, and distinctive customs. Tourism trends are influenced by the spatial distribution of cultural attractions, including historical monuments, museums, and temples. A destination's appeal is influenced by the accessibility of its tourism infrastructure, which includes lodging, dining options, entertainment venues, and medical care. The entire tourist experience is improved by well-developed infrastructure. Tourism is impacted by a region's economic and political stability. Tourists are more willing to visit locations that are seen as secure and prosperous. On the other hand, economic downturns and political upheavals might discourage tourists.

An essential component is the natural environment, which includes biodiversity, landscape preservation, and the quality of the air and water. Eco-conscious travellers are increasingly choosing destinations that place a high priority on environmental sustainability and conservation. Tourists are drawn to urban regions with a variety of attractions, entertainment venues, retail establishments, and cultural events. Tourism can be greatly impacted by the degree of urban development and the existence of famous cityscapes. Tourism may suffer in areas vulnerable to natural disasters including hurricanes, floods, earthquakes, and volcanic eruptions. Important factors are the likelihood of such occurrences and the destination's capacity for disaster management and recovery.

A destination's appeal may be influenced by its geographic location in relation to other well-known tourist destinations. Increased visitor flow might be advantageous for locations that are connected to other tourist destinations or have a number of neighbouring attractions. The evolution of tourist sites and patterns of travel are influenced by the intricate interactions between these geographic elements. Planners and legislators may more effectively oversee and encourage the growth of sustainable tourism by being aware of these elements.

Relationship between Tourism and Geography

The geography of tourism covers several aspects. It connects the two ideas of geography and tourism, which is a novel idea. Despite the fact that tourism is an application in the study of geography for many years, the geography of tourism can be dated back to the early 1900s. By the 1950s, tourism geography started to gain recognition as a distinct field, particularly in American and German scholarly publications. The role of tourism in geography and its research expanded along with its growth. Books used to incorporate tourist-related data sparingly, but no geographical description would be complete without mentioning tourism. At its core, tourism is a geographical phenomenon. It is the movement of individuals and services across time and location. There has always been a relationship between geography and tourism. The origins of the relationship between geography and travel can be found in antiquity, when geographers had no alternative but to travel and see the globe in order to describe it.

Fundamentals of Tourism Geography

The following categories apply to the foundations of tourism geography. These make it possible for tourism geography to be implied in a meaningful way. The spatial features of tourism, such as how it is dispersed among various locales, how visitors migrate, and how it affects local communities, are examined by tourism geography.

Demand and Supply for Tourism: Recognising the factors that influence travel, such as adventure, culture, business, and leisure, evaluating the amenities, activities, transportation, lodging, and other services that are provided to tourists determine the demand and supply.

Tourism Types:

Domestic and International travel within one's own country versus traveling to foreign destinations. While niche tourism targets certain interests like ecotourism, historic tourism, and adventure tourism, mass tourism involves vast numbers of travellers visiting well-known locations. Identifying popular tourist destinations and comprehending the elements that influence their appeal are key components of the spatial distribution of tourism. Mapping the travel patterns and trends of travellers from their starting point to their final destination is a significant feature of tourism.

Geographical aspects affecting travel:

Physical elements that draw tourists include geography, climate, and scenic vistas. Human elements such as political stability, infrastructure, economic growth, and cultural heritage are also elements that affect travel.

Effects of Travel:

Environmental effects on natural habitats, including both beneficial conservation initiatives and detrimental ones (pollution, habitat destruction), contributes to local economies in the form of infrastructure development, income generating, and job creation. Cultural exchange, preservation, and occasionally cultural degradation are examples of social and cultural impacts on local communities and cultures. The goal of sustainable tourism is to reduce adverse effects while encouraging beneficial contributions to the environment and culture. putting eco-friendly procedures into action, helping out the community, and making sure tourist sites are sustainable over the long run are part of it.

Methods of Tourism Geography Research:

Statistical data is used in quantitative methods to examine trends and patterns in tourism. Qualitative methods are used to learn about the behavior and experiences of tourists through surveys, interviews, and case studies.

Future Trends and Challenges:

Digital marketing, online reservations, virtual tourism, and other technological advancements and their impact on the travel industry are trends in tourism. The effects of globalisation and interconnection on travel markets and cross-cultural interactions, are challenges related to climate change, excessive tourism, and preserving cultural integrity. These foundational concepts offer a thorough review of tourism geography, emphasising the interaction of human and physical factors in forming tourist experiences and landscapes.

The Economic Effects of Geographical Tourism

The geography of tourism has a significant and diverse economic influence that affects local, regional, and national economies in different ways. Direct jobs are created by tourism in industries including entertainment, transportation, and hospitality. Industries that support the tourism sector, such as manufacturing services, and agriculture, generate indirect employment. Tourism provides significant income for businesses and governments. Tourist spending on accommodations, food, attractions, and services boosts local economies. Taxes collected from tourism-related activities contribute to government revenue.

Enormous funds are spent on infrastructure development to have better roads, airports, and public services. These results in raising the living standards of local communities in addition to promoting tourism. By stimulating investment in underdeveloped areas, tourism supports a balanced regional development. It lessens reliance on conventional industries and aids in economic diversification. One of the main sources of foreign exchange profits is international tourism. For nations with a robust tourism industry, this is essential since it supports economic growth and stabilises the balance of payments.

Local companies, such as restaurants, retail stores, and artisan markets, benefit from tourism. It encourages small enterprises and entrepreneurship, which results in resilience and economic diversification. The economy is impacted in multiple ways by tourism. Tourist spending ripples across the economy, creating additional revenue and economic activity. Both direct and indirect economic advantages are included in this.

Cultural tourism also generates economic benefits when visitors spend money on cultural experiences, which helps to preserve and promote cultural heritage sites and customs. Seasonal economic increases brought about by tourism can be both a benefit and a drawback. Strategic planning is necessary to manage economic stability during off-peak periods, even when seasonal peaks provide substantial revenue. By guaranteeing that tourism development protects the environment and cultural assets, which are important attractions, sustainable tourism practices can have long-term positive economic effects.

Environmental Impact of Tourism Geography

There are both positive and negative impacts of the environment as a result of tourism. The following are some detrimental effects on the environment. Overuse of food, energy, and water to accommodate tourists can put a strain on local resources, particularly in places where commodities are scarce. Pollution of the air, water, and land can result from tourism. Emissions from transportation, garbage from lodging and visitors, and pollution from leisure activities are common causes. The construction of tourist infrastructure, such as roads, hotels, and resorts, may result in the loss of natural habitats, endangering the local wildlife and plants. More visitors frequently mean more garbage, including sewage and solid waste, which might overload the capacity of the local waste management systems. Tourism can disturb wildlife and ecosystems, leading to a loss of biodiversity. Particularly dangerous activities include hunting, fishing, and gathering trinkets from natural areas. Climate change is exacerbated by tourism, which contributes heavily to greenhouse gas emissions, especially air travel and upscale lodging. Due to high foot traffic and recreational activities, popular tourist destinations may experience soil erosion, corrosion, and other environmental wear and tear.

The positive effects on the environment are very striking. Natural environments can be preserved by reinvesting tourism-related income in conservation initiatives like marine sanctuaries, wildlife reserves, and protected areas. By encouraging conservation initiatives and sustainable practices, tourism may increase awareness of environmental issues among both visitors and local people. Eco-tourism and sustainable tourism practices aim to minimize environmental footprints by promoting responsible travel, energy efficiency, waste reduction, and community involvement. In order to attract tourists, local communities may be encouraged to preserve their natural and cultural heritage assets through the provision of financial incentives.

Remedies for the Harmful Environmental Effects

Several steps can be made to lessen the detrimental effects of tourism on the environment. Putting into practice strategic plans that give sustainable growth first priority and take environmental carrying capabilities into account will help safeguard the environment. Encouraging companies and visitors to adopt eco-friendly habits such using renewable energy sources, cutting back on waste, and saving water, fostering ethical behavior and teaching visitors and residents the value of protecting the environment, putting into practice laws that restrict the negative effects of tourism on the environment, such as those pertaining to resource use, pollution prevention, and protected area management. It is feasible to reap the rewards of tourism while reducing its adverse effects on the environment by striking a balance between its demands and environmental sustainability.

Geographical aspects of Tourism's Social Impact

Destinations and their local communities may have significant social effects as a result of tourism. The exchange of cultures, customs, and ideas are facilitated by tourism, which is one of the positive social impacts. While inhabitants are exposed to many cultures, tourists learn about the habits, dialects, and lifestyles of the area. Both visitors and locals can gain from the growth of community amenities and services including public utilities, healthcare, and education brought about by tourism. By giving local communities, the chance to take part in and profit from tourism-related activities, tourism may promote a feeling of pride and ownership. To ensure that cultural heritage is preserved for future generations, tourism-related revenue can be utilised to maintain and repair historical and cultural sites. Better roads, communication systems, and recreational opportunities are just a few examples of how the growth of tourism infrastructure and services may enhance the standard of living for locals.

The detrimental effects on society and the environment include local customs and cultures that may be eroded as a result of tourism-induced exposure to outsiders. Commercialisation or abandonment of traditional aspects in favour of tourism-driven activities are possible outcomes. Social and economic upheavals may result from the displacement of local residents brought on by the expansion of tourism infrastructure. To provide room for additional hotels, resorts, and attractions, residents might have to move. Living expenses in destinations may rise as a result of tourism. Rising costs for goods, services, and real estate could make it harder for locals to pay for needs. Seasonal employment brought up by tourism frequently causes local workers' incomes to fluctuate. While there may be plenty of job openings during the busiest travel seasons, there may be few during the other times. Social tensions between visitors and locals may result from the influx of tourists. Relationships can be strained by problems like noise, crowding, and disregard for regional traditions.

Remedies for the Adverse Social Effects

Several tactics can be used to minimise the negative social effects of tourism and optimise its beneficial ones. Engaging local communities in tourism planning and decision-making processes to ensure their needs and concerns are addressed.

Fostering respect and cultural awareness among travellers and travel agencies in order to preserve regional customs and history, implementing eco-friendly tourism strategies that strike a balance between local communities' welfare, economic expansion, and the protection of natural and cultural resources, supplying locals with educational and training opportunities to improve their abilities and empower them to engage in tourism activities in an efficient manner. Ensuring that everyone in the community, particularly disadvantaged and marginalised groups, receives an equitable share of the economic advantages of tourism, better planning and management of tourist-related activities is made possible by these social implications, guaranteeing that tourism growth is inclusive, considerate, and advantageous for all parties.

The importance of Geography and Tourism

Geography and tourism are closely related, and each greatly influences the other. Due to its ability to provide income and job opportunities, tourism is a key contributor to economic growth. By bringing in money for governments and companies through taxes and visitor expenditure, it boosts regional economies. Cultural exchange and understanding are fostered by tourism. By experiencing many cultures, customs, and ways of life, travellers might develop tolerance and a global perspective. Better roads, airports, and public facilities are frequently the result of the necessity to accommodate tourists, which helps both visitors and locals. Sites of cultural and natural heritage can be preserved financially through tourism. Tourism-related income can be used to support historical landmark preservation and conservation initiatives. By giving local populations access to new services, amenities, and social interaction possibilities, tourism can improve their quality of life. Natural resource protection initiatives are sparked by ecotourism and sustainable tourism practices, which increase public awareness of environmental problems and the value of conservation.

Significance of Geography in Tourism

Recognising spatial patterns is crucial, and Geography aids in comprehending how tourism activities are distributed geographically. It examines how location, accessibility, and destination appeal affect tourist flows. Assessment of the environmental impact is unavoidable. Geographical studies evaluate how tourism affects the environment, directing conservation and sustainable development initiatives. Geography aids in locating regions that are susceptible to pressure from tourists. It is necessary to manage the resources. In order to ensure that tourism development is sustainable and does not deplete or harm local resources, geography offers insights into the management of natural resources and landscapes. The best tourism geography comes from planning and development.

Geographic principles are used in tourism planning to optimize land use, design infrastructure, and develop policies that balance tourism growth with environmental and social considerations. Examining the attitude and needs of tourists is the need of the hour. Geographers investigate why and how tourists behave, as well as what kinds of places and activities they choose. This data aids in customising marketing plans and travel-related items. In order to comprehend how tourism supports regional growth and economic diversification, geography looks at the economic effects of tourism on various locations. When evaluating the dangers and natural hazards related to tourism, geography is essential. In order to safeguard visitors and local populations, it supports disaster preparedness and mitigation measures. Understanding and protecting the cultural landscapes that draw tourists is made easier by geography. It guarantees that the growth of tourism honours and advances the local cultural heritage.

Geography and tourism are closely related, with geography offering the frameworks and instruments for managing and analysing tourism activities. Stakeholders can create plans that optimise tourism's positive effects while reducing its negative ones by comprehending the geographical, environmental, and cultural aspects of the industry. The development of prosperous and sustainable tourism industries that favourably impact the local and global economies, society, and environment depends on this collaboration.

Conclusion

The complex and profound relationship between geography and tourism affects the global development, sustainability, and spatial distribution of tourist-related activities. The fundamental knowledge of physical landscapes, cultural settings, and environmental dynamics that influence travel destinations and experiences is provided by geography. In turn, tourism promotes cultural interchange, stimulates economic growth, and calls for the expansion of services and infrastructure. We can better plan by gaining insights into the trends and effects of tourism through a thorough examination of regional elements. This mutually beneficial relationship emphasises how crucial it is to incorporate spatial knowledge into tourism development plans in order to guarantee that travel supports sustainable practices, protects cultural and natural heritage, and boosts local economies.

The task going forward is to strike a balance between the economic advantages of tourism and its effects on society and the environment in order to create a sustainable, responsible, and egalitarian tourism model. We can negotiate this complicated terrain and strive towards a tourist industry that benefits both visitors and host communities, promoting understanding and sustainability on a worldwide scale, by utilising the concepts of geography.

TOURISM AND ENVIRONMENT

Dr. D. Benitha Golda
Assistant Professor,
Department of Advanced Zoology and Biotechnology,
Women's Christian College

Introduction

The intricate relationship between tourism and the environment is deeply rooted in the complex nature of tourism itself. As a multifaceted phenomenon, tourism is shaped by a dynamic interplay of factors in both the tourists' home environments and the destinations they visit. This chapter explores the evolution of tourism, tracing its history and examining how societal shifts since the Industrial Revolution have contributed to the rise of mass tourism. The growth in demand for tourism, although a relatively recent phenomenon, is a hallmark of global society. Several factors have converged to fuel this growth, transforming tourism into an activity of mass participation. This chapter delves into the history of tourism, unravelling the reasons behind its rapid expansion. A significant development in the latter half of the twentieth century was the emergence of international mass tourism, which has profoundly impacted the environment. As a consequence of mass participation in global tourism, an increasing number and variety of natural environments are being exposed to tourism, leading to various environmental consequences. This chapter aims to explore the intricate relationship between tourism and the environment, examining the concepts and theories behind the far-reaching impacts of this phenomenon.

Historical Context and Development of Tourism and Environment

The relationship between tourism and the environment has undergone significant transformations over the centuries. In the pre-industrial era, tourism was a privilege reserved for the wealthy, with minimal environmental impact. However, the Industrial Revolution marked a turning point, as improved transportation made travel more accessible, leading to the growth of mass tourism. This, in turn, resulted in habitat destruction, pollution, and resource degradation.

The post-World War II period saw the rise of international mass tourism, fuelled by advancements in air transportation and package tours. While this growth brought economic benefits, it also led to substantial environmental consequences, including habitat destruction, pollution, and climate change. The tourism industry's reliance on natural resources, such as water and energy, further exacerbated these issues.

In recent decades, the tourism industry has acknowledged its environmental footprint and begun to adopt sustainable practices. Initiatives like eco-tourism, responsible travel, environmental certification programs, and community-based tourism have gained traction. However, the industry still faces significant environmental challenges, including climate change, over-tourism, and resource depletion. Addressing these challenges will require continued innovation, collaboration, and a commitment to sustainability.

Tourism approaches in Modern Times and their environmental consequences

The approach to tourism can be categorized as hard- and soft tourism based on the travel style, duration, transport modes, planning, guidance, lifestyles, focus, engagement, preparation, cultural learning, attitude, exchange, activities, emotions and ambiance. **(Table 1)** Hard tourism is structured, fast-paced, and commodified, emphasizing convenience and sightseeing. It focuses on mass tourism with significant infrastructure development, often resulting in higher environmental impacts. Soft tourism on the other hand is more flexible, immersive, and experiential, prioritizing cultural understanding, local interactions, and sustainability. It emphasizes low-impact activities, small-scale operations, and sustainable practices.

Table 1 Comparison of Hard Tourism and Soft Tourism

Aspect	Hard Tourism	Soft Tourism
Travel Style	Mass tourism, institutionalized	Individual travel, with family or friends
Duration	Short duration, limited time in the area	Long duration, extended time spent in the area
Transport Modes	Fast vehicles, quick travel modes	Slow vehicles, suited to purpose
Planning	Fixed, pre-prepared tour programs	Spontaneous decisions during the trip
Guidance	External guidance	Internal guidance
Lifestyles	Imported lifestyles	Common rural lifestyles
Focus	"Sights"	Experiences
Engagement	Passive, comfortable, effortless	Active, requires effort and involvement
Preparation	Minimal or no preparation	Pre-travel learning about the destination
Cultural Learning	No attempt to learn the local language	Learning the local language
Attitude	Feeling of superiority	Joy of learning
Exchange	Souvenirs, shopping	Bringing gifts, gaining knowledge and skills
Activities	Taking pictures, buying postcards	Photography, drawing, painting
Emotions	Curiosity	Sensitivity and understanding
Ambiance	Noisy	Quiet and reflective

Source: Fekete, M. (2006) and Bacsi, Zsuzsanna & Tóth, Éva. (2019).

Key Concepts and Theories

- The relationship between tourism and the environment is complex and multifaceted. Understanding this relationship requires an examination of the key concepts and theories that underpin it. The major concepts underlying the intersection of tourism and the environment are condensed for the benefit of the reader with the relevant theories in parenthesis
- One of the fundamental concepts in this context is sustainability. Sustainable tourism refers to tourism that is economically viable, socially responsible, and environmentally friendly. This concept recognizes that tourism can have both positive and negative impacts on the environment, and seeks to minimize the negative impacts while maximizing the positive ones **(Sustainable Tourism Development Theory)**. Further, it emphasizes that tourism development should be balanced with community well-being and ecological preservation **(Doxey's Irritation Index (Irridex)** to make it sustainable.
- Another important concept is the carrying capacity of a destination. Carrying capacity refers to the maximum number of tourists a destination can accommodate without suffering environmental degradation or loss of its cultural identity. Understanding the carrying capacity of a destination is crucial for sustainable tourism planning and management and growth **(Tourism Carrying Capacity Theory).**
- Unchecked Tourism, especially in developing nations that become economically dependent on tourism results in fragile environments **(Dependency Theory).**
- Emphasis on a dynamic approach involving acceptable levels of environmental and social change can help to manage the impact of tourism on the environment **(Limits of Acceptable Change Theory).**
- Eco-friendly practices, specifically focussed on the natural environment promoting conservation and sustainability promoted as 'Ecotourism' should be integrated into tourism development **(Ecological Modernisation Theory).**

- Sustainable tourism requires cooperation, accountability, and collaboration among various stakeholders **(Stakeholder Theory in Tourism)**
- Regulations and collective actions are needed to prevent over-exploitation of natural environments as tourist destinations **(Tragedy of Commons).**
- Ecosystems and communities have the capacity to recover from disturbances caused by tourism activities **(Resilience Theory).**
- A holistic approach to tourism planning that integrates conservation with socio-economic goals must be encouraged **(Ecological Systems Theory).**

Theoretical Frameworks to understand the concepts about relationship between tourism and the environment

1. Tourism Impact Model

Several theoretical frameworks have been developed to understand the relationship between tourism and the environment. One of the most influential frameworks is the **Tourism Impact Model,** envisioned by Mathieson and Wall (1982), and modified later by multiple researchers which identifies the various impacts of tourism on the environment, including economic, social, and environmental impacts. Economically, tourism boosts local economies through revenue generation, job creation, and infrastructure development, benefiting both visitors and residents. However, challenges include economic leakage (profits going to external entities), over-reliance on tourism, and inflation, which can raise living costs for locals. Socio-culturally, tourism supports cultural preservation, fosters cross-cultural exchange, and funds community development projects. Conversely, it can lead to cultural commodification, overcrowding, and the loss of authenticity in traditions and practices. Environmentally

Tourism contributes positively by supporting conservation efforts and raising environmental awareness. However, it can strain natural resources, cause pollution, and degrade habitats due to infrastructure expansion and high tourist activity.

The model functions as a **feedback loop**:

1. Tourism development attracts visitors.
2. Their activities interact with the economy, society, and environment, leading to positive and negative impacts.
3. Authorities analyse these effects and implement strategies to enhance benefits and mitigate harm.
4. Destinations evolve to maintain sustainability and long-term appeal.

Measurement tools include economic (GDP and employment data), socio-cultural (community satisfaction surveys), and environmental indicators (carbon footprint and biodiversity metrics).

The model is essential for identifying areas needing intervention, promoting sustainable strategies, and balancing tourism growth with conservation and community well-being. When effectively applied, it serves as a framework for responsible and equitable tourism development

2. **Sustainable Tourism Development Model**

Another important framework is the **Sustainable Tourism Development Model**, which provides a holistic approach to sustainable tourism planning and management. The core idea of the sustainable development theory/ model is that tourism must meet the needs of current tourists and host communities while protecting and enhancing environmental resources for future generations.

The basic tenets of this theory are conserving biodiversity and ecosystems, promoting equitable economic benefits for local communities, and ensuring a balance between environmental conservation and tourist satisfaction. Sustainable tourism initiatives such as ecotourism, green certifications, and carbon offset programs align with this theory.

Sustainable Tourism Model

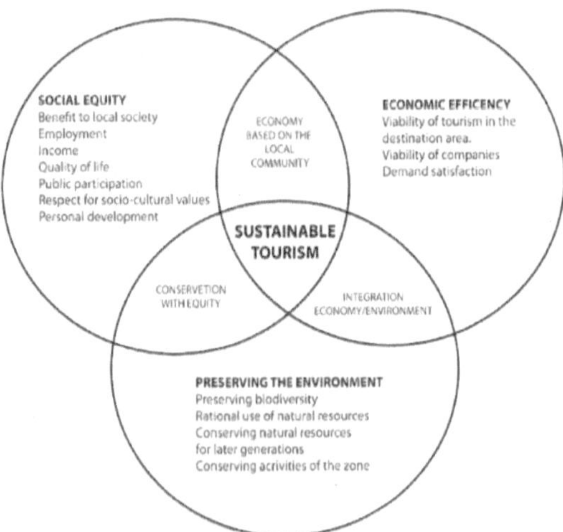

Tourism Carrying Capacity Theory

The Carrying Capacity theory in tourism is an adaptation from the original theory proposed by Thomas Robert Malthus (1766-1834). The concept of carrying capacity focuses on the maximum number of visitors a destination can accommodate without causing unacceptable environmental, economic, or social impacts. Carrying capacity theory groups carrying capacity as Physical Carrying Capacity that has limits based on infrastructure (e.g., number of hotel rooms or parking spaces), Environmental Carrying Capacity with thresholds for environmental damage (e.g., wildlife disturbances or water pollution), and Social Carrying Capacity the point at which local communities or tourists feel crowded or stressed. This theory is crucial for sustainable tourism planning and environmental preservation.

3. Doxey's Irritation Index (Irridex) to balance growth and conservation

Doxey's Irritation Index, or Irridex Theory, introduced by George Doxey in 1975, is a framework that illustrates the changing attitudes of local communities toward tourism and tourists as tourism development progresses. The model highlights how unchecked tourism can lead to social and environmental challenges, affecting the host community's perception of the industry.

In the early stages of a destination's development, locals typically feel a sense of excitement and anticipation, enjoying informal interactions with tourists. Over time, as tourism expands, these interactions become more formal, and the industry is viewed positively as a source of income and investment. However, as the number of tourists increases and external investments dominate, residents may begin to express concerns about the growing pressures on their community. Eventually, these concerns escalate to frustration, often verbal or physical, with tourists perceived as the root of the issues.

This theory provides a valuable lens for understanding how tourism impacts host communities and underscores the need for proactive measures. By addressing these challenges early, stakeholders can balance tourism growth with the preservation of local culture, community well-being, and environmental sustainability.

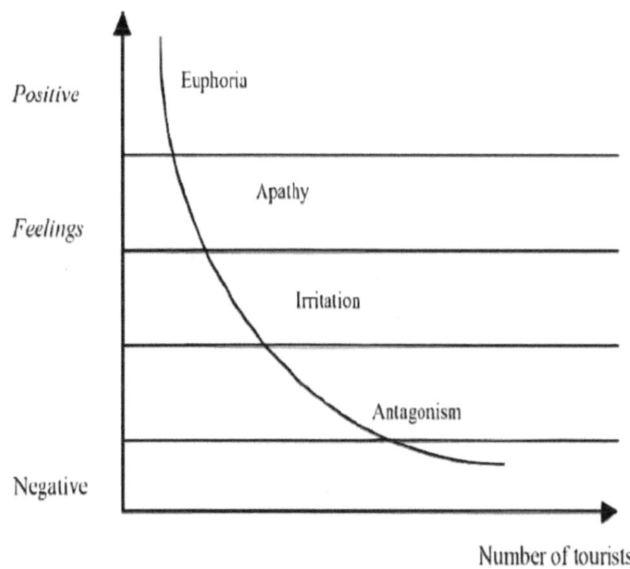

4. **Dependency theory**

Dependency Theory, introduced by Raul Prebisch in the 1960s, examines the unequal power relationships between developed and developing countries, particularly in the context of economic systems like international tourism. The theory highlights how wealthier nations and multinational corporations often benefit disproportionately from tourism, exploiting the natural and cultural resources of economically backward nations, frequently at the expense of the local environment and communities. A simplified example illustrates this imbalance: Country A, a resource-rich but economically poor nation, is exploited by Country B, a wealthier nation. Country B extracts raw materials from Country A at low prices, destabilizing it through colonialism or neocolonialism. Country B then refines the materials and sells the finished goods back to Country A at much higher prices, creating a cycle of dependence and debt for Country A. Developing countries often rely heavily on tourism for economic growth, but this dependency can result in overexploitation and unsustainable practices driven by external capitalist enterprises.

Dynamic and novel approaches are needed to embrace the rapid changes happening in the tourism sector globally to develop this as an environmentally sustainable enterprise. The following theories propose to mitigate the environmental impacts reasonably.

5. **The Limits of Acceptable Change (LAC) Theory**

Developed during the 1970s and 1980s, this theory offers a modern approach to managing tourism impacts on destinations. Unlike traditional Tourism Carrying Capacity models that focus on visitor numbers, LAC evaluates the environmental, social, and ecological changes a destination can sustainably accommodate. The framework involves three key stages: defining destination objectives, identifying measurable indicators for social, economic, and environmental conditions, and setting standards to maintain these conditions. Effective governance and collaboration among stakeholders are critical for determining acceptable limits and ensuring sustainable visitor management. Further, it emphasizes maintaining the quality of the environment and visitor experience rather than adhering to rigid numerical thresholds. LAC promotes adaptable management by defining acceptable conditions based on a destination's specific objectives. It shifts the discussion from visitor counts to the desired state of the area, making it a more dynamic and goal-oriented model. Despite its theoretical strengths, the LAC framework presents practical challenges, such as balancing varying stakeholder perspectives and distinguishing between tolerable and ideal conditions, integrating complex variables and limited data availability, requiring careful planning and adaptive strategies for effective application.

6. **The Ecological Modernisation Theory,**

This theory conceptualised by Christoff Peter (1996) emphasizes adopting environmentally sustainable practices in business operations and economic development while laying the foundation for innovative approaches such as sustainable supply chain management and cleaner technologies. The theory highlights the importance of diversity, as ecological modernization functions within a multi-level framework involving markets, entrepreneurs, society, and government and integrates it with the socio-cultural dimensions of the economy.

7. **Stakeholder theory in tourism**

Effective management models, such as Freeman's stakeholder theory (1984), emphasize understanding the interests and relationships of all parties, guiding the sustainable tourism process. By fostering joint management and participation from all stakeholders, tourism development can become more inclusive and balanced, ensuring that future generations benefit from a thriving, sustainable tourism industry. Stakeholder engagement is crucial for sustainable tourism, as it involves integrating various agents—such as local populations, tourists, and management entities—who each have distinct needs and interests. A sustainable model should satisfy these diverse interests by ensuring that tourism development benefits all involved parties. The concept of sustainability requires a collective effort, where stakeholders work together to achieve a common goal: **the conservation and long-term viability of the destination**. This requires consensus-building and collaborative decision-making, often based on ethical principles like solidarity and social equality.

8. **Tragedy of Commons theory**

The concept of the "Tragedy of the Commons" (TOC), introduced by Garrett Hardin in 1968, describes the over-exploitation and degradation of shared resources like oceans, rivers, and parklands. Hardin's argument illustrates a scenario where a common pasture is open to all herders. Each herder benefits individually by selling their animals, while only incurring a small cost from over-grazing. As the number of animals increases beyond the pasture's capacity, each herder continues adding more animals to maximize personal profit, despite contributing to the shared destruction of the resource. Hardin concludes that this self-interest in an unrestricted system leads to inevitable ruin: "Freedom in a common brings ruin to all." This theory highlights the challenges of managing resources that are accessible to all but owned by none. The Tragedy of the Commons occurs when it is costly or difficult to prevent individuals from exploiting common resources, leading to their depletion. In the context of sustainable tourism, this concept is crucial, as tourism often places pressure on natural and cultural assets that are shared by multiple stakeholders. Without proper management and regulation, over-tourism can lead to resource degradation, undermining the very attractions that sustain the tourism industry. Therefore, sustainable tourism must address the balance between individual interests and the collective responsibility to protect and conserve shared resources for long-term benefit.

9. **Resilience theory in tourism**

This theory was notably developed and applied by **Timothy Beatley** and **Brian R. Walker**, who integrated it into the field of sustainable tourism management. They extended the concept of resilience from ecological systems to human-influenced systems, stressing that tourism destinations, much like ecosystems, need to have the flexibility and capacity to adjust to ongoing changes and shocks. The application of resilience thinking in tourism is important in designing sustainable, long-term tourism strategies that are responsive to environmental, social, and economic shifts. The theory suggests that resilience is not just about bouncing back to the status quo after a disturbance but also about building adaptive capacity to evolve and improve over time. This involves maintaining the functionality of key tourism systems (e.g., the environment, community, infrastructure, and economy), learning from past experiences, and adapting management practices to better handle future challenges. Resilience theory in tourism is a framework that emphasizes the ability of tourism systems—whether natural, economic, or social—to absorb disturbances and adapt to changes, while maintaining the ability to evolve and thrive in the long term. It draws from ecological and systems theory, focusing on the capacity of tourism destinations to cope with shocks (like natural disasters, economic downturns, or crises) and stresses (such as overtourism), and to recover or transform in response to these challenges.

After that comprehensive overview of the theories concepts and frameworks in tourism that focus on the environment, let us now shift our focus to understanding whether there is an effective tool that can help nations predict and prevent environmental degradation because of tourism

A Diagnostic Aid to Highlight the Interconnectedness of Tourism Growth and Environmental Carrying Capacity

Richard Butler's Tourism Area Life Cycle (TALC) Model (Butler, 1980). TALC model is relevant as the first "port of call" for any serious analysis of a particular tourist area. It highlights the environmental risks associated with unplanned growth and over-tourism and underscores the need for sustainable management. This model describes the evolution of a tourism destination and how tourist attractions change over time through six stages.

1. **Exploration**

Exploration is the first stage in this model. A few adventurous tourists usually the nonlocal ones visit irregularly for its culture and scenic beauty and the environment remains largely untouched. At this stage, local communities interact with tourists yet are not economically involved.

2. **Involvement:**

Tourism infrastructure develops and tourist seasons get demarcated as efforts to market these destinations begin. Further local communities start providing services and basic facilities such as food, accommodation, guides and transport. As the stage progresses, local and national authorities are pressurised to contribute to the development of the area by providing and improving transport infrastructure and other facilities for visitors.

3. **Development:**

The area becomes widely recognized as a tourist attraction because of enhanced promotion, advertising, and marketing strategies by tourist companies and the government at the regional, national, and international levels for greater financial gains. Rapid tourist influx coupled with increased facilities subject the destination to environmental pressures.

4. **Consolidation:**

This is the stage where the numbers of visitors is higher than permanent residents. Tourism becomes a major contributor to the local economy and to environmental degradation as businesses push for further expansion. However, locals not involved in tourism start opposing tourism activities as they witness socio-cultural and environmental degradation

5. **Stagnation:**

As the name suggests, the tourist attraction relies heavily on repeat visitations. Tourist destinations can no longer expand as they have reached their maximum capacity leading to noticeably polluted environments, loss of biodiversity, and social issues leading to reduced tourist satisfaction.

6. Post stagnation:

The destination either adopts sustainable practices by developing artificial attractiveness such as casinos or by using previously unused natural resources and creating a new tourist market and rejuvenates or faces reduced appeal, declines and is incompetent with newer attractions. This decline stage is characterized by weekend and day trips as the attraction has lost its appeal. Example of decline include but not limited to Porcelain Tower of Nanjing (China).

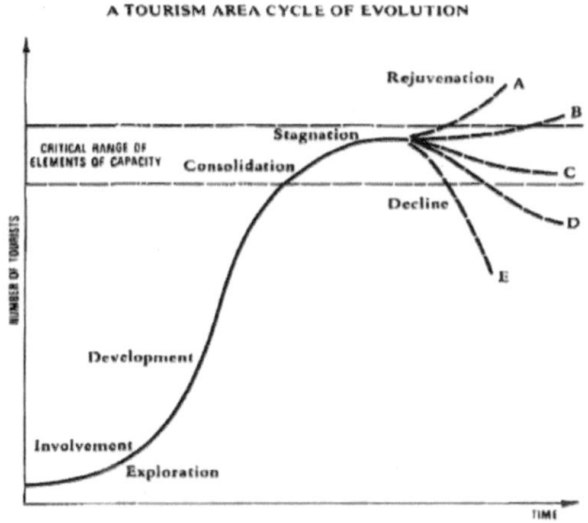

Source: Richard Butler's Tourism Area Life Cycle Model (Butler, 1980, p.7)

Major Types of Tourism in India and its Impacts

Various types and forms of tourism have emerged over the years, each with its unique characteristics and environmental implications. One of the most popular forms of tourism is mass tourism, which involves large numbers of tourists visiting popular destinations. While mass tourism can generate significant economic benefits, it can also lead to environmental degradation, pollution, and strain on local resources.

In contrast, alternative forms of tourism, such as ecotourism and sustainable tourism, prioritize environmental conservation and cultural sensitivity. Ecotourism, for example, involves responsible travel to natural areas that conserves the environment and promotes the well-being of local communities. Sustainable tourism, on the other hand, aims to minimize the negative impacts of tourism on the environment and local cultures, while maximizing economic benefits.

Other forms of tourism that have gained popularity in recent years include adventure tourism, wildlife tourism, and geo-tourism to name a few. Adventure tourism involves traveling to remote or exotic destinations to participate in outdoor activities such as hiking, climbing, or rafting. Trekking hotspots include Ladakh, Sikkim, and the Himalayas, while Himachal Pradesh and Jammu & Kashmir are known for skiing. Whitewater rafting is also popular in Uttarakhand, Assam, and Arunachal Pradesh. Wildlife tourism, on the other hand, involves observing and interacting with wildlife in their natural habitats. Geo tourism, a relatively new form of tourism, involves exploring and appreciating the unique geological features of a destination.

Special interest tourism is another type of tourism that has emerged in recent years. This form of tourism involves traveling to destinations that cater to specific interests or hobbies, such as food and wine tourism, cultural tourism, or sports tourism. While special interest tourism can provide unique and enriching experiences for tourists, it can also have negative environmental impacts if not managed sustainably.

India's vast coastline supports beach tourism, with destinations like Kerala, Goa, the Andaman & Nicobar Islands, and Lakshadweep offering year-round appeal. Cultural tourism thrives due to India's rich heritage, attracting visitors to events like the Pushkar Fair (Rajasthan) and sites such as the Taj Mahal (Uttar Pradesh) and Ajanta & Ellora Caves (Maharashtra). Eco-tourism focuses on sustainability, with notable spots including Kaziranga National Park (Assam) and Gir National Park (Gujarat). Medical tourism has positioned India as a global healthcare hub, especially in Chennai, offering affordable, quality treatments. Finally, India's biodiversity boosts wildlife tourism in areas like Corbett National Park (Uttarakhand) and Sariska Wildlife Sanctuary (Rajasthan).

Overall, the various types and forms of tourism offer a range of opportunities for tourists to experience and appreciate different environments and cultures. However, it is essential to recognize the potential environmental impacts of tourism and to adopt sustainable tourism practices that minimize harm and promote conservation.

Benefits and Impacts

Tourism's environmental impact is multifaceted, yielding both benefits and drawbacks. While it can generate substantial economic benefits for local communities, supporting conservation efforts and promoting cultural exchange, it also poses significant environmental risks. The degradation of natural habitats, pollution, and climate change are notable concerns, exacerbated by inadequate waste management and transportation emissions. Nevertheless, sustainable tourism practices, such as ecotourism and responsible travel, offer a promising solution, enabling the industry to mitigate its negative impacts while preserving the environment and supporting local communities.

Challenges and Constraints

The tourism industry confronts numerous intricate challenges in its pursuit of sustainable practices and minimized environmental impacts. Key obstacles include tourists' lack of awareness about their ecological footprint, inadequate infrastructure and resources in destinations, and the prohibitively high costs of implementing sustainable measures. Moreover, climate change, rapid tourism growth, and balancing economic, social, and environmental considerations further complicate the industry's sustainability endeavours. Addressing these multifaceted challenges necessitates a collaborative effort from governments, tourism operators, local communities, and tourists to foster environmentally conscious practices and mitigate the industry's ecological consequences.

Technology and Innovation

The tourism industry is harnessing technology and innovation to propel sustainable practices and mitigate its ecological footprint. Digital platforms, mobile apps, and renewable energy solutions are being leveraged to promote eco-friendly behaviors, reduce energy consumption, and track environmental metrics. Data analytics, virtual and augmented reality, and blockchain technology are also being explored to enhance the tourist experience, verify sustainability credentials, and promote environmentally responsible travel choices. By embracing these technological advancements, the tourism industry can transform into a more sustainable, efficient, and environmentally conscious sector, ultimately reducing its impact on the planet while enriching the travel experience.

Policy and Regulatory Framework

The policy and regulatory framework governing tourism and environment plays a vital role in promoting sustainable tourism practices and mitigating the industry's ecological footprint. Governments worldwide have established guidelines and regulations to manage tourism's environmental impacts, such as the UNWTO's sustainable tourism guidelines and national policies like the US's National Environmental Policy Act. India, too, has a robust framework, including the National Tourism Policy 2002, the Sustainable Tourism Criteria for India, and regulatory laws like the Environment (Protection) Act 1986. Effective implementation and enforcement of these policies require collaborative efforts from governments, tourism boards, and local stakeholders to promote sustainable tourism practices, protect the environment, and ensure the industry's long-term sustainability.

Future Directions and Prospects

The future of tourism and the environment is poised for transformative change, driven by escalating demand for sustainable experiences, growing climate change awareness, and emerging technologies. Key directions include adopting sustainable tourism practices that balance environmental stewardship with economic benefits, as exemplified by the UNWTO's Sustainable Tourism for Development Guidebook. Governments worldwide, including India, are integrating tourism and environmental policies, launching initiatives like the Swachh Bharat Abhiyan and Incredible India 2.0 campaign to promote eco-tourism, conservation, and community involvement, thereby unlocking opportunities for sustainable entrepreneurship and innovation. Overall, the future of tourism and environment globally and in India looks promising, with a growing recognition of the importance of sustainable tourism practices. With governments, stakeholders, and tourists working together to promote sustainable tourism, the industry is expected to emerge as a leader in sustainable development, providing economic benefits while minimizing environmental impacts.

Conclusion

In conclusion, the relationship between tourism and environment is complex and multifaceted. While tourism can have significant environmental impacts, such as pollution, habitat destruction, and climate change, it also has the potential to promote conservation, sustainable development, and community empowerment. Effective management of tourism's environmental impacts requires a comprehensive approach that involves governments, stakeholders, and tourists. This includes adopting sustainable tourism practices, implementing policies and regulations, and promoting education and awareness. By working together, we can minimize the negative impacts of tourism on the environment and maximize its benefits, ultimately contributing to a more sustainable and responsible tourism industry. India, with its rich natural and cultural heritage, has a significant role to play in this endeavour, and its efforts to promote sustainable tourism practices are a step in the right direction.

TOURISM AND MARKETING

Dr. P. Senkathir Selvi
Assistant Professor,
Department of History,
Stella Maris College (Autonomous)
Chennai – 600086

Introduction

Tourism is a dynamic global industry that contributes significantly to economic growth, cultural exchange, and social development. It encompasses a wide range of activities, including leisure travel, business trips, and pilgrimage, making it a complex sector that touches diverse aspects of human life. Marketing plays a crucial role in tourism business by creating awareness, promoting destinations, and influencing travel decisions. Through strategic marketing, destinations and tourism-related commerce can attract and engage travellers, ultimately enhancing their economic viability and cultural visibility.

Historically, tourism marketing has evolved alongside technological advancements, shifting from traditional print advertisements to sophisticated digital campaigns. In today's competitive global landscape, tourism marketing is not just about selling a destination but about creating meaningful experiences that resonate with travellers. It involves understanding consumer behavior, tailoring messages to specific audiences, and leveraging technology to expand reach and impact.

The interplay between tourism and marketing is essential for sustainable growth. Effective marketing strategies can help destinations manage tourism flows, reduce environmental impacts, and preserve cultural heritage. This paper examines the interdependence of tourism and marketing, exploring key concepts, challenges, and innovations while highlighting best practices and future directions for the industry to thrive in a rapidly changing world.

Definition

Tourism encompasses the activities of people travelling to and staying in places outside their usual environment for leisure, business, or other purposes, typically for less than a year. It involves a complex network of stakeholders, including travellers, destination management organizations, governments, and service providers. Marketing, on the other hand, is the strategic process of promoting and selling products or services to target audiences. In tourism, marketing involves creating awareness, building appeal, and persuading travellers to choose specific destinations or experiences. By understanding customer needs and preferences, tourism marketing helps create memorable and satisfying journeys, ensuring long-term benefits for destinations and stakeholders alike.

Kotler, Bowen and Makens define marketing as creating superior value for your customers and delivering customer satisfaction at a profit. Peter Drucker has said that the aim of marketing is to make selling superfluous. 'The aim is to know and understand customers so well that the product or service fits them and sells itself.' Anurag Kothari defines tourism marketing as 'systematic and coordinated efforts exerted by the national tourist organizations and/or tourist enterprises at the international, national, and local levels to optimize the satisfaction of tourists, groups, and individuals, in view of sustained tourism growth.'

Historical Context and Development

The relationship between tourism and marketing has undergone a profound transformation over time, reflecting broader social, economic, and technological changes. In ancient civilizations, tourism was limited to elite classes who travelled for religious pilgrimages, cultural exchanges, or trade. Early forms of marketing were rudimentary, relying on word of mouth and the reputation of destinations such as the Egyptian pyramids, Greek temples, or Roman baths, which attracted visitors seeking spiritual or intellectual enrichment.

The medieval period saw a continuation of pilgrimage tourism, with destinations like Mecca, Canterbury, and Santiago de Compostela emerging as significant travel hubs. Marketing during this time was informal, often relying on religious institutions to promote sacred sites through stories, manuscripts, and word of mouth. The lack of accessibility and infrastructure meant tourism was primarily regional and limited to those with resources and time.

The Renaissance and Enlightenment periods brought a surge in leisure and cultural tourism. Wealthy Europeans embarked on "Grand Tours" to explore art, architecture, and classical heritage, particularly in Italy and Greece. During this era, guidebooks, maps, and paintings began serving as early marketing tools, highlighting the allure of prominent destinations. The Industrial Revolution in the 18th and 19th centuries marked a turning point in tourism marketing. Advances in transportation, including railways and steamships, made travel more accessible, while the rise of the middle class created a broader audience for leisure tourism. Travel agencies, such as Thomas Cook in the mid-19th century, pioneered organized tours and promotional campaigns through brochures and advertisements, laying the foundation for modern tourism marketing.

Subsequently, in the early years of the 20th century, tourism marketing was limited to print media, brochures, and posters, which highlighted exotic destinations and appealed to the affluent classes. The 20th century witnessed the democratization of travel, with air transportation, automobiles, and improved infrastructure enabling global tourism. Post-World War II saw destinations embracing mass marketing to attract international visitors, supported by television and print media. The mid-20th century brought significant changes with the rise of mass tourism, as air travel became affordable and accessible to a broader demographic. Marketing campaigns during this period were often standardized, focusing on popular attractions and package deals.

The late 20th and early 21st centuries witnessed a digital revolution that transformed tourism marketing. Websites, social media platforms like Facebook, Twitter and Instagram, and online travel agencies (OTAs) transformed the way destinations and experiences were promoted, with user-generated content playing a pivotal role in influencing travel decisions. Personalization and interactivity emerged as key trends, enabling marketers to engage directly with potential travellers. Today, tourism marketing operates in a highly competitive and dynamic environment. Marketing strategies are increasingly data-driven, leveraging artificial intelligence and big data analytics to predict consumer behavior and tailor offerings to individual preferences. The integration of technology, sustainability concerns, and the growing demand for unique experiences continue to shape its development. By understanding its historical evolution, stakeholders can better appreciate the strategies and innovations that drive modern tourism marketing efforts.

Key Concepts and Theories

- **Destination branding** is one of the foundational ideas in tourism marketing which involves creating a unique identity for a place to differentiate it from its competitors. Effective branding not only highlights a destination's unique features but also creates an emotional connection with potential tourists. For instance, campaigns such as "Incredible India" and "100% Pure New Zealand" have successfully positioned these countries as must-visit destinations.

- **Travel motivators:** Another important theory is tourist motivation, which examines the psychological and sociological drivers behind travel decisions. Push factors, such as the desire for relaxation or adventure, and pull factors, like the appeal of a destination's attractions, are central to understanding why people travel. Marketers use these insights to design campaigns that align with travellers' aspirations and preferences.

- **Marketing mix**, commonly known as the 'Four Ps— product, price, place, and promotion' — also plays a crucial role in tourism. In this context, the 'product' refers to the tourist experience, the 'price' reflects affordability and value, the 'place' concerns distribution channels, and 'promotion' encompasses advertising and communication strategies. Adapting these principles to the tourism industry helps ensure comprehensive and effective marketing.

- **Experiential marketing:** More recent concept in tourism marketing, which focuses on delivering memorable and emotionally engaging experiences. In tourism, this might involve promoting cultural festivals, immersive activities, or local culinary experiences. Coupled with the rise of digital platforms, experiential marketing has become a powerful tool for capturing the imagination of modern travellers.

Types and Forms

Tourism marketing manifests in various types and forms, tailored to meet the diverse needs of travellers and destinations. These classifications allow marketers to target specific audience segments effectively and align their strategies with consumer preferences.

- **Mass Tourism Marketing:** Targets a broad audience and promotes general travel packages. This form often focuses on affordability, convenience, and popular destinations, appealing to large groups seeking standard experiences. For example, all-inclusive vacation packages marketed by large tour operators represent mass tourism marketing.

- **Niche Tourism Marketing:** Caters to specialized interests and smaller audience segments. Examples include eco-tourism, adventure tourism, cultural tourism, and wellness tourism. Niche marketing emphasizes unique and personalized experiences, appealing to tourists with specific preferences, such as wildlife safaris, pilgrimage tours, or spa retreats.

- **Digital Tourism Marketing:** The rise of the internet and social media has given birth to digital tourism marketing, which leverages online platforms to reach a global audience. Techniques such as search engine optimization (SEO), pay-per-click (PPC) advertising, and social media campaigns are used to enhance visibility and engagement. This type of marketing also enables destinations to interact directly with potential tourists through user-generated content, reviews, and influencer partnerships.

- **Integrated Marketing Communications (IMC):** Another important form is IMC, which combines traditional and digital marketing tools to deliver a consistent message across multiple channels. This approach ensures integrated marketing efforts that work together, creating a cohesive brand image for the destination.

- **Experiential and Sustainable Marketing:** Emerging forms of tourism marketing include experiential and sustainable marketing, which focus on creating meaningful and eco-friendly experiences. Experiential marketing seeks to engage tourists emotionally, while sustainable marketing highlights environmental and cultural preservation, appealing to ethically conscious travellers.

Benefits

Tourism marketing offers numerous benefits, ranging from economic growth to cultural preservation and global connectivity. These advantages underscore the importance of well-executed marketing strategies in driving the success of the tourism sector. One of the primary benefits of tourism marketing is its contribution to economic development. By attracting tourists, destinations generate revenue through accommodation, transportation, dining, and entertainment. This influx of spending creates jobs, supports local businesses, and stimulates regional economies. Additionally, tourism marketing helps diversify income sources, particularly in regions reliant on a single industry.

The promotion of cultural exchange and preservation is another significant benefit in tourism marketing. Effective marketing showcases a destination's traditions, history, and way of life, fostering global awareness and appreciation for diverse cultures. This cultural promotion not only enriches the tourist experience but also encourages local communities to preserve their heritage. Tourism marketing also plays a pivotal role in infrastructure development, as increased tourist demand often prompts investments in transportation, utilities, and public amenities, which benefit both visitors and residents. For example, promoting a destination may lead to improved airports, roads, and communication networks, enhancing overall accessibility and quality of life.

Also, tourism marketing enhances a destination's global reputation, building brand equity and long-term appeal. By positioning itself as a safe, welcoming, and vibrant location, a destination can attract repeat visitors and foster loyalty among tourists. Correspondingly, tourism marketing supports the development of sustainable practices, as campaigns increasingly emphasize eco-friendly and community-based initiatives. This not only attracts environmentally conscious travellers but also contributes to the long-term viability of the tourism industry.

Impacts

While tourism marketing yields significant benefits, it also has far-reaching impacts, both positive and negative - on destinations, communities, and the environment. Understanding these impacts is essential for developing responsible and sustainable marketing strategies. One notable impact is the potential for environmental degradation. Aggressive marketing campaigns can lead to over-tourism, where the number of visitors exceeds a destination's carrying capacity. This results in pollution, habitat destruction, and strain on natural resources such as water and energy. For instance, heavily marketed coastal destinations often face issues like beach erosion and marine ecosystem disruption.

On the social front, tourism marketing can contribute to cultural commodification. Over-commercialization of cultural practices and traditions to attract tourists may dilute their authenticity. Local communities might feel pressured to perform or alter their customs to meet tourist expectations, leading to a loss of cultural integrity. Economically, while tourism marketing drives growth, it can also lead to inequalities. The benefits of increased tourist activity may not be evenly distributed, with large corporations often reaping the majority of profits while local businesses struggle to compete. Additionally, rising property values and living costs in popular tourist destinations can marginalize local residents.

However, tourism marketing also has positive impacts. It raises awareness about conservation, promoting eco-tourism initiatives and encouraging tourists to adopt sustainable practices. Furthermore, it fosters cross-cultural understanding, reducing prejudices and building global solidarity through meaningful interactions. In addressing these impacts, it is crucial for stakeholders to adopt a balanced approach. Integrating sustainability into marketing strategies and actively involving local communities can mitigate negative effects while maximizing the positive outcomes. This ensures that tourism remains a force for good, benefiting all stakeholders without compromising the well-being of destinations and their inhabitants.

Challenges and Constraints

Tourism marketing, while essential for promoting destinations and driving economic growth, faces several challenges and constraints that can hinder its effectiveness. These challenges arise from external factors, evolving market dynamics, and operational limitations, requiring innovative solutions from stakeholders. One of the foremost challenges is global competition. With innumerable destinations contending for the attention of travellers, differentiating a destination and maintaining its appeal becomes increasingly difficult. Also to be noted that the less prominent or lesser-known destinations often find it difficult to compete with globally renowned locations that have well-established brands and significant marketing budgets.

Sustainability is a significant concern, as marketers must balance growth with environmental conservation and cultural preservation. Another critical constraint is the complexity of consumer behavior. Tourists' preferences are influenced by diverse factors such as cultural trends, social media, and economic conditions, making it challenging to predict and meet their expectations consistently. For instance, the growing demand for personalized and experiential travel requires marketers to adapt their strategies and offer tailored solutions.

The seasonality of tourism poses additional difficulties. Many destinations experience fluctuating visitor numbers, with high and low seasons impacting revenue and resource allocation. Marketing campaigns must therefore address these variations by promoting low season travel or diversifying offerings to maintain a steady flow of tourists throughout the year. Likewise, tourism marketing must navigate the constraints of limited resources. Smaller destinations or businesses may lack the financial and technical resources to execute large-scale campaigns or adopt advanced technologies, placing them at a disadvantage in the global market. Also, the need for crisis management has become increasingly apparent.

Events such as pandemics, natural disasters, and political instability can severely disrupt tourism marketing efforts. The COVID-19 pandemic underscored the vulnerability of the tourism sector to global disruptions, emphasizing the importance of resilience and adaptability in marketing strategies. For instance, the COVID-19 pandemic, enforced marketers to rethink strategies, focusing on domestic tourism and virtual engagement while preparing for recovery. Marketers must stay attuned to these trends to remain relevant and effective in the field of tourism marketing throughout their stay in the business.

Best Practices

Implementing best practices in tourism marketing ensures that destinations and businesses can attract tourists effectively, while fostering sustainability and inclusivity. These practices are grounded in research, innovation, and collaboration, creating a framework for successful marketing efforts. One such essential practice is the use of data-driven marketing. By analysing consumer behavior, preferences, and trends, marketers can create targeted campaigns that resonate with specific audiences. For instance, segmenting travellers based on demographics or travel motivations allows for more personalized and impactful messaging.

Authentic storytelling is another best practice, highlighting unique cultural narratives, local traditions, and the human aspect of a destination that creates emotional connections with potential tourists. Authenticity not only builds trust but also distinguishes a destination from its competitors. For example, promoting indigenous crafts or community-led tourism initiatives can enhance a destination's appeal.

Collaboration among stakeholders, including governments, local communities, and private operators, is crucial for effective tourism marketing. Public-private partnerships enable the pooling of resources, expertise, and networks, resulting in cohesive and comprehensive campaigns. Additionally, involving local communities ensures that marketing efforts align with their interests and values. Adopting a sustainability focus in marketing practices is increasingly important. Highlighting eco-friendly accommodations, carbon-neutral activities, and responsible travel behaviors not only attracts ethically conscious travellers but also supports the long-term health of the tourism industry. Leveraging digital platforms is vital for modern tourism marketing. Social media, websites, and email campaigns offer cost-effective ways to engage with global audiences. Tools like virtual tours and influencer collaborations provide immersive and relatable content, encouraging travellers to explore new destinations.

Case Study 1: Tourism Marketing in Thailand

Thailand provides an exemplary model of effective tourism marketing, showcasing how a destination can use strategic campaigns to attract and retain a global audience. Launched in 1998 by the Tourism Authority of Thailand (TAT), the country's iconic "Amazing Thailand" campaign highlighted the country's rich heritage, natural beauty and modern attractions to appeal to a wide range of travellers. It emphasized Thailand's identity as a welcoming and affordable destination, catering to both luxury travellers and budget-conscious tourists. Over the years, the campaign has evolved, incorporating wellness tourism, adventure activities, and eco-friendly travel to diversify its offerings.

One of the strengths of Thailand's marketing approach is its **use of digital platforms**. Social media campaigns, influencer partnerships, and user-generated content have played a significant role in promoting Thailand's attractions. For instance, Instagram hashtags like '#AmazingThailand' have allowed travellers to share their experiences, creating authentic and relatable content that inspires others. Another factor contributing to the campaign's success is its focus on **personalization**. Thailand markets itself as a destination that offers something for everyone, from beach vacations and cultural explorations to adventure sports and culinary tours. This inclusivity has helped the country maintain its status as a top tourist destination. Thailand has embraced **sustainability** in its marketing efforts. Initiatives like promoting community-based tourism and conservation-focused travel demonstrate a commitment to preserving the environment and supporting local communities.

Case Study 2: Tourism Marketing in India

India's tourism marketing has significantly evolved, adapting to global trends while promoting its rich cultural heritage, diverse landscapes, and emerging digital capabilities. Historically, India's tourism campaigns, such as 'Incredible India,' launched in 2002, focused on the country's cultural diversity and natural beauty. The campaign successfully utilized traditional advertising methods, including print media and television, to showcase India's unique offerings. In recent years, India's tourism marketing has embraced digital tools to engage with a tech-savvy demographic. Platforms like Instagram, YouTube, and Twitter have enabled destinations to highlight lesser-known attractions and experiences such as wellness retreats, adventure tourism, and rural tourism. This shift aligns with the global preference for experiential travel, emphasizing unique, personalized encounters with both nature and culture.

A significant feature of India's tourism marketing is the promotion of its diverse natural attractions, which range from the towering peaks of the Himalayas in the north to the serene beaches of Goa and Kerala in the south. National parks such as Kaziranga, home to the endangered one-horned rhinoceros, and Jim Corbett National Park, famous for its tiger reserves, are central to wildlife tourism efforts. India's backwaters in Kerala, Thar Desert in Rajasthan, and hill stations like Darjeeling and Shimla offer visitors a diverse range of natural experiences. The Sundarbans, the largest mangrove forest in the world, and the Andaman and Nicobar Islands are further examples of the country's unique ecosystems, attracting eco-tourists and nature lovers.

A key aspect of India's present tourism marketing is its emphasis on sustainability and eco-tourism. Campaigns now highlight eco-friendly practices, responsible tourism, and the promotion of rural and heritage tourism, thus ensuring that tourism benefits local communities and preserves natural resources. The integration of the *Swachh Bharat Abhiyan* (Clean India Mission) into tourism initiatives has further reinforced India's commitment to a cleaner, more environmentally conscious tourism sector. Looking forward, AI and VR are expected to play an increasingly significant role in India's tourism marketing. These technologies will offer immersive experiences, such as virtual tours of cultural landmarks, and provide personalized travel recommendations based on individual preferences. Furthermore, the promotion of inclusive tourism will become central, as India looks to offer accessible travel experiences for people with disabilities, elderly travellers, and marginalized groups.

Technology and Innovation

Technological advancements have revolutionized tourism marketing, enabling greater efficiency, personalization, and engagement. These advancements have transformed how destinations connect with potential travellers, offering personalized experiences and real-time interactions that drive interest and bookings. One of the most significant developments is the use of data analytics. Advanced tools enable marketers to analyze consumer preferences, search behavior, and spending patterns, providing insights that inform targeted campaigns. Platforms like Google Analytics and CRM software help destinations tailor their messaging to specific demographics, ensuring greater relevance and impact.

Social media platforms such as Facebook, Twitter and Instagram have become indispensable in tourism marketing. Visual content, including photos and videos of the influencers experiencing the tourist locations, allows destinations to showcase their attractions in a compelling way. The rise of influencer marketing has also added a layer of authenticity, as travellers are more likely to trust recommendations from experiences of the relatable personalities than scripted and filmed traditional advertisements.

Virtual Reality (VR) and Augmented Reality (AR) technologies are redefining how destinations are promoted. Virtual tours and immersive experiences enable potential tourists to explore attractions before booking, offering a preview of what they can expect in the tourist destinations. For instance, museums and heritage sites increasingly use AR to provide interactive exhibits that enhance visitor engagement. Artificial intelligence (AI) and machine learning have introduced chatbots and personalized recommendations. These tools streamline customer interactions by offering tailored suggestions, answering queries, and guiding users through the booking process. For example, AI-powered assistants on travel websites or apps can suggest itineraries based on individual preferences and past behavior. Blockchain technology and secure payment gateways used by the travel agencies and hotels have enhanced trust and transparency in tourism transactions, enabling seamless booking experiences. Meanwhile, innovations in eco-friendly technologies such as carbon footprint trackers helps in supporting sustainable tourism marketing efforts.

Policy and Regulatory Framework

The success of tourism marketing is closely tied to the policy and regulatory frameworks that govern the tourism sector. These frameworks provide guidelines for ethical practices, sustainability, and the equitable distribution of benefits, ensuring that tourism contributes positively to destinations and their communities. Governments play a pivotal role in shaping tourism policies. National tourism boards often set regulations that define marketing standards, including the promotion of cultural heritage, environmental conservation, and community welfare. For example, the UNESCO guidelines for World Heritage Sites emphasize responsible marketing practices that balance tourism growth with the preservation of historical and natural resources. International organizations like the United Nations World Tourism Organization (UNWTO) also influence tourism marketing through global standards and initiatives. Programs such as the UNWTO's 'Global Code of Ethics for Tourism' encourage destinations to adopt ethical marketing strategies that respect local cultures and minimize environmental impacts.

At the regional and local levels, policies often focus on niche tourism development and infrastructure enhancement. Some governments provide financial incentives for marketing campaigns that promote eco-tourism or off-season travel. In addition, regulatory measures ensure that marketing content is truthful and not misleading, protecting tourists from deceptive practices. Emerging policies address challenges such as over-tourism and climate change. For instance, regulations limiting the number of visitors to sensitive ecological areas help prevent environmental degradation.

Likewise, policies promoting carbon-neutral tourism campaigns align marketing strategies with global sustainability goals. Collaborative frameworks between public and private sectors further strengthen tourism marketing efforts. By aligning government policies with private enterprise initiatives, destinations can create cohesive campaigns that maximize impact while adhering to regulatory requirements.

Future Directions and Prospects

Looking ahead, tourism marketing is poised for further transformation, shaped by emerging technologies, evolving consumer behaviors, and global sustainability goals. The future of tourism marketing will be defined by a greater emphasis on innovation, inclusivity, and adaptability, reflecting the needs of modern travellers and the industry's drive for sustainable practices. One of the most promising areas for future growth is the integration of artificial intelligence (AI) and machine learning in tourism marketing, as these technologies will not only help in data collection but also enhance predictive capabilities by qualitative and quantitative research, allowing destinations to anticipate shifts in consumer preferences and tailor their offerings accordingly.

To understand this better, AI could enable hyper-personalization, where marketing campaigns are dynamically adjusted in real-time based on a traveller's past behaviors, current trends in tourism, and predicted future preferences. This personalization will likely become a standard in future campaigns, ensuring that tourists receive highly relevant recommendations throughout their travel journey. Sustainability will continue to be a defining feature of tourism marketing, as global environmental awareness grows. Tourists are increasingly seeking eco-friendly and responsible travel options, which means that destinations will need to adopt marketing strategies that highlight their commitment to sustainability. Future tourism campaigns will likely focus on promoting green tourism, carbon offset programs, and environmentally conscious activities. Additionally, the integration of sustainability-focused innovations—such as eco-friendly accommodations, transportation options, and responsible visitor management systems—will be essential in addressing both consumer demand and the industry's environmental footprint.

The rise of the metaverse is another emerging direction for tourism marketing. This Virtual Reality (VR) space allows tourists to engage with destinations and experiences before physically travelling, creating opportunities for destinations to present themselves in novel and immersive ways. As metaverse technologies mature, tourism marketers will be able to offer virtual travel experiences that could encourage real-world visits or expand tourism into new virtual realms.

Similarly, Augmented Reality (AR) is expected to play a larger role, enhancing in-person experiences through interactive, real-time digital overlays that provide additional information and context to physical spaces. Additionally, inclusive marketing practices will gain prominence as tourism destinations strive to cater to a broader spectrum of travellers. Future tourism marketing will focus on ensuring 'accessibility for all', including the elderly, those with disabilities, and travellers from underrepresented groups. Emphasizing inclusivity in campaigns will not only meet the needs of these communities but also open up new market segments for the tourism industry. Also, the adoption of smart technologies such as Internet of Things (IoT) devices, contactless systems, and real-time data will further streamline the tourist experience, from seamless check-ins at accommodations to enhanced mobility solutions. These innovations will simplify travel logistics, reduce friction points, and improve safety and convenience for tourists, contributing to a smoother, more enjoyable travel experience.

Conclusion

Tourism marketing has evolved into a sophisticated and dynamic field, driven by technological advancements, shifting consumer preferences, and the imperative of sustainability. As the tourism industry continues to grow and diversify, effective marketing strategies will play a vital role in promoting destinations, fostering cultural exchange, and driving economic development. By embracing innovation, inclusivity, and environmental responsibility, tourism marketers can create compelling campaigns that resonate with modern travellers, while contributing to a more sustainable and equitable tourism ecosystem. Ultimately, the future of tourism marketing will be shaped by its ability to adapt to emerging trends, technologies, and consumer values, ensuring that the industry remains a positive force for global connectivity, cultural understanding, and environmental stewardship.

TOURISM AND STAGED CULTURE

Author
Ashwin Prakash
Lecturer, D.B.Jain College,
Thuraipaakam, Chennai

Co-Author
Lara Chamberlain
Founder, Tida-Ryu Karate Association,
California, USA

Introduction

Tourism and Staged Culture denotes the deliberate presentation and performance of local cultures and traditions for the benefit of tourists, often resulting in a sterilized and commercialized rendition of reality. This phenomenon is reminiscent of sociologist Erving Goffman's notion of "life as theatre," where cultural practices, rituals, and everyday life are transformed into a spectacle for tourist consumption.

The staged nature of cultural experiences in tourist settings raises pertinent questions about the commodification of culture, authenticity, and the impact of tourism on local communities. As locals assume the role of "performers" and tourists become the "audience," the boundaries between reality and artifice become increasingly blurred. This phenomenon warrants a critical examination of the complex dynamics between tourism, culture, and identity.

Key Concepts and Theories

Goffman's Dramaturgy

Erving Goffman's sociological theory, "The Presentation of Self in Everyday Life" (1959), posits that life is a performance, and individuals play roles to create impressions. This concept is crucial in understanding tourism as a staged culture, where locals perform their cultural identities and practices for tourist consumption. Goffman's dramaturgy highlights the distinction between the "front stage" (the public performance) and the "back stage" (the private, authentic self), illustrating the tension between authenticity and performativity.

Staged Authenticity

Staged authenticity refers to the creation of an authentic experience for tourists through deliberate performances, rituals, and cultural practices. This concept challenges the notion of authenticity, suggesting that cultural experiences can be staged and manipulated to meet tourist expectations. Staged authenticity raises questions about the commodification of culture, the role of tourism in shaping cultural identity, and the impact of staged performances on local communities.

Commodification of Culture

The commodification of culture refers to the process of transforming cultural practices, traditions, and artifacts into marketable products for tourist consumption. This phenomenon is driven by the tourism industry's demand for unique and exotic cultural experiences. The commodification of culture raises concerns about cultural exploitation, the loss of cultural heritage, and the homogenization of local cultures.

Cultural Performance

Cultural performance refers to the deliberate presentation of cultural practices, rituals, and traditions as a form of entertainment for tourists. This concept highlights the performative nature of cultural experiences, where locals play the role of "performers" and tourists assume the role of "audience." Cultural performance raises questions about the authenticity of cultural experiences, the impact of tourism on local cultures, and the power dynamics between locals and tourists.

Tourist Gaze

The tourist gaze refers to the way tourists perceive and interpret the local culture, often through a lens of exoticism and stereotyping. This concept, coined by John Urry (1990), highlights the power dynamics between tourists and locals, where tourists often hold the gaze and locals are subject to their scrutiny. The tourist gaze raises questions about the representation of local cultures, the impact of tourism on local identities, and the ethics of cultural consumption.

Host-Guest Relations

Host-guest relations refer to the complex dynamics between locals (hosts) and tourists (guests), including issues of power, identity, and cultural exchange. This concept highlights the tension between the host's desire to showcase their culture and the guest's desire to experience authenticity. Host-guest relations raise questions about cultural hospitality, the politics of cultural exchange, and the impact of tourism on local communities.

Cultural Homogenization

Cultural homogenization refers to the process of standardizing and simplifying local cultures to cater to tourist expectations, resulting in the loss of cultural diversity. This phenomenon is driven by the tourism industry's demand for familiar and comfortable cultural experiences. Cultural homogenization raises concerns about the erosion of local cultures, the loss of cultural heritage, and the impact of globalization on local identities.

Authenticity and Inauthenticity

The tension between authenticity and inauthenticity is a central theme in tourism studies. Authenticity refers to the genuine and unmediated cultural experience, while inauthenticity refers to the staged and manipulated cultural experience. This dichotomy raises questions about the nature of cultural experiences, the impact of tourism on local cultures, and the ethics of cultural consumption.

Emotional Labour

Emotional labour refers to the effort exerted by locals to create a welcoming and authentic atmosphere for tourists, often masking their true feelings and emotions. This concept, coined by Arlie Hochschild (1983), highlights the emotional demands placed on locals in the tourism industry. Emotional labor raises questions about the impact of tourism on local well-being, the politics of emotional exchange, and the ethics of cultural hospitality.

Performative Identity

Performative identity refers to the way locals perform and negotiate their cultural identities for tourist consumption, often blurring the lines between reality and performance. This concept highlights the tension between the authentic and performed self, raising questions about the nature of cultural identity, the impact of tourism on local identities, and the ethics of cultural representation.

Forms of Tourism as a Staged Culture

Heritage Tourism - A Sanitized Representation of the Past

Heritage tourism involves the deliberate preservation and showcasing of cultural heritage sites, such as historic monuments, museums, and traditional villages. This type of tourism often perpetuates a sanitized and nostalgic representation of the past, reinforcing dominant narratives and eliding marginalized voices. As a result, the cultural heritage is reduced to a commodity, stripped of its original context and significance.

Ethnic Tourism: Commodification of Ethnic Cultures

Ethnic tourism revolves around the commodification of ethnic cultures, where tourists are invited to experience the "exotic" and "authentic" traditions of indigenous communities. This form of tourism frequently raises concerns about cultural appropriation, exploitation, and the homogenization of local cultures. The staged performances of ethnic cultures often reinforce stereotypes and perpetuate the "othering" of indigenous communities.

Festival Tourism: Superficial Spectacles or Cultural Exchange?

Festival tourism has emerged as a significant phenomenon, where tourists flock to experience vibrant cultural festivals, such as the Tomatina festival in Spain or the Holi festival in India. While these events can foster cross-cultural understanding and exchange, they also risk being reduced to superficial spectacles, stripped of their original cultural significance. The commercialization of festivals can lead to the erosion of traditional practices and the exploitation of local cultures.

Rural Tourism: Performing Rural Authenticity

Rural tourism involves tourists visiting rural areas to experience traditional ways of life. This type of tourism often relies on the performance of rural authenticity, where locals are expected to embody traditional roles and practices. However, this can lead to the reinforcement of romanticized notions of rural life, obscuring the complexities and challenges faced by rural communities. The staged performances of rural authenticity can perpetuate stereotypes and limit the opportunities for genuine cultural exchange.

Dark Tourism: Ethics of Cultural Consumption

Dark tourism involves tourists visiting sites associated with death, tragedy, or suffering, such as concentration camps or disaster zones. This form of tourism raises important questions about the ethics of cultural consumption, the representation of trauma, and the impact on local communities. The commodification of tragedy and suffering can perpetuate voyeurism and disrespect for the victims, highlighting the need for responsible and respectful tourism practices.

Benefits

Economic Benefits

Tourism as a staged culture can generate significant economic benefits for local communities. The creation of cultural performances, festivals, and heritage sites can attract tourists, creating jobs and stimulating local economies. The revenue generated from tourism can also be invested in the preservation and promotion of cultural heritage, supporting the development of local infrastructure and services.

Cultural Exchange and Understanding

Tourism as a staged culture can facilitate cultural exchange and understanding between locals and tourists. Cultural performances and festivals can provide a platform for the sharing of traditions, customs, and values, promoting cross-cultural understanding and respect. This exchange can also foster greater appreciation and empathy for local cultures, challenging stereotypes and misconceptions.

Preservation of Cultural Heritage

Tourism as a staged culture can support the preservation of cultural heritage by providing a financial incentive for the protection and promotion of cultural sites and traditions. The revenue generated from tourism can be invested in the restoration and maintenance of cultural heritage sites, ensuring their preservation for future generations.

Community Empowerment

Tourism as a staged culture can empower local communities by providing them with a platform to showcase their culture and traditions. This can foster a sense of pride and ownership among community members, promoting cultural revitalization and community development.

Negative Impacts

Tourism as a staged culture can also have negative impacts on local communities. The commercialization of cultural heritage can lead to the exploitation and commodification of local cultures, perpetuating stereotypes and cultural appropriation. The influx of tourists can also disrupt local ways of life, causing cultural and environmental degradation.

Cultural Homogenization

The staged nature of cultural performances and festivals can also contribute to cultural homogenization, where local cultures are reduced to a standardized and superficial representation. This can erase the unique characteristics and traditions of local cultures, promoting a bland and uniform cultural landscape.

Environmental Degradation

The development of tourism infrastructure and the influx of tourists can also lead to environmental degradation, causing strain on local resources and ecosystems. The pollution, waste, and destruction of natural habitats can have devastating impacts on local environments, threatening the long-term sustainability of tourism development.

Loss of Authenticity

The staged nature of cultural performances and festivals can also lead to the loss of authenticity, where local cultures are reduced to a superficial and commercialized representation. This can erode the cultural significance and meaning of local traditions, promoting a shallow and artificial cultural experience.

Challenges and Constraints

The burgeoning phenomenon of tourism as a staged culture presents a myriad of challenges and constraints. One of the paramount concerns is the precarious balance between authenticity and commodification, wherein the cultural heritage of local communities is transformed into marketable commodities, risking the erosion of their inherent significance and meaning. Furthermore, the lack of cultural sensitivity and respect can lead to cultural clashes and misunderstandings, undermining the potential benefits of cross-cultural exchange. The power dynamics between locals and tourists also necessitate careful management, as the economic and cultural disparities can result in exploitation and inequality.

The sustainability and environmental impact of tourism as a staged culture also warrant attention, as the development of tourism infrastructure and the influx of tourists can lead to environmental degradation and strain on local resources. Effective regulation and management strategies must be implemented to mitigate these negative consequences and ensure that the benefits of tourism are shared equitably among all stakeholders. Ultimately, a nuanced understanding of these challenges and constraints is essential for developing responsible and sustainable tourism practices that prioritize the well-being of local communities and the preservation of their cultural heritage.

Case Study

Okinawa, the birthplace of karate, has emerged as a hub for karate enthusiasts, with numerous karate trainers and schools capitalizing on the island's rich martial arts heritage. As a prime example of tourism as a staged culture, Okinawa's karate industry has become a major draw for tourists, who flock to the island to experience the "authentic" Okinawan karate culture. Karate trainers and schools have adapted to this demand, offering staged performances, training sessions, and cultural workshops that cater to tourists' expectations. By packaging and selling their cultural heritage as a tourist product, Okinawa's karate community has created a staged culture that blurs the lines between authenticity and performance, raising questions about the commodification of culture, the impact of tourism on local communities, and the preservation of traditional practices in the face of commercialization.

The wise words of O' Sensei Shoshin Nagamine, a renowned Okinawan karate master, underscore the importance of understanding the rich cultural heritage of Okinawa in order to truly appreciate the art of karate. He emphasizes that grasping the intricacies of Okinawan culture is a lifelong pursuit, requiring patience, dedication, and immersion. However, in the context of tourism as a staged culture, this nuanced understanding is often sacrificed for the sake of convenience and commercialization. Many karate enthusiasts flock to Okinawa's numerous dojos, seeking a superficial experience that barely scratches the surface of the island's cultural depth. In contrast, O' Sensei Nagamine's approach encourages a more holistic and immersive experience, one that involves engaging with the local community, appreciating the natural beauty of the island, and exploring the interconnectedness of karate with other Okinawan art forms. Ironically, the very cultural practices that are most valuable and authentic are often the ones that are deliberately concealed from tourists, in order to protect them from the corrosive effects of commercialization. This paradox highlights the tension between preserving cultural integrity and catering to the demands of tourism, a challenge that Okinawa's karate community must navigate in order to maintain the authenticity and richness of their cultural heritage.

Irei Hiroshi, a well-known karate master in Okinawa, poignant remarks on the globalization of Ryukyu karate underscore the imperative of preserving the cultural integrity of this ancient martial art. As karate is disseminated worldwide, the risk of cultural homogenization and intellectual property rights infringement looms large. Hiroshi's concerns are well-founded, as the proliferation of karate has led to its commodification, with various interpretations and adaptations emerging that often deviate from the traditional practices of the Ryukyu people. The Okinawan government and industries must develop strategies to safeguard the cultural heritage of Ryukyu karate, ensuring that its dissemination is accompanied by a deep respect for its historical and cultural context.

The parallels between the globalization of karate and the impact of tourism on Okinawa's cultural landscape are striking. As tourists flock to the island to experience its unique culture, including karate, there is a risk of cultural degradation and the erosion of traditional practices. The influx of visitors can also lead to the commercialization of sacred sites, such as the Sefa Utaki, which, while generating revenue, can compromise the cultural and spiritual significance of these locations. However, as Hiroshi notes, the sharing of Okinawa's cultural treasures with the world can also have a positive impact, as it can foster greater appreciation and respect for the island's unique heritage. Ultimately, striking a balance between cultural preservation and sharing is crucial, ensuring that the dissemination of Ryukyu karate and Okinawan culture is accompanied by a deep respect for its historical and cultural context.

The pursuit of authenticity in karate is a nuanced and multifaceted endeavour. The worthy practitioner must navigate through a maze of illusions, avoiding the superficial trappings of fame and prestige. In Okinawa, the birthplace of karate, the culture itself is guarded, and only reveals its secrets to those who approach with reverence and humility. The commercialization of karate has led to a proliferation of superficial practitioners, who prioritize photo opportunities with famous karate masters over genuine mastery. The emphasis on spectacle over substance has created a culture of superficiality, where the true essence of karate is lost amidst the noise of ego and self-promotion. As Jokei Kushi astutely observes, "We should not withdraw into a shell of Karate... but rather give physical consideration to other sports to sort out the quality... of them." This sentiment echoes the need for karate practitioners to remain adaptable, open-minded, and committed to the pursuit of excellence. By embracing this mindset, we can ensure that karate remains a vibrant, living tradition, rather than a stagnant relic of the past. Ultimately, the true treasure of karate lies not in its external trappings, but in the depth of its spiritual and cultural heritage.

Technology and Innovation

The synergy between technology and innovation has transformed the tourism landscape, particularly in the realm of staged culture. In Okinawa, karate schools and cultural centres are harnessing digital platforms to showcase their traditions and attract tourists. Virtual and augmented reality experiences, social media, and influencer marketing are being leveraged to provide immersive and interactive cultural experiences. Digital museums and archives are also being created to preserve and showcase Okinawan cultural heritage, providing tourists with a deeper understanding of the island's rich history and traditions.

The strategic integration of technology has enhanced the authenticity and cultural sensitivity of staged cultural experiences in Okinawa. Mobile apps and online booking platforms have streamlined the process of booking karate lessons and cultural workshops, while digital storytelling platforms have facilitated community engagement and cultural exchange. By embracing innovation, Okinawan karate schools and cultural centres can promote their traditions, engage with tourists, and contribute to the preservation of their cultural heritage, ultimately enriching the tourist experience and fostering a deeper appreciation for Okinawan culture.

Policy and Regulatory Framework

Effective policy and regulatory frameworks are crucial in managing the complexities of tourism as staged culture, particularly in sensitive cultural and environmental contexts like Okinawa. A well-crafted framework can help strike a balance between preserving cultural heritage, promoting economic development, and ensuring the well-being of local communities. This requires careful consideration of the potential impacts of tourism on local cultures and environments, as well as the development of strategies to mitigate any negative effects.

To achieve this balance, governments and local authorities must establish regulations governing the commercialization of cultural heritage sites and traditions. This includes implementing cultural impact assessments and monitoring mechanisms to prevent cultural degradation and exploitation. Additionally, community-based tourism initiatives can empower local stakeholders and ensure fair distribution of benefits. By prioritizing the needs and concerns of local communities, policymakers can help ensure that tourism as staged culture is developed and managed in a responsible and sustainable manner.

Conclusion

As the tourism industry continues to evolve, the concept of tourism as staged culture is likely to undergo significant transformations. One potential future direction is the increasing emphasis on authenticity and immersive experiences. Tourists are seeking more meaningful and engaging encounters with local cultures, which may lead to a shift away from superficial and commercialized staged cultural experiences. Another prospect is the growing importance of sustainability and responsible tourism practices. As concerns about climate change, cultural degradation, and social inequality continue to mount, tourists are becoming more discerning about the environmental and social impact of their travel choices. This may lead to a greater demand for staged cultural experiences that prioritize sustainability, community engagement, and cultural sensitivity.

The integration of technology and innovation is also likely to play a significant role in shaping the future of tourism as staged culture. Virtual and augmented reality experiences, for example, may become increasingly popular, allowing tourists to engage with cultural heritage sites and traditions in new and immersive ways. Additionally, social media and digital platforms may continue to transform the way tourists interact with and experience staged cultural events. Ultimately, the future of tourism as staged culture will depend on the ability of industry stakeholders, policymakers, and local communities to work together to create experiences that are authentic, sustainable, and respectful of cultural heritage. By prioritizing these values, it may be possible to create a more equitable and responsible tourism industry that benefits both tourists and local communities.

TOURISM AND HUMAN TRAFFICKING

Dr. Marilyn Gracey Augustine
Assistant Professor of History
Madras Christian College (Autonomous)
Tambaram, Chennai – 600 059

Introduction

Human trafficking within the global tourism industry is a pervasive and often hidden problem, where the movement of people across borders for leisure and business creates opportunities for exploitation. As the tourism sector continues to grow, it inadvertently facilitates trafficking in various forms, including sex trafficking, forced labour, and involuntary servitude. Vulnerable individuals, often from marginalized communities, are preyed upon by traffickers who exploit their desire for better economic opportunities or escape from difficult circumstances.

Tourism-related infrastructure such as hotels, resorts, and transportation networks provide cover for trafficking operations, while tourists themselves may unwittingly contribute to the demand for exploitative services. Despite efforts to combat this issue through law enforcement, industry initiatives, and public awareness campaigns, challenges persist due to the complexity of trafficking networks, lack of training, and resource constraints. This paper explores the intersection of tourism and human trafficking, examining the roles of various stakeholders, the impact on victims, conditions in India and the strategies necessary to address this global crisis.

An Overview of Human Trafficking

The United Nations (UN) Protocol to Prevent, Suppress, and Punish Trafficking in Persons, Particularly Women and Children, also known as the Palermo Protocol, was adopted by the UN General Assembly on November 15, 2000. It defines human trafficking in persons as "the recruitment, transportation, transfer, harbouring or receipt of persons, by means of the threat or use of force or other forms of coercion, of abduction, of fraud, of deception, of the abuse of power or of a position of vulnerability or of the giving or receiving of payments or benefits to achieve the consent of a person having control over another person, for the purpose of exploitation. Exploitation shall include, at a minimum, the exploitation of the prostitution of others or other forms of sexual exploitation, forced labour or services, slavery or practices similar to slavery, servitude or the removal of organs". This definition applies to both adults and children. The Protocol further elaborates that the consent of a trafficked person will be considered irrelevant if obtained through improper means. In the case of trafficked children (below the age of 18years), the Protocol elaborates that even if the child has consented, it will be not be considered valid regardless of whether it was taken by proper means or not.

Human trafficking is widely recognized as a horrific form of modern slavery and a severe violation of fundamental human rights. On 1 September 2010, the United Nations Global Plan of Action to Combat Trafficking in Persons was adopted by the General Assembly. Secretary General Ban Ki-Moon said "It is slavery in the modern age". He continued "every year thousands of people, mainly women and children, are exploited by criminals who use them for forced labour or the sex trade. No country is immune. Almost all play a part, either as a source of trafficked people, transit point or destination."

It involves treating individuals as commodities to be bought and sold as slaves, where traffickers exploit their victims by confiscating passports and visas, withholding earnings, and controlling them completely. This crime is among the fastest-growing global offenses, driven by massive profits and supported by international criminal networks that treat human trafficking like the trade in arms, drugs, or money. Regions with unstable social and economic conditions, where there is a demand for illegal labour, including sex workers, quickly become targets for trafficking activities. This was evident in the rapid emergence of criminal gangs in Central and Eastern Europe after the Cold War.

Although trafficking has become a global issue in recent decades, certain areas are more affected due to various push and pull factors, such as poverty, illiteracy, unemployment, weak or corrupt governments, the demand for illegal labour, shortage of brides, and the growth of sex tourism. Currently, Western and Northern Europe, North America, the UAE, Saudi Arabia, Turkey, and Japan are considered major destination countries for trafficking victims. However, the distinction between supply and demand regions has become increasingly blurred. While traditional trafficking routes still follow South-North and East-West patterns, trafficking also occurs between countries within the same regions, such as from Brazil to Thailand, Romania to Cambodia, Mozambique to South Africa, and Nepal to India. People are even trafficked within their own countries.

The perpetrators of trafficking are diverse, ranging from large transnational criminal organizations that profit significantly, to smaller agencies, including employment bureaus, transit hotels, travel and transport companies, local brothels, bars, nightclubs, and massage parlours, all operating at the grassroots level. Many individuals, including recruiters, middlemen, pimps, and employers, facilitate the movement and exploitation of trafficked persons. Tragically, often those who fall victim to trafficking are sold by people they know—such as parents, spouses, or relatives—who exploit their vulnerability, trust, and ignorance. According to some NGOs, more than 80% of trafficked individuals were sold by someone they personally knew, who profited from their desperation.

This phenomenon, especially the trafficking of children, is a sad reflection of a world where economic gain is prioritized over basic ethical principles, leaving vulnerable individuals, particularly children, at the mercy of exploitation.

Data Speaks

Human trafficking is a global issue, affecting millions worldwide. Although precise statistics are difficult to obtain due to the covert nature of the crime, the International Labour Organization (ILO) estimated that in 2016, over 40 million people were victims of trafficking, including 25 million in forced labour, 15 million in forced marriage, and 71% women or girls. In 2020, the total number of victims of trafficking detected around the world by the UN Office on Drugs and Crime (UNODC) declined for the first time in twenty years due to the pandemic which restricted the movement of the people across the borders. Compared to 2019, there was a 24 per cent decline in the detection of the victims of trafficking in 2020. The UNODC's 2020 Global Report on Trafficking in Persons confirmed a 15-year trend of shifting victim demographics, with the proportion of adult women decreasing and the share of children, especially boys, increasing. The UNODC's Report on Trafficking in Persons, 2024, reports that the number of victims of trafficking detected is on the rise again and the child victims are increasingly detected. According to the Report 202,478 are the detected cases of trafficking during the period of 2020-23 of whom 62% are adults and 38% are children.

The Counter Trafficking Data Collective (CTDT) of the International Organisation for Migration reports that highest number of trafficking happens for sexual exploitation followed by forced labour. CTDT also reports that a large number trafficked are women and girls for sexual exploitation and recently trends show that men and boys are also vulnerable to many forms of human trafficking, including sexual exploitation.

Intersection of Tourism and Trafficking of Humans

Tourism, while economically beneficial, can create opportunities for traffickers to exploit vulnerable individuals, particularly women and children, for sex tourism and forced labour. In areas with high tourist traffic, such as resorts, entertainment districts, or during major events, traffickers often use the anonymity provided by tourism to move victims across borders and conceal their activities. The intersection between tourism and trafficking will include sex tourism, child sex tourism, and the use of hotels in the sex trade. The discussion of labour exploitation will include child labour and beggars, hospitality staff, construction staff, and labour trafficking in the supply chain.

Although sex trafficking occurs globally and affects people from all demographics, around 71% of trafficking victims are women. The Asia and Pacific region comprise more than two-thirds of the world's trafficking victims with more than 25 million trafficking victims.

Sex Tourism

The connection between sex trafficking and the tourism industry is particularly complex due to the presence of legal sex tourism. In many places where prostitution is legalized, a booming sex tourism industry exists, offering tourists opportunities to attend sex shows, hire sex workers, and engage in other exploitative activities. Sex tourism is prevalent in nearly every region of the world, with destinations like Thailand and the Netherlands being among the most well-known. Despite these countries' efforts to reshape their image and distance themselves from such associations, some tourism agencies continue to promote sex tourism in places like Thailand and Amsterdam. This ongoing promotion complicates efforts to address the broader issue of human trafficking in the tourism sector.

While the sex tourism industry exists at the crossroads of legal prostitution and sex trafficking, with child sex tourism always being classified as a form of sex trafficking. Worldwide, it is estimated that 20% of sex trafficking victims are children, with this percentage being even higher in regions like Southeast Asia. The exploitation of children for sex with tourists is a significant issue, with estimates suggesting that as many as 250,000 tourists annually engage in sexual activity with minors while visiting Southeast Asia.

Among these sex tourists, up to 25% are believed to come from the United States, while 13% are from Australia.

Labour Exploitation

In places of improper welfare policies and laws for labour protection, the risk of labour trafficking and other exploitation. In Europe alone, it is estimated that around 4,500 individuals fall victim to labour trafficking within the hotel sector. Several factors contribute to labour trafficking and exploitation being more prevalent in the tourism and travel industry than in other sectors. Many hotels rely on recruiters or subcontractors to meet local staffing needs for roles such as housekeeping, maintenance, security, and restaurant positions. These recruiters and subcontractors may use tactics like debt bondage, excessive recruitment fees, or the confiscation of passports and visas to control and exploit workers. Indirectly, humans are also trafficked for labour for construction industry. Places that are popular for tourism rely on trafficked labour for construction of their infrastructure. It is the same when international events like Olympics, World Cups or other tourism related events happen.

Forced child labour in the tourism industry manifests at various levels, from children trafficked and exploited in construction, housekeeping, and hospitality roles to those coerced into begging at popular tourist attractions. Children from disadvantaged backgrounds, including those with disabilities, refugees, or orphans, are particularly vulnerable to exploitation and trafficking. Forced begging is recognized as one of the "worst forms" of child labour due to its dangerous nature, which jeopardizes the child's safety. Additionally, the physical and emotional abuse these children endure from their exploiters when they fail to meet begging quotas adds to the severity of the issue. In tourist areas, particularly in developing countries, children are often forced to beg, sell goods, or engage in pickpocketing, driven by the perception of tourists as wealthy and easy targets.

The Case of Thailand

In the late 1960s, Thailand's economy became increasingly reliant on the presence of U.S. and other foreign military personnel. The large American airbases and the investments and labour needed to establish, staff, and support them were further supplemented by contracts that Thailand signed with the U.S. Department of Defence in 1967. Such agreements provided Rest and Recreation (R and R) for thousands of servicemen who were on rotation basis stayed in Thailand while fighting in Vietnam. While R and R officially stood for Rest and Recreation, many U.S. soldiers referred to it as "I and I," meaning "Intercourse and Intoxication," as these were the primary activities for which it was used. Along with food, lodging, transportation, entertainment, and other comforts these soldiers also received sexual services.

Following the prospective end of Indo-China War and the subsequent withdrawal of the American troops, a delegation from the World Bank visited Thailand in 1971. The report was issued in 1975 which recommended that Thailand's post-war economy should focus on the development of mass tourism. This recommendation was significant because it ensured loans and funding would be provided for the tourism initiative, while other economic proposals would not receive the same support. Mass tourism primarily involved package tours, which included airfare, hotel, transportation, meals, and guides, all bundled into a single price. However, even at discounted rates, Thailand was still a long and expensive flight for most people. As a result, the tourism focus shifted toward single male travellers wanting for the similar R and R breaks which were given to the U.S. soldiers.

Thai cities, especially Bangkok, Pattaya, and Phuket, have become renowned for their lively nightlife, which includes bars, clubs, and entertainment venues that attract sex tourists. Cultural pressures for young women to repay their families, high rates of poverty, corruption and support by local politicians, and high demand from international tourists all contribute to the thriving sex tourism industry in Thailand.

Thailand serves as a source, transit, and destination country for the trafficking of children for sexual exploitation. While the exact number of children forced into prostitution is not definitively known, estimates from 2007 by the government, university researchers, and NGOs suggested that up to 60,000 children under 18 were involved in prostitution. The Children's Rights Protection Center in Thailand also reports that 40 percent of individuals engaged in prostitution are minors. Although many victims are still drawn into exploitation due to poverty, discrimination, and legal vulnerability, there is a growing number of children who are pushed into sexual exploitation by materialism, with some not even recognizing their situation as prostitution.

Prostitution is illegal in Thailand and there are attempts made by the Government to curb sex tourism. However, Thailand in 2024 is still placed in Tier – II in Trafficking in Persons Report of the U.S. Government. As per the report:

"As reported over the past five years, human traffickers exploit domestic and foreign victims in Thailand, and traffickers exploit Thai victims abroad. Labor and sex traffickers exploit women, men, LGBTQI+ individuals, and children from Thailand, other Southeast Asian countries, Sri Lanka, Russia, Uzbekistan, and increasingly some Northern African and Sub-Saharan African countries, including Kenya, Tanzania, and Uganda, in Thailand. Members of ethnic minorities, highland persons, and stateless persons in Thailand experience instances of abuse indicative of trafficking. Children from Thailand, Burma, Cambodia, and Laos are increasingly victims of sex trafficking in brothels, massage parlours, bars, karaoke lounges, hotels, and private residences. Traffickers induce Thai children to perform sex acts through videos and photos on the Internet, sometimes by blackmailing victims with explicit images. Children are lured by traffickers into commercial sex through the Internet, chat and dating applications, as well as other social networking platforms. Children in orphanages are at risk of trafficking. Children of families that lost employment because of the impacts of the pandemic, including among migrant families, were increasingly at risk of trafficking."

Case studies in India

In India, child sex tourism is not often viewed as a significant social problem. This is partly because it is believed that the issue is not as severe as in some Southeast Asian countries, and also because the problem is often linked only to poverty. Additionally, the social acceptance of child marriage and the perception of women from certain social groups as "inferior" contribute to the belief that their sexual exploitation is not inherently wrong in parts of Indian society. The perception of the commercial sexual exploitation of children in India is largely influenced by the "poverty syndrome."

Child sex tourism in India became widely recognized only recently. Before the arrest of Freddy Peats, a 76-year-old man of unknown origin on April 3, 1991, there was little awareness of organized sexual abuse of children, especially involving young boys, despite the known involvement of female minors in prostitution. Peats' arrest shocked the nation, and in March 1996, he was convicted of sex crimes against young boys in Goa, marking India's first conviction for running an organized paedophilia ring. However, both the Goan government and the tourism industry continued to view the issue as an anomaly. Shortly after the Peats case, in 1999, the case of HB, a 57-year-old German paedophile, came to light when he was arrested by the Calangute police station. He was convicted under Sections 373 and 377 for hiring a minor for immoral purposes and committing unnatural sexual offenses, receiving a six-year prison sentence.

In recent years, the growth of tourism in Goa has had a detrimental effect on local children living along the coast. There has been an increase in prostitution and the trafficking of women and children for sex tourism and labour. Kerala and Delhi-Agra-Jaipur are other places that have also potential cases of sex-tourism. The boat houses of Kerala are mentioned as "sex on the water". They are safe haven as the boats are in the backwaters without any monitoring.

Remedies and Recommendations

Through collaboration across the tourism industry, government agencies, and civil society, it is possible to mitigate the impact of trafficking and ensure that tourism becomes a force for positive social and economic change, free from exploitation. Addressing this complex crime requires coordinated, multidisciplinary efforts. In the Travel & Tourism sector, this involves engaging stakeholders, including survivors, civil society organizations, and establishing collaborative initiatives. The sector must focus on enhancing awareness of human trafficking, improving identification and prevention strategies, and fostering public-private cooperation to ensure that appropriate actions are taken when trafficking is detected.

The World Travel & Tourism Council (WTTC) is committed to leveraging its position to facilitate information sharing and coordination across the private sector. By building on the experiences of its members and external coalitions, WTTC has developed a framework to proactively combat human trafficking. This framework consists of four key pillars: Awareness, Education & Training, Advocacy, and Support.

Public awareness campaigns can help educate both locals and tourists about the harmful effects of sex tourism. This includes teaching communities about the signs of trafficking and exploitation, as well as the risks and legal consequences of engaging in such activities.

The tourism sector must take responsibility by implementing ethical practices and monitoring for exploitation. This includes training tourism providers, such as hotel staff and tour operators, to identify and report suspicious activities. Tourists should also be educated on the ethical implications of engaging in sex tourism. The Ministry of Tourism, India, UNODC, the Pacific

Asia Travel Association, and Save the Children collaborated to create and implement a Code of Conduct "to protect the dignity, safety, and freedom from exploitation of all tourists and local residents affected by tourism." On World Tourism Day, September 27, 2010, nearly 250 tourism professionals in India committed to following the Code of Conduct for Safe and Honourable Tourism. India's Minister of Tourism, Kumari Selja, emphasized, "By signing this pledge, we are sending a clear message to the world that neither we nor our organizations will participate in activities that exploit women and children." The Code was designed to ensure that individuals working in the hospitality industry are not subjected to drug use or sexual exploitation, crimes that the UNODC is dedicated to combating, particularly in relation to human trafficking. This was done before the commencement of the Commonwealth Games in 2010 which was hosted by India.

Governments must enact and enforce stricter laws against child trafficking, prostitution, and sex tourism. This includes ensuring that perpetrators, whether tourists or local facilitators, face severe penalties. Strengthening the monitoring and regulation of the tourism industry is essential to detect and prevent such crimes. Trafficking in Human Beings or Persons is prohibited under the Constitution of India under Article 23 (1). Special Acts that are passed are The Immoral Traffic (Prevention) Act, 1956, Protection of Children from Sexual offences (POCSO) Act, 2012 etc.

Providing adequate resources and support for victims of sex tourism, such as safe shelters, counselling, legal assistance, and rehabilitation programs, is crucial. Empowering these individuals through education and skills training can help them reintegrate into society and avoid being re-exploited. NGOs play a vital role in combating sex tourism, particularly in regions with high trafficking rates. Governments should collaborate with organizations that work on prevention, victim protection, and legal advocacy.

International cooperation, particularly with countries that are both source and destination points for trafficked individuals, is also crucial. Since sex tourism often involves international travel, countries need to collaborate in order to monitor and restrict the movement of perpetrators. Joint efforts, such as information sharing and coordinated law enforcement actions, can help combat the global nature of this issue.

Conclusion

In conclusion, human trafficking within the global tourism industry remains a pressing and complex issue that requires urgent attention and action. As tourism continues to grow, so too does the exploitation of vulnerable individuals, particularly women and children, who are trafficked for sexual and labour exploitation. The involvement of both organized crime networks and local facilitators in perpetuating these abuses highlights the systemic nature of the problem. Addressing human trafficking in tourism demands a multifaceted approach, including stronger legal frameworks, greater international cooperation, and a commitment to holding both perpetrators and facilitators accountable. Additionally, education and awareness programs for both tourists and the tourism industry can play a pivotal role in preventing exploitation. The need for reform is clear—governments, the tourism industry, and civil society must work collaboratively to create an environment where trafficking is no longer tolerated, and where ethical, responsible tourism practices are the standard. Only through comprehensive reforms and concerted efforts can we hope to reduce human trafficking and ensure that tourism becomes a force for good, fostering opportunities and respect for human dignity worldwide.

TOURISM AND PUBLIC ADMINISTRATION

Author
Dr. Esther Buvana C
Associate Professor,
Government Arts College
(Autonomous),
Bharathiar University,
Coimbatore, Tamil Nadu

Co-Author
Manikandan M L
Research Scholar,
Government Arts College
(Autonomous),
Bharathiar University,
Coimbatore, Tamil Nadu

Introduction

The intersection of tourism and public administration presents a complex and multifaceted landscape, replete with challenges and opportunities. As a significant contributor to national economies and local livelihoods, tourism necessitates effective governance and administrative frameworks to ensure its sustainable development and equitable distribution of benefits. Public administration plays a pivotal role in this context, as it is responsible for crafting and implementing policies, regulations, and strategies that facilitate the growth of tourism while mitigating its negative impacts on the environment, culture, and society. Effective public administration in tourism requires a nuanced understanding of the sector's dynamics, as well as the ability to balance competing interests, manage resources efficiently, and engage with diverse stakeholders. By examining the confluence of tourism and public administration, we can gain insights into the ways in which governments can harness the potential of tourism to drive economic development, promote cultural exchange, and enhance the well-being of communities.

Historical Context and Development

The historical context and development of tourism and public administration are deeply intertwined, with the evolution of tourism as an industry closely tied to the growth of government involvement and regulation. In the early stages of tourism development, governments played a limited role, with the industry driven primarily by private sector initiatives. However, as tourism grew in importance, governments began to recognize its potential as a tool for economic development and job creation.

In the mid-20th century, governments started to take a more active role in tourism development, establishing national tourism organizations and implementing policies to promote the industry. This period also saw the emergence of international tourism organizations, such as the World Tourism Organization (UNWTO), which played a key role in promoting cooperation and knowledge-sharing among governments.

As tourism continued to grow, governments faced increasing pressure to manage its impacts, including environmental degradation, cultural commodification, and social displacement. In response, governments began to develop more sophisticated policies and regulatory frameworks, aimed at balancing the economic benefits of tourism with its social and environmental costs. This shift towards more sustainable and responsible tourism practices has been driven in part by the growing recognition of the importance of tourism in achieving the United Nations' Sustainable Development Goals (SDGs). Today, public administration plays a critical role in shaping the tourism industry, from developing and implementing policies to regulating and monitoring industry practices.

Key Concepts and Theories

The study of tourism and public administration encompasses a range of key concepts and theories that shed light on the complex relationships between government, tourism, and society. Some of the key concepts and theories include:

Governance and Policy-Making

Governance and policy-making are critical components of tourism and public administration. Effective governance ensures that tourism development is aligned with national and local priorities, and that the needs of diverse stakeholders are taken into account. Policy-making involves the formulation, implementation, and evaluation of policies that promote sustainable tourism development, manage tourism impacts, and enhance the overall quality of the tourism experience. Governments use various policy instruments, such as laws, regulations, and incentives, to influence the behavior of tourism stakeholders and achieve desired outcomes. For instance, governments may establish regulations to protect environmental and cultural heritage sites, or offer incentives to encourage the development of sustainable tourism infrastructure.

Sustainable Tourism Development

Sustainable tourism development is a key concept in tourism and public administration. It recognizes that tourism can have significant environmental, social, and economic impacts, and that these impacts must be managed to ensure the long-term viability of tourism destinations. Sustainable tourism development involves adopting practices that minimize negative impacts and maximize positive benefits. This includes implementing measures to reduce energy consumption, waste, and pollution, as well as promoting cultural heritage conservation, community engagement, and fair labour practices. Governments play a crucial role in promoting sustainable tourism development by establishing policies, regulations, and incentives that encourage stakeholders to adopt sustainable practices. For example, the government of Costa Rica has implemented a certification program for sustainable tourism businesses, which recognizes companies that meet rigorous environmental and social standards.

Tourism Planning and Management

Tourism planning and management are essential components of tourism and public administration. Effective planning and management ensure that tourism development is aligned with local and national priorities, and that the needs of diverse stakeholders are taken into account. Tourism planning involves identifying tourism resources, assessing tourism impacts, and developing strategies to manage tourism growth. Management involves implementing plans, monitoring progress, and evaluating outcomes. Governments use various planning and management tools, such as tourism master plans, zoning regulations, and impact assessments, to guide tourism development and ensure that it is sustainable and responsible. For instance, the government of Singapore has developed a tourism master plan that outlines strategies for managing tourism growth, enhancing the quality of the tourism experience, and promoting sustainable tourism practices.

Public-Private Partnerships

Public-private partnerships (PPPs) are collaborative relationships between government agencies and private sector organizations that aim to promote tourism development and improve the quality of tourism services. PPPs can take various forms, including joint ventures, concessions, and management contracts. These partnerships can help leverage resources, expertise, and risk-sharing to achieve common goals. Governments can use PPPs to finance and deliver tourism infrastructure, such as airports, hotels, and attractions. PPPs can also facilitate the development of sustainable tourism practices, such as energy-efficient accommodations and environmentally-friendly transportation systems. For example, the government of Australia has established a PPP to develop and manage a sustainable tourism precinct in the Kakadu National Park.

Stakeholder Theory

Stakeholder theory emphasizes the importance of identifying and engaging with key stakeholders in tourism development. Stakeholders include individuals, groups, and organizations that have a vested interest in tourism development, such as local communities, tourism operators, government agencies, and environmental groups. Effective stakeholder engagement involves understanding the needs, concerns, and expectations of diverse stakeholders and developing strategies to address them. Stakeholder theory recognizes that tourism development can have significant impacts on stakeholders, and that these impacts must be managed to ensure the long-term viability of tourism destinations.

For instance, the government of New Zealand has established a stakeholder engagement framework that involves consulting with local communities, Maori tribes, and environmental groups to develop sustainable tourism strategies.

Network Theory

Network theory highlights the importance of relationships and networks in shaping tourism development. Tourism development involves complex relationships between diverse stakeholders, including government agencies, private sector organizations, local communities, and tourists. Network theory recognizes that these relationships can influence the flow of resources, information, and knowledge, and that they can impact the overall quality of the tourism experience. Effective network management involves understanding the structure and dynamics of tourism networks and developing strategies to build and maintain relationships. For example, the government of Thailand has established a network of tourism stakeholders, including local communities, tourism operators, and government agencies, to promote sustainable tourism development and enhance the quality of the tourism experience.

Institutional Theory

Institutional theory emphasizes the role of institutions and institutional frameworks in shaping tourism development. Institutions include formal rules, regulations, and laws, as well as informal norms, values, and practices. Institutional theory recognizes that institutions can influence the behavior of tourism stakeholders and impact the overall quality of the tourism experience. Effective institutional management involves understanding the institutional framework that governs tourism development and developing strategies to build and maintain institutions. For instance, the government of South Africa has established a national tourism policy framework that outlines the institutional arrangements for tourism development, including the roles and responsibilities of government agencies, private sector organizations, and local communities.

Benefits

Economic Benefits

The symbiotic relationship between tourism and public administration can yield a plethora of economic benefits for destinations, communities, and tourists alike. By harnessing the potential of tourism, local economies can experience a significant surge in revenue, thereby stimulating entrepreneurship, creating employment opportunities, and contributing substantially to GDP growth. Effective public administration plays a vital role in maximizing these economic benefits by investing in tourism infrastructure, promoting destination marketing, and streamlining regulatory frameworks to facilitate a conducive business environment.

Sustainable Development

The integration of tourism and public administration can also foster sustainable development, a paradigm that prioritizes environmental conservation, cultural heritage preservation, and community engagement. By adopting sustainable tourism strategies, destinations can mitigate negative impacts, such as environmental degradation, cultural commodification, and social displacement, while maximizing long-term benefits. Public administration can play a crucial role in promoting sustainable tourism practices by implementing policies, regulations, and incentives that encourage stakeholders to adopt environmentally-friendly and socially-responsible practices.

Improved Infrastructure

The confluence of tourism and public administration can also lead to improved infrastructure, a critical component of a destination's competitiveness in the global tourism market. Public administration can facilitate the development of tourism infrastructure, including transportation systems, accommodations, and attractions, thereby enhancing the overall quality of the tourism experience. This, in turn, can increase visitor satisfaction, encourage repeat visits, and foster a positive word-of-mouth reputation for the destination.

Community Engagement

The intersection of tourism and public administration can facilitate community engagement, cultural exchange, and social interaction. Public administration can promote community-based tourism initiatives, support local entrepreneurship, and ensure that benefits are shared equitably among stakeholders. This can lead to increased community participation, enhanced cultural heritage preservation, and improved social cohesion, ultimately contributing to a more resilient and sustainable tourism industry.

Tax Revenue Generation

In addition, tourism can generate significant tax revenue for governments, which can be reinvested in public services, infrastructure, and community development. This can create a virtuous cycle of economic growth, improved public services, and enhanced quality of life for local communities. Effective public administration is essential in ensuring that tax revenue is allocated efficiently and effectively, thereby maximizing the benefits of tourism for local communities.

Destination Competitiveness

The synergy between tourism and public administration can also enhance a destination's competitiveness in the global tourism market. Public administration can facilitate strategic marketing, product development, and service quality improvement, thereby differentiating the destination from its competitors. This can lead to increased market share, improved brand reputation, and enhanced economic benefits for local communities.

Environmental Conservation

The integration of tourism and public administration can promote environmental conservation and sustainable tourism practices, protecting natural resources and preserving cultural heritage sites for future generations. Public administration can implement policies, regulations, and incentives that encourage stakeholders to adopt environmentally-friendly and socially-responsible practices, thereby minimizing negative impacts and maximizing long-term benefits.

Challenges and Constraints

Despite the numerous benefits of tourism and public administration, there are several challenges and constraints that can hinder the effective management of tourism destinations. Some of the key challenges and constraints include:

Institutional and Governance Challenges

One of the primary challenges facing tourism and public administration is the need for effective institutional and governance frameworks. This includes the development of clear policies, laws, and regulations that govern the tourism industry, as well as the establishment of effective institutional arrangements for tourism management.

Infrastructure and Resource Constraints

Tourism destinations often face significant infrastructure and resource constraints, including inadequate transportation systems, insufficient accommodation capacity, and limited access to basic services such as water and sanitation. These constraints can limit the ability of destinations to accommodate growing numbers of tourists.

Environmental and Cultural Degradation

The rapid growth of tourism can lead to environmental and cultural degradation, including the destruction of natural habitats, the pollution of air and water, and the erosion of cultural heritage sites. Public administration must balance the economic benefits of tourism with the need to protect the environment and preserve cultural heritage.

Community Engagement and Participation

Effective community engagement and participation are critical to the success of tourism development initiatives. However, many tourism destinations struggle to engage local communities in the planning and decision-making process, leading to conflicts over resource use and benefits distribution.

Economic Leakage and Unequal Distribution of Benefits

Tourism can generate significant economic benefits, but these benefits are often unevenly distributed, with local communities receiving a small proportion of the revenue generated. Economic leakage, where tourism revenue is repatriated to external companies or individuals, can exacerbate this problem.

Climate Change and Disaster Risk Management

Tourism destinations are increasingly vulnerable to the impacts of climate change, including sea-level rise, more frequent natural disasters, and changing weather patterns. Public administration must develop effective strategies for climate change adaptation and disaster risk management to protect tourism infrastructure and ensure the long-term sustainability of the industry.

Technological and Digital Challenges

The tourism industry is undergoing rapid technological and digital transformation, with the rise of online booking platforms, social media, and big data analytics. Public administration must develop the capacity to leverage these technologies to enhance the tourism experience, improve destination management, and increase competitiveness.

Policy and Regulatory Framework

The policy and regulatory framework of public administration towards tourism in India plays a pivotal role in shaping the development and management of the tourism industry.

This framework is designed to promote sustainable tourism development, ensure the protection of the environment and cultural heritage, and provide a conducive business environment for tourism stakeholders. In India, various regulations govern the tourism industry, including the Wildlife (Protection) Act, 1972, the Environment (Protection) Act, 1986, the Tourism and Hospitality Industry (Regulation of Service) Act, 2011, the Right to Information Act, 2005, and the Foreign Exchange Management Act, 1999. These regulations cover various aspects, including environmental protection, wildlife conservation, consumer protection, and foreign exchange management.

Public administration plays a crucial role in ensuring that tourism development aligns with India's broader economic, social, and environmental goals. The government has established a robust regulatory framework to promote sustainable tourism practices, protect the environment and cultural heritage, and ensure that the benefits of tourism are shared equitably among stakeholders. Effective governance and regulation are critical in ensuring that tourism development is environmentally sustainable, socially responsible, and economically viable. Public administration must balance the needs of diverse stakeholders, including tourists, local communities, tourism businesses, and the environment.

By complying with regulations and adhering to sustainable tourism practices, tourism businesses in India can contribute to the country's sustainable development goals, promote eco-friendly practices, and provide quality services to tourists. Public administration must provide support and incentives to encourage tourism businesses to adopt sustainable practices and comply with regulations. Ultimately, the successful development and management of the tourism industry in India require a collaborative effort between public administration, tourism businesses, local communities, and other stakeholders. By working together, these stakeholders can promote sustainable tourism development, protect the environment and cultural heritage, and ensure that the benefits of tourism are shared equitably among all.

Conclusion

The intersection of tourism and public administration is a complex and multifaceted field that requires careful consideration of economic, social, and environmental factors. Effective public administration plays a vital role in promoting sustainable tourism development, protecting the environment and cultural heritage, and ensuring that the benefits of tourism are shared equitably among stakeholders. By adopting a collaborative and inclusive approach, governments can work with tourism businesses, local communities, and other stakeholders to develop and implement policies and regulations that support the long-term sustainability of the tourism industry. Ultimately, the successful integration of tourism and public administration can contribute to the achievement of broader economic, social, and environmental goals, while enhancing the quality of life for local communities and promoting a positive and enriching experience for tourists.

TOURISM AND HUMAN RIGHTS

Dr. Dolly Thomas
Associate Professor
Department of History
Stella Maris College(Autonomous)
Chennai-86

Introduction

Tourism and Human Rights are both well-established concepts of the modern age. Spurred by the need for recreation and leisure, tourism has become a mass phenomenon post-Second World War. It is part of the consumption pattern of developed as well as developing countries, a major employer and income generator across the world. The capacity of tourism to reduce poverty levels, induce development and transfer of cash from highly developed to lesser developed regions is a proven fact. Virtually every country is trying to develop tourism as it results in economic growth, prosperity and results in better standard of living for its citizens.

The concept of Human Right ever since the Universal Declaration of Human Rights has gradually found acceptance in the far corners of the world. The rampant exploitation of weaker sections of the population is in the present age prevented through protective legislation, largely due to global acceptance of human rights. All through history one has witnessed the rampant abuse of rights of the rich over the poor and the haves over the have nots. Moving on to the question of tourism and human rights, with growing number of people becoming tourists and traveling all of the world, it often negatively impacts the rights of people in destination communities. This chapter will focus on various aspects of the impact of tourism on human rights and explore how tourism can work in tandem with human rights organisations to minimise violations and make tourism growth a blessing for all stakeholders.

Historical Context and Development

Human beings have been traveling since time immemorial, driven initially by the need for survival. The nomadic traits of our ancestors instilled in us an innate desire to explore, discover, and experience new environments and cultures. As civilizations evolved, so did the purpose and nature of travel. Ancient Rome played a pivotal role in laying the foundations of modern tourism. The Roman Empire's impressive network of roads, roadside inns, and maintenance of law and order created a conducive environment for travel. Prosperity and stability enabled the wealthy to indulge in leisure travel, visiting magnificent monuments and experiencing different cultures. However, this also led to the exploitation of local communities, who were often forced to provide labour and services to cater to the needs of wealthy travellers.

The concept of the Grand Tour, originating in England, became a rage throughout Europe. Young men from affluent families embarked on extended journeys to explore the famous sites of Europe, thereby completing their formal education. While this promoted cultural exchange and appreciation of art, architecture, and history, it also perpetuated social and economic inequalities. The Grand Tour was a privilege reserved for the wealthy, while the local populations were often relegated to secondary roles, providing services and entertainment for the tourists. During the Middle Ages, pilgrimage tourism gained prominence. Travellers would embark on arduous journeys to sacred sites, such as the Holy Land, Rome, and Santiago de Compostela. While this type of tourism satisfied the spiritual needs of travellers, it also raised concerns about cultural appropriation, exploitation of local resources, and disregard for human rights.

The industrial revolution brought in long hours of work, polluted and crowded industrial towns but eventually it brought in more money and more leisure, which enabled a greater number of people to travel. The need to escape the polluted and crowded industrial towns became a felt need and people flocked to seaside and hill resorts and other places of interest. The Holidays with Pay Act was yet another important milestone in the history of travel. It was in the post-World War period with the remarkable advances made in travel technology that proved to be the turning point in the concept of travel. As the modes of transportation became faster, safer and more affordable, it enabled a greater number of people to become tourists. Aircrafts constructed for the war efforts began to carry passengers across continents.

Today, tourism is a global phenomenon, with millions of people traveling every year. While tourism has the potential to promote cultural exchange, economic growth, and environmental sustainability, it also raises critical human rights concerns. The exploitation of local communities, displacement of indigenous peoples, and abuse of workers' rights are just a few examples of the human rights issues that arise in the context of tourism. As the tourism industry continues to grow, it is essential to recognize the inherent linkages between tourism and human rights. Ensuring that tourism is developed and managed in a responsible and sustainable manner, with respect for human rights and dignity, is crucial for promoting equitable and just tourism practices. In India as well travel existed from ancient times, the earliest known reasons being pilgrimage, trade and commerce. Benevolent kings built sarais (rest houses) for the safety of travellers. Post independence efforts were made to promote tourism, with the formation of the Ministry of Tourism and the evolution of a National Tourism Policy, tourism in India has come of age. India with its rich heritage and culture is a treasure trove and with careful and sustainable development practices has much to gain from the development of tourism.

Human Rights as a concept does not have a definition that is universally accepted but they are the basic standards without which people cannot live with dignity (Donnelly 2003). According to the United Nations human rights are inherent to the nature of human beings. Human rights include our fundamental freedoms of speech, thought and expression, it refers to an individual's right to equality, dignity and wellbeing. The Universal Declaration of Human Rights that was passed by the United Nations in 1948 is accepted as a universal standard that all nations are bound to use in implementing their national laws. The right to rest and leisure (tourism) and freedom of movement (travel) also fall within the ambit of human rights.

Key concepts

Tourism is a significant contributor to economic development globally, it is a major earner of forex and helps improve the balance of payments. As people from different parts of the world get to interact with others culturally and racially different, it fosters mutual respect and understanding thereby promoting peace and goodwill. Tourism has resulted in multidimensional "good change" leading to self-sufficiency, self-determination and empowerment, as well as improved standards of living (Scheyvens, 2003). Tourism has significantly contributed to the development of backward regions. Improvement of infrastructure to support tourism has had a positive impact on the lives of communities. Tourism is a labour-intensive industry, which supports skilled, semi-skilled as well as unskilled labour. The large scope for unskilled labour has resulted in poverty alleviation and also the opportunity of local people to participate in a positive manner in promoting and protecting the cultural heritage of a region. Women and several marginalised communities have found jobs due to the growth of opportunities ushered in by tourism.

Despite the positive changes brought about by tourism, it also has several negative impacts. If there is unregulated and unplanned growth in tourism it can damage the environment of a region detrimentally affecting the livelihoods of the local communities. Tourism is often driven by big businesses that are only interested in profit, they pay scant attention to the over exploitation of resources with scant regard for sustainable practices. The large inflow of tourists into a region pushes up the cost of basic amenities thereby increasing the financial burden on the local people. International tourism is also dominated by trans-national corporations with large stakes and political clout, who are able to dictate terms and operate in a monopolistic way, elbowing out local and regional operators. Such organizations are also driven by profits and have no long-term loyalty to the destinations they promote.

Their mantra is to maximise their profits by maximising the exploitation of a popular destinations, they wrap up their business and head elsewhere when a region reaches its carrying capacity and begins to deteriorate as a tourist destination. There are several dimensions to the relationship between tourism and human rights which will be explained as the chapter unfolds.

Types and Forms

Since its early inception as an important dimension of recreational leisure, tourism has evolved into myriad forms and types, each new type a surprising and innovative addition to the ever-growing list of tourism types. Traditional forms of tourism are being rejected by the new age travellers. Some of the recent trends in tourism include, Noctourism or nocturnal tourism, which includes stargazing and other nocturnal recreations. There is a greater drive among vacationers to focus on vacations that are themed on extending lifespan and well-being. People are even looking at travel as an opportunity to trigger personal growth. Slum tourism, voluntourism, wellness tourism, destination weddings are the new age fads with a growing number of takers.

Human rights have several dimensions to it as well – the civil and political side. The economic, social and cultural aspects of human rights are equally important as well. Human rights are universal, inalienable and indivisible. Despite the UDHR, the covenants, the optional protocols and conventions like the CERD and CEDAW, for the poor and the marginalised access to a life of respect and dignity still remains a distant dream. Tourism is also contributing to the exploitation and marginalization therefore it is the need of the hour for governments to recognize the problem and take the necessary steps for redressal.

Benefits and impact

The economic and cultural benefits of tourism promotion are undeniable. Tourism has become a significant contributor to the GDP of many countries, providing employment opportunities and helping to balance regional disparities. However, the negative impact of tourism on human rights cannot be ignored. Tourism generates significant revenue for local economies, creating jobs and stimulating economic growth. It also promotes cultural exchange between visitors and local communities, fostering greater understanding and appreciation of diverse cultures. Furthermore, tourism can drive investment in infrastructure development, such as roads, airports, and public services. In many cases, tourism has provided economic opportunities for marginalized communities, helping to reduce poverty and inequality.

Despite these benefits, tourism development can have devastating consequences for local communities. The displacement of local communities is a common phenomenon, as their lands are converted into tourist infrastructure. Tourism workers, including those in the hospitality and service sectors, are often exploited, facing low wages, long working hours, and poor working conditions. Cultural appropriation is also a significant concern, where local cultural practices and traditions are commodified and exploited for tourist consumption. The environmental impact of tourism is also a pressing issue. Tourism can contribute to environmental degradation, including pollution, deforestation, and climate change. In addition, tourism can also contribute to human trafficking, particularly in the sex tourism industry. To mitigate these negative impacts, it is essential to adopt sustainable and responsible tourism practices.

Community-based tourism is a critical approach, where tourism development is community-led, ensuring that local communities benefit from tourism and have control over their lands and resources. Fair labour practices are also essential, providing decent wages, safe working conditions, and social protections for workers. Cultural sensitivity is vital, respecting local cultural practices and traditions, and avoiding cultural appropriation. Finally, environmental sustainability should be a top priority, minimizing waste, reducing energy consumption, and promoting conservation.

By adopting these practices, tourism can become a force for good, promoting economic development, cultural exchange, and human rights, while minimizing its negative impacts. It is essential for governments, tourism businesses, and local communities to work together to ensure that tourism is developed and managed in a responsible and sustainable manner.

Challenges and constraints

One dark side of tourism is sex tourism. Sex is very often the motivating factor for travel. Also called as tourism prostitution, sex tourism is defined as tourism for which the main motivation or purpose is to consummate commercial sexual relations (Graburn, 1983: Hall, 1991a) South East Asian countries especially Thailand and Philippines are the most popular destinations for sex tourism, though it exists in virtually every country. There are also cases of children involved in sex tourism in places. It is poverty that pushes children and adults into the tourist flesh trade.

Tourism has the potential of affecting human rights in many ways, such as an impact on working conditions. Since there is a lot of scope for unskilled labour, tourism can result in the creation of exploitative working conditions with poor pay, and dependence on child labour. Tourism also impacts access to resources. Tourism often leads to inequitable access to basic need like water, food and housing. Big hotels and resorts enjoy unlimited supply of water, food and electricity to pamper and entertain the rich tourists, while local residents might lack access to portable water. Items of food become expensive as there a growing demand to cater to the needs of tourists. In regions of high tourism demand accommodation also becomes expensive for the non-tourists. Another blight caused by tourism is cultural erosion. Commodification in tourism leads to loss of culture and traditions. While tourism helps preserve dying arts and traditions, often to cater to tourist needs the real traditions and culture gets corrupted. For instance, the original Kathakalli performances of Kerala were performances that lasted all night long but to suit the entertainment of tourists the Kathakalli performances have been reduced to 15-minute affairs. Therefore, what is offered to tourists is very often not the authentic culture but something tailormade to suit their preferences.

A significant blot on tourism is the sexual exploitation. Women and children are sometimes pushed into prostitution. The link between sex and tourism is well known but often ignored by governments. There are instances when government covertly support sex tourism as it brings in much needed forex. This is a clear violation of rights; governments are willing to sacrifice the well-being of their citizens for the profits that are coming through tourism. Closely linked to sex tourism is the blatant selling of drugs to tourists. Yet another human rights violation is the displacement and forced relocation that sometimes happens due to tourism. When big companies purchase land for major tourism projects not only does it inflate land and property prices making it unaffordable for locals it also leads to forced relocation. People are displaced and very often poor people who don't have proper land documents are removed to make way for tourism businesses. Political nexus with big businesses can also lead to illegal land acquisitions.

Pollution and lack of sustainable development as a result of tourism has caused ill health and even loss of livelihoods. When tourism is promoted only for short term profits without assessing the carrying capacity of a region or analysing the environmental impact, the result can be disastrous. Several tourist regions have faced a backlash as a result of unregulated tourism. The floods and avalanches in Uttarakhand several years ago and the Wayanad floods of 2024 are all examples of environmental disasters because of over exploitation by tourism businesses. At the end of the day, it is the poor residents of a region who suffer the brunt of environmental disasters. There have also been instances of indigenous tribes being put on display for tourists. Tourism sometimes results in a source of conflict between tourists and locals.

Policy and regulatory framework

The tourism sector has a critical role to play in protecting human rights, particularly for vulnerable groups such as women, children, people below the poverty line, tribals, indigenous people, migrant workers, and people with disabilities. One key step towards achieving this is by establishing a human rights-based policy that is binding on all tourism businesses. This policy should be integrated into business management, ensuring that human rights are respected and protected throughout all operations.

Agencies should be established to monitor the impact of business activities on the human rights of local communities. These agencies can help identify areas of concern and provide guidance on how to address them. Furthermore, the ministry of tourism should implement a grievance mechanism that provides all citizens with access to report human rights abuses. This mechanism should also review the progress of legislative measures protecting rights, ensuring that they are effective and enforced. It's essential for governments to take a proactive approach to addressing human rights issues in the tourism sector. Instead of ignoring problems like sex tourism, governments should encourage reporting of such abuses and hold perpetrators accountable. International frameworks, such as the UN international human rights instruments and the International Labour Organisation Conventions, can provide valuable guidance and support in protecting human rights in the tourism sector.

The Roundtable Human Rights in Tourism is an excellent example of an initiative promoting human rights in the tourism industry. This international multi-stakeholder initiative provides incentives for enterprises to respect human rights in tourism, in accordance with the UN Guiding Principles on Business and Human Rights. By working together, governments, businesses, and civil society can ensure that the tourism sector promotes and respects human rights for all. In addition to these measures, it's crucial to address the specific human rights risks faced by workers in the tourism sector. This includes ensuring fair labour practices, preventing exploitation and abuse, and promoting decent work. The International Labour Organisation's (ILO) Guidelines on Decent Work and Socially Responsible Tourism provide a valuable framework for achieving this.[3] By prioritizing human rights and fair labour practices, the tourism sector can contribute to sustainable development and promote the well-being of local communities.

Future directions and prospects

Despite the overwhelming evidence of the intrinsic link between tourism and human rights exploitation, this critical issue remains woefully neglected by policymakers worldwide. Even among human rights advocates, the exploitation resulting from tourism has yet to garner the attention it warrants, failing to secure a spot on the list of pressing priorities. Tourism is still not perceived as a significant or influential sector in the realm of human rights protection, leaving a gaping void in the quest for justice and equality.

Consequently, the onus rests squarely on the shoulders of tourism businesses to make a paradigm shift, embracing a moral obligation to prioritize human rights. Rather than perpetuating exploitation, tourism enterprises must become allies in the protection and promotion of human rights, harnessing their influence to drive positive change. By doing so, tourism can evolve into a transformative force, fostering a culture of respect, empathy, and inclusivity.

Imagine a tourism paradigm where children are safeguarded from the scourge of labour and sexual exploitation, their innocence and dignity protected. Envision a tourism industry where access to services is equitable and inclusive, where diversity is celebrated, and gender identity is respected. Picture a tourism sector where the intangible heritage of a nation is revered and preserved, its cultural essence intact.

If tourism can navigate this path, eschewing exploitation and embracing responsibility, it can become a beacon of hope for a brighter, more equitable future. By marrying economic growth with social justice and environmental stewardship, tourism can emerge as a powerful catalyst for sustainable development, enriching the lives of individuals and communities worldwide. Ultimately, tourism can become a shining exemplar of humanity's capacity for compassion, empathy, and kindness, illuminating the path towards a more harmonious and equitable world.

Conclusion

The intricate relationship between tourism and human rights demands urgent attention from policymakers, tourism businesses, and civil society. As the tourism sector continues to grow, it is imperative to recognize the inherent linkages between tourism and human rights. By adopting sustainable and responsible tourism practices, prioritizing human rights, and promoting fair labour practices, the tourism sector can transform into a powerful catalyst for sustainable development, enriching the lives of individuals and communities worldwide. Ultimately, the future of tourism depends on its ability to balance economic growth with social justice and environmental stewardship, ensuring that the benefits of tourism are equitably shared among all stakeholders, and that the rights and dignity of local communities are respected and protected.

TOURISM AND FIVE-YEAR PLANS

Dr. M. Sabeera Sulthana Bijli
Assistant Professor of History,
Madras Christian College, Chennai

Introduction

From the 16th century, the world saw significant changes in global travel patterns, particularly with the expansion of European empires. The development of tourism was influenced by the policies, economic interests, and cultural exchanges promoted by colonial powers. The modern concept of tourism, with mass travel and leisure as its central focus, emerged in the 19th and 20th centuries. Prior to that, people across the world travelled for pilgrimage centres, acquiring new knowledge, spreading their ideas and ideologies, but they had made their travels without any facilities as of now and travelled amid various hardships.

Colonialism and Tourism

Colonialism led to the creation of vast networks connecting Europe with Asia, Africa, and the Americas. These interactions created opportunities for Europeans to travel to the colonies, not just for administrative or economic purposes, but also for leisure. The infrastructure laid by the colonial powers like construction of railways, roadways also support tourism development: Further The colonial period was also marked by the romanticization of colonised lands. Books, paintings, and photography depicted the colonies as picturesque landscapes, creating a demand for visits to this location. The wealthy Europeans from Britain and France travelled to the colonies for leisure or health reasons.

Tourism in Colonial India

In the colonial period, tourism was influenced by several factors related to colonial governance, economic interests, and the cultural attitudes of the time. Although the tourism industry was not fully developed during this period, British laid the foundation step for tourism in India, particularly catering to European tastes and needs. The concept of tourism evolved in India, was confined to the colonial elite, such as British officials, traders, and settlers, as well as a few wealthy Indians who had adopted Western lifestyles British colonial administrators and military officers frequently visited India for work, but they also travelled for leisure and health. Hill stations, such as Mussoorie, Darjeeling, became popular destinations for Europeans to take respite from the tropical heat of Indian plains. These places were often used by the British as places to retreat during the summer month. Many of these hill stations were developed with Western-style infrastructure, such as colonial-style bungalows, churches, and social clubs, catering to the British elite.

Infrastructure Development and Transportation

A major catalyst for tourism in British rule was the development of transportation networks, which allowed easier access to various regions of the country. The British established an extensive railway network across India starting in the 1850s. Railways facilitated not only the movement of goods and troops but also made travel within India much easier for Europeans, as well as for Elite Indians. The railways connected major cities to hill stations, ports, and tourist destinations, making it convenient for British officials and others to travel for leisure. The introduction of the railways also paved the way for the creation of hotels and resorts around key railway stations.

In addition to railways, roads and ports were developed to improve the colonial economy and facilitate trade. The roads also made it easier for tourists to access other parts of the country, such as coastal regions and sites of historical or cultural significance. During the colonial period, European tourists were encouraged to visit India to experience its culture, landscapes, and historical monuments. Many historical sites, such as the Taj Mahal, ancient temples, forts, and palaces, were promoted as part of India's heritage. British colonial officials were often responsible for preserving these monuments, though their focus was frequently on presenting these sites as relics of India's past glory, separate from the contemporary

Indian society they controlled. Some tourists were drawn to these monuments, as they symbolized India's cultural richness. The colonial authorities invested in the creation of infrastructure for tourists, especially in areas popular among the British. Along with the development of hill stations, like Darjeeling, Ooty, and Nainital hotels, and resorts were built to accommodate and attract he European visitor

Tourism Development in Independence Era

The first effort to promote tourism in India was made in the year 1945, when a Committee was set up by the Government of India under the Chairmanship of Sir John Sargent ,To recommend what action should be taken for providing the necessary facilities by Indian and or Local Governments Various departments of Central Government to facilitate tourism in India .The Sargent Committee submitted its interim report in October, 1946 It suggested successful steps in the promotion· of tourism would result in substantial addition to India.

Separate Tourist Traffic Branch was created in the Ministry of Transport in the year 1949. Further regional tourist offices. were established in the four major cities, Bombay, Calcutta, Delhi and Madras. There was a better 'means of communication, specially' air travel growing interest in India by foreign countries; and greater publicity and better facilities to foreign tourists, partly due to the recommendations of Sargent Commission. Tourism development in India has gone through many stages. The Five-year Plan started by the Government of India also booted the tourism industry.

Circumstances laid for introducing Five Year Plan in India

When India gains independence in the year in 1947, there were lots of socio-economic problems prevailed in India such as poverty, famines, low yield due to commercialisation of agriculture in the British period, poor industrial growth. To overcome these problems and to build its economy, in the year 15th March 1950 the Government of India initiated the National Planning Commission. It assesses all the resources of the country, and formulate the Five-year plans to achieve economic growth etc.

Importance of Five-Year Plans in India

Five-Year Plans were launched by the government to achieve specific socio-economic goals. They were designed to address India's economic challenges, boost industrialization, improve infrastructure, and reduce poverty.

- The Five-Year Plans provided a road map for the country's economic development, setting out clear targets and priorities. These plans enabled the government to systematically allocate resources, monitor progress, and adjust policies as needed to meet the long-term goals of industrialization, infrastructure development, and poverty reduction.
- The key priorities were given to industrialization. The establishment of heavy industries, power plants, and steel plants (e.g., Bhilai Steel Plant) laid the foundation for India's industrial growth.
- The plans also focused on the infrastructure, including transportation (railways, roads), communication, and energy generation. This laid the groundwork for modernization in these sectors, which contributed to economic growth and connectivity.
- To ensure food security, improve rural livelihoods, and address poverty.
- The plans also aimed at addressing rural healthcare, education
- The Five-Year Plans, emphasized the development of domestic industries, reducing dependence on foreign imports.
- The Five-Year Plans played an important role in promoting education at all levels—primary, secondary, and higher education.
- It contributed to the healthcare sector, leading to the construction of hospitals, clinics, and health programs that

focused on improving public health and reducing infant mortality rates.

- The plans supported programs for S.C and S.T, and other underprivileged sections through affirmative action and welfare scheme
- The Five-Year Plans sought to, improve trade policies, and encouraging foreign investments.
- The Five plans aimed at bridging regional disparities by allocating resources to both urban and rural areas, and various states, ensuring balanced development.
- By setting national priorities, the plans ensured that all sectors of the economy moved in a coordinated manner toward a common goal.

First Five-Year Plan (1951-56)

In this plan much focus was given to economic needs, development of agriculture, infrastructure and industries. Tourism was not a major priority during this period, there were some early efforts that indirectly contributed to the growth of tourism in India such as upgradation of tourist traffic branch as the Tourist Traffic Division in 1955-56.

Although the First Five-Year Plan did not specifically target tourism as a major sector, A significant focus of the plan was on improving transport and communication infrastructure, including roads, railways, and airports. This directly impacted the accessibility of different parts of India, which was crucial for the growth of tourism. Better transportation made easier for both domestic and international travellers to explore various regions of India. Further, the government, recognizing the importance of India's cultural heritage, took initial steps towards promoting the country's rich history and architectural landmarks, to attract tourists in the future. As it said earlier, though tourism was not an official focus, some early investments were made in developing basic tourism infrastructure, such as hotels and rest houses in popular tourist locations.

Second Five-Year Plan (1956-1961) primarily focused on industrialization, with a significant development of heavy industries and the expansion of infrastructure. Significant investments were made in transportation, energy, and communication infrastructure to support industrial growth and economic development One of the key features of the plan was the development of transportation infrastructure, including roads, railways, and airports. This was essential for improving connectivity within India and with the rest of the world, thereby making travel more accessible for tourists.

Third Five-Year plan 1961-66 focused on self-reliance, industrial development, and economic growth. This was known as Gadgil yojna, the deputy charman of this plan was D.R. Gadgil. The potentiality of tourism has been realized. In order to attract foreign tourist and to promote tourism, historical sites like Bodhgaya, Khajuraho, Konark, Mahabalipuram, Sanchi, Tiruchirapalli, Kanchipuram were provided with accommodation facilities for foreign tourists. The government started to recognize that tourism could also provide employment opportunities and contribute to regional development.

The outbreak of the Sino-Indian War in 1962 severely strained India's economic situation. spending for defence increased by diverting resources from development projects. This disrupted the goals of the 3rd Five-Year Plan and contributed to a delay in initiating the 4th Plan. For consecutive three years1966-1969 the Government of India shifted from Five-year plan to yearly annual plan. Stabilizing the economy, controlling the inflation, recovery in agriculture were the aim of Annual plans. The fund allocated for 1st annual plan (1966-67) is2217rs crore, the fund allocated for second (1967-68) and the third annual plan (1968-69) is Rs 2300 crores and Rs 2400 crores. Economic stabilisation, food security and agricultural recovery through Green revolution are the impacts of the annual plans.

Fourth Five-Year Plan (1969–1974) focused on achieving self-reliance and economic growth, industrial development, agricultural progress, and social welfare. Tourism, although not a primary focus of the plan, was recognized for its potential in contributing to the economic and cultural development. The tourism industry was seen as a means to earn foreign exchange, create employment, and foster infrastructure development .The government established as well as strengthened organizations such as the India Tourism Development Corporation (ITDC), which acted a crucial part in promoting tourism, developing tourist destinations, and managing hotel facilities. This was an early step toward institutionalizing tourism promotion in India.

Fifth Five-Year plan (1974-79) was focused on agricultural development, rural employment, poverty alleviation, and infrastructural improvements. It marked a significant turning point in India's tourism development. It recognized the tourism as a major economic contributor and a tool for social and cultural exchange Special attention was given to the promotion of rural and eco-tourism, allowing tourists to associate with the traditional lifestyles of India's rural population and its natural beauty.

Sixth Five-Year plan sets goal on self-reliance, poverty alleviation, and improvements in social infrastructure. The plan also recognized the importance of promoting key sectors, including tourism, as a means of generating foreign exchange, and improving India's global image. Tourism became more central to India's development strategy during this period, with increasing attention paid to its economic potential and its role in fostering national and international goodwill. The promotion of regional tourism was emphasized, with particular focus on improving accessibility to rural and heritage sites, ensuring that lesser-known destinations could be explored by tourists, thereby promoting economic growth in less-developed region. In the year1986, the plan setup a National Committee on Tourism to formulate a long-term perspective plan for the tourism sector. Furthe tourism circuits were given importance.

Seventh Five-Year plan (1985-1990) placed significant emphasis on preserving and promoting India's rich cultural heritage. Historical sites, monuments, and places of religious significance received more attention. Efforts were made to safeguard these cultural assets and promote them as tourist attractions. The promotion of India's heritage helped increase both domestic and international interest in India's tourism offerings. One of the key objectives of the 7th Plan was to create employment opportunities across different sector

Eighth Five-Year Plan 1992-97 The early 1990s marked a turning point for India with the adoption of economic liberalization ppolicies. It opened up the Indian economy to global markets, leading to an influx of foreign investments and a growing middle class with higher incomes. Both domestic and international tourism began to flourish, driven by increased global connectivity, improved transportation, and better infrastructure. This Plan highlighted the growing role of State Tourism Agencies (STAs) in promoting regional tourism. As central government under the Ministry of Tourism was responsible for national-level promotions, the **STAs** became more proactive in developing regional attractions, and implementing state-level tourism initiatives.

Nineth Five-Year Plan (1997–2002) of India was focused on developing human resources, poverty alleviation, and **i**nfrastructure development while promoting economi**c** growth. The launch of the *Incredible India* campaign in 2002, is a major tourism marketing campaign, was part of the government's strategy to place India as a global tourist destination. The plan also seeks to expand the tourism product by 'encouraging rural and village tourism, adventure and eco-tourism, indigenous and natural health tourism, heritage tourism and youth and senior citizen's packages.

Tenth Five Year Plan (2002–2007) was focused on sustainable growth, poverty, employment generation, and infrastructure development. The plan recognized the importance of tourism as a means to enhance India's global image, preserve its cultural tourism. A significant feature of the 10th Five-Year Plan was the increased focus on Public-Private Partnerships (PPP) in tourism infrastructure development. The government recognized the need for private sector involvement to accelerate tourism growth and improve services. This led to the establishment of numerous joint ventures in the development of hotels, resorts, and transportation services, as well as the promotion of tourism through advertising campaigns and digital media. To enhance local tourism many training programs were introduced for local communities, focusing on hospitality, language skills, and cultural knowledge, thus providing employment and promoting social inclusion.

Eleventh Five-Year plan (2007-2012) recognized tourism as a key driver of economic development. It highlighted the sector's potential to create jobs, particularly in hospitality, transportation, and service sectors, and contribute significantly to foreign exchange earnings. The plan aimed to double foreign tourist arrivals by 2012 and enhance India's share in global tourism. The tourism sector was also seen as an avenue for boosting regional economic development, especially in rural and less-developed area

The **Twelfth Five-Year Plan** (2012–2017) placed a strong emphasis on inclusive growth, sustainable development, and human development. It also emphasized eco-tourism and heritage tourism as core elements to promote India as a responsible tourist destination. The twelfth plan also emphasized the need for public-private partnerships (PPP) in the tourism sector. This included collaborating with private stakeholders to build and upgrade infrastructure, develop tourism products, and promote destinations. The 12th Five-Year Plan emphasized the importance of strategic **branding and marketing** to position India as a top global tourist destination. Government initiatives, such as the Incredible India campaign, continued to play a key role in enhancing the country's image globally.

Conclusion

Five-Year Plans performed a significant part in the development of tourism industry in India. They provided the necessary infrastructure, policy frameworks, and fund is to transform tourism into a major economic sector. In the year 2017 The Five-Year Plans were officially discontinued and India adopted a new framework for growth under the NITI Aayog (National Institution for Transforming India), which replaced the Planning Commission. The present government's approach to tourism development in India is multi-faceted and holistic, focusing on infrastructure development, sustainability, digital innovation, and the promotion of diverse tourism niche.

TOURISM AND INTERNATIONAL REGULATIONS

Dr. K.S. Beena
Assistant Professor & Head
Department of Travel & Tourism
SDNB Vaishnav College for Women
Chennai

Introduction

Tourism regulations are a set of legal standards and practices that govern the tourism industry, both nationally and internationally. These regulations are important for ensuring that tourism operations are sustainable and responsible, and that they adhere to local and international laws.

Here are some key areas covered by tourism regulations:

Licensing and permits- Businesses in the tourism industry, such as hotels, restaurants, and tour agencies, need specific permits and licenses to operate legally.

Health and safety-Regulations ensure the safety of tourists and staff in tourism facilities, including fire safety, sanitation, and emergency protocols.

Environmental protection-Guidelines are in place to minimize the environmental impact of tourism. For example, regulations might limit the number of accommodations in coastal areas to prevent beach erosion and preserve marine life.

Consumer rights-Regulations protect tourists from fraud, ensuring fair pricing and quality service.

Customs and visa policies-These policies facilitate or restrict entry of travellers across international borders.

Traveler rights:

These regulations ensure the protection and security of tourists. Tourism regulations are important because they help balance the interests of tourists, businesses, and local communities. They also help to protect cultural and natural resources, and ensure orderly growth and development in the tourism sector. Tourism regulation refers to the set of rules and guidelines established by governments to manage and control the tourism industry, ensuring sustainable development and the preservation of cultural and environmental assets.

Travel regulations definition:

Rules and guidelines that govern the movement across borders to ensure safety, legality, and efficiency. Importance of travel regulations: They are essential for maintaining security, public health, economic stability, and legal compliance during travel.

The term "tourism laws" refers to a collection of national, state, and international laws that govern many facets and operations of the travel industry. For instance, travel legislation may include rules governing work, hospitality, or public health. The ISO standards for tourism industry play a vital role in ensuring quality, safety, and sustainability across the sector. These international standards provide a framework that helps tourism businesses improve their services and offer consistent experiences to travellers worldwide.

Historical Context and Development

Tourism regulations have evolved over time to address economic, social, and environmental concerns, and to meet the needs of the industry. Here are some examples of how tourism regulations have developed:

Early regulations

In ancient times, tourism regulations were rudimentary and focused on basic safety and security.

International Air Transport Association (IATA)

Established in 1945, the IATA regulated commercial aviation to ensure safe and efficient air travel.

India's first tourism policy

In 1982, India announced its first tourism policy, which focused on coordination and the importance of tourism as a "common endeavor".

India's tourism policy in 2002

This policy aimed to increase the number of domestic and international tourists. It also led to the launch of the "Incredible India" international marketing campaign.

Tourism regulations in the United States

Tourism laws in the United States come from a variety of sources, including federal and state constitutions, common law, administrative law, treaties, and statutes. Tourism regulations are adaptive and have evolved to meet the needs of the industry as it has grown and changed. For example, as tourism has become a significant economic driver, regulations have become more comprehensive to address new challenges, such as digital technology and environmental impacts.

Key Concepts and Theories

This area of law is still relatively unknown to the general public, but it's important for the tourism sector. It governs the rights and obligations of tourists and tourism workers, and is linked to constitutional law in many destinations.

Global Code of Ethics for Tourism

As a fundamental frame of reference for responsible and sustainable tourism, the **Global Code of Ethics for Tourism** (GCET) is a comprehensive set of principles designed to guide key-players in tourism development. Addressed to governments, the travel industry, communities and tourists alike, it aims to help maximise the sector's benefits while minimising its potentially negative impact on the environment, cultural heritage and societies across the globe.

Adopted in 1999 by the General Assembly of the World Tourism Organization, its acknowledgement by the United Nations two years later expressly encouraged UN Tourism to promote the effective follow-up of its provisions. Although not legally binding, the Code features a **voluntary implementation mechanism** through its recognition of the role of the **World Committee on Tourism Ethics** (WCTE), to which stakeholders may refer matters concerning the application and interpretation of the document.

Types and Forms:

Types of Regulations: Inbound and Outbound Regulations

- **Passport**

Every international passenger requires a valid passport or other official document of identity issued by a competent authority. These documents establish the identity and nationality of the bearer and authorize travel outside their own country.

Types of Passports:

- Alien passport
- Children's identity cards
- Diplomatic or consular passports
- Official, special or service passports
- International Red Cross passports
- Joint passports (Family Passports)
- Laissez-Passer (United Nations document)
- National Identity book/card
- Seaman's discharge books
- Military identity Documents
- Travel Certificates.

Visa

A Visa is an entry in a passport or other travel document made by a consular official of a government to indicate that the bearer has been granted authority to enter or re-enter the country concerned.

Characteristics of Visas:

- Visas are normally issued by a consulate of such country and will only, in rare cases, be issued on arrival. A visa appears on one page of the passport either as a stamp or as a sticker with stamp and the signature of the issuing consulate.
- Visas could be for single, double or multiple entries and they usually have a period of validity. Some visas could also be valid for a lengthy period of time or for the holder's lifetime or throughout the validity of the passport.
- There are different types of visas: business visa, visitor's visa, immigrant visa and the visa for special purpose (Eg. Pilgrims, students, etc.,). Countries can impose different individual conditions on these visas.
- A visa issued in a family passport is valid only for those family members in the passport who are expressly mentioned in the visa.
- For transit in a country, a transit visa with much shorter validity is issued to those requiring a visa. For some nationals, transit visas are issued on arrival, and some passengers may be allowed to transit without a visa (TWOV).

Health regulations – Vaccinations

Proof of certain vaccinations and /0r health certificates are only required by a few countries, against certain diseases, especially in times of health crises. Generally, a vaccination certificates in an international format as legislated by the World Health Organization (WHO) containing confirmation of these vaccinations is recognized. Different vaccinations have different period of validity.

Check-in and Check-out for Passengers and Baggage

- To provide quick and efficient check-in for passengers and their baggage.
- To guide passengers to their embarkation point.
- To guide passengers upon arrival and during transfer stops.
- To provide appropriate, up-to-date and accurate information concerning flights and services.

Customs regulations

Custom Rules for India. Visitors are usually required to make an oral baggage declaration of the baggage and foreign currency in their possession. They also have to obtain the Currency Declaration Form from the Customs department. You must declare specific items when crossing borders, like food, weapons, or large amounts of money, to comply with customs regulations.

Legal Compliance regulations:

They ensure that travellers adhere to local laws, maintaining order and respecting the rights of citizens in the traveler's destination.

Foreign travel Tax regulations

All passengers who have dutiable goods in their possession or goods in excess of their eligible Duty-Free allowance must fill up the Customs Declaration Card clearly mentioning the quantity and value of goods that he has brought. On his/her arrival the passenger is first cleared by Immigration Officer.

Accommodations and catering regulations

Many countries have legislation covering the hospitality sector as a sequel to common law, constitutional law or penal codes enacted by Central or State Governments.

Legislation for Hospitality Sector Legaf duties and responsibilities covered by legislation can be as listed here:

a) Right to accept or refuse lodging to a person or a group
b) Duty to protect person and property of a guest or patron.
c) Entry of police is to be purely investigatory.
d) Locking out of a guest is permissible
e) Acceptance of valuables for safe-keeping is permissible
f) Hotel Manager's lien to demand proper charges for accommodation and meals and any other extras.
g) Guest's right of privacy cannot be violated
h) The management is responsible for: guests, invitees of guests, employees and any other persons lawfully on the premises or property.

Environmental protection and conservation

Cultural resources, both natural and man-made, have great value for tourism. They should be properly listed and documented with the help of available technology and the concerned organizations. There is a lot of pressure on these resources and pollution emanating from different human activities, like settlements, industries, mining etc., requires special study and attention if the ancient cultural heritage of the destination is not to be damaged.

Conservation and Pollution Control Measures Suggested By WTO

i) Providing for pedestrian zones at holiday resorts (shopping malls, public parks, playgrounds etc.)
ii) Encouraging the resident population, through contests and other activities, to decorate their houses and balconies.
iii) Co-ordinating tourist recreation with the social and cultural activities of the local population, through information and publicity campaigns.
iv) Applying multiple-use concepts of facilities wherever possible.

v) Awarding National Quality seals of approval for tourist recreation facilities to operators of accommodation units and other travel services.

vi) Many countries have also initiated the formation of Heritage Bodies and Art and Cultural funds, which then serve to identify conservation heritage zones, and co-ordinate funding, for which tax reliefs to contributors are given by the concerned governments.

Impacts of International tourism regulations:

- Economic impacts- The importance of the economics of this sector could be judged by the number of people involved in it as well the income generated. Directly or indirectly, large number of people is involved in the tourism sector. It includes areas like transportation, accommodation, food, ticketing, guiding, boating, rafting, trekking, maintenance of the tourist sites etc.

- Socio-cultural impacts - Society is a community or broad grouping of people living in a certain area that has common traditions, institutions, activities and interests. In fact, society is a system of relationship of people who share some sense of common identity. When more and more people come from far flung places and interact with local residents of any area, the social and cultural impacts are bound to take place.

- Political impacts- are he a set of rules, regulations, guidelines, and directives for development and promotion of tourism by the government. It provides a framework with which the collective and individual decisions affect the tourism development. Government can create a code of conduct for a tourist. There are some outlooks which encourage tourism and some create obstacles.

- Environmental impacts-Environment is the total surroundings or conditions in which a person, animal or plant lives or interacts More and more infrastructures are created to accommodate them due to which great changes in the landscape of the area are made. Some of the environmental improvements are also observed to attract more and more tourists. Therefore, tourism helps in preserving the environment.

Challenges and Constraints:

International tourism regulations face many challenges, including:

- Security and cross-border regulations: Security concerns can disrupt travel plans and impact the tourism industry.
- Climate change: Climate change and its environmental impacts are a major challenge for the tourism sector.
- Overcrowding: Overcrowding in popular destinations can strain local infrastructure.
- Geopolitical uncertainties: Geopolitical uncertainties can impact the tourism industry.
- Economic fluctuations: Economic fluctuations can impact the tourism industry.
- Inflation: Inflation can impact the tourism industry.
- Extreme weather: Extreme weather can impact the tourism industry.
- Balancing growth with sustainability: Balancing growth with sustainability is a major problem.
- Equity and inclusion: Equity and inclusion are persistent concerns.
- Gender parity: Gender parity remains a major issue for regions such as MENA and South Asia.

Case Studies

International Code for the Protection of Tourists

The COVID-19 crisis has revealed the absence of an international legal framework to assist international tourists in emergency situations and a lack of uniformity at the international level regarding tourism consumer protection rights. During the crisis, the closure of borders with little or no notice left hundreds of thousands of tourists stranded abroad, with millions of flights being cancelled and the situation soon deteriorating. Many of these travellers were left in a foreign environment without assistance, including safety and security, health services and consular assistance, and sometimes without sufficient resources to meet their basic needs, such as food and shelter.

The lack of clarity regarding one another's obligations, duties, and responsibilities to provide care and assistance in emergency situations created great uncertainty around tourists' rights, impacting negatively on the confidence of tourists in international travel. This experience has highlighted significant failings in the current legal and regulatory frameworks, and the existing disparities regarding the consumer rights of tourists from country to country. Moreover, the introduction of measures such as vouchers and the boom of new digital tourism services without a clear, transparent, and harmonized framework, along with the sharp increase of litigation in travel and tourism disputes, present additional challenges for restoring consumers' confidence. In order to support the recovery of the tourism sector, the ICPT was created with a view to restoring tourist confidence by developing and harmonizing minimum international standards, and providing sufficient guarantees for the protection of international tourists in the post COVID-19 world.

Digitalization in Tourism regulations

Digitalization has had a significant impact on tourism regulations, including:

- **Smart travel:** Digitalization has made travel more convenient and secure through smart visas, automated security, and digital boarding passes.
- **Smart destinations:** Digitalization can help destinations become more sustainable, accessible, and inclusive by using data.

- **New job roles:** Digitalization has created new technology-based jobs and expertise.
- **Startups and small businesses**: Digitalization has helped startups and small businesses foster innovation and job creation.
- **Digital governance:** Digital governance can help the economy by allowing online information sharing and controlling network security risks. However, too much digital control can limit freedom of speech and economic development.
- **Data privacy:** Digitalization has raised concerns about data privacy.
- **Overreliance on technology:** Excessive use of technology can make tourism services less personalized.

Other impacts of digitalization on tourism include: improved customer experiences, increased efficiency, new business models, job displacement, and the digital divide.

Policy and Regulatory Framework

- **Article 1 - Tourism's contribution to mutual understanding and respect between peoples and societies ;** The understanding and promotion of the ethical values common to humanity, with an attitude of tolerance and respect for the diversity of religious, philosophical and moral beliefs, are both the foundation and the consequence of responsible tourism; stakeholders in tourism development and tourists themselves should observe the social and cultural traditions and practices of all peoples, including those of minorities and indigenous peoples and to recognize their worth.

- **Article 2- Tourism as a vehicle for individual and collective fulfillment;** Tourism, the activity most frequently associated with rest and relaxation, sport and access to culture and nature, should be planned and practised as a privileged means of individual and collective fulfilment; when practised with a sufficiently open mind, it is an irreplaceable factor of self-education, mutual tolerance and for learning about the legitimate differences between peoples and cultures and their diversity.

- **Article 3- Tourism, a factor of sustainable development;** All the stakeholders in tourism development should safeguard the natural environment with a view to achieving sound, continuous and sustainable economic growth geared to satisfying equitably the needs and aspirations of present and future generations.

- **Article 4-Tourism, a user of the cultural heritage of mankind and contributor to its enhancement;** Tourism resources belong to the common heritage of mankind; the communities in whose territories they are situated have particular rights and obligations to them. Tourism policies and activities should be conducted with respect for the artistic, archaeological and cultural heritage, which they should protect and pass on to future generations; particular care should be devoted to preserving and upgrading monuments, shrines and museums as well as archaeological and historic sites which must be widely open to tourist visits.

- **Article 5- Tourism, a beneficial activity for host countries and communities;** Local populations should be associated with tourism activities and share equitably in the economic, social and cultural benefits they generate, and particularly in the creation of direct and indirect jobs resulting from them.

- **Article 6- Obligations of stakeholders in tourism development;** Tourism professionals have an obligation to provide tourists with objective and honest information on their places of destination and on the conditions of travel, hospitality and stays; they should ensure that the contractual clauses proposed to their customers are readily understandable as to the nature, price and quality of the services they commit themselves to providing and the financial compensation payable by them.

- **Article 7- Right to tourism;** The prospect of direct and personal access to the discovery and enjoyment of the planet's resources constitutes a right equally open to all the world's inhabitants; the increasingly extensive participation in national and international tourism should be regarded as one of the best possible expressions of the sustained growth of free time, and obstacles should not be placed in its way.

- **Article 8-Liberty of tourist movements;** Tourists and visitors should benefit, in compliance with international law and national legislation, from the liberty to move within their countries and from one State to another.

- **Article 9- Rights of the workers and entrepreneurs in the tourism industry;** The fundamental rights of salaried and self-employed workers in the tourism industry and related activities, should be guaranteed under the supervision of the national and local administrations.

- **Article 10- Implementation of the principles of the Global Code of Ethics for Tourism;** The public and private stakeholders in tourism development should cooperate in the implementation of these principles and monitor their effective application;

Conclusion

Tourism and international regulations are inextricably linked, with the latter playing a crucial role in shaping the former. The complex and multifaceted nature of tourism necessitates a comprehensive regulatory framework that balances the interests of tourists, businesses, and local communities. The Global Code of Ethics for Tourism, the International Code for the Protection of Tourists, and other international instruments provide a foundation for responsible and sustainable tourism practices.

As the tourism industry continues to evolve, it is essential that international regulations adapt to emerging challenges, such as digitalization, climate change, and pandemics. By fostering cooperation, collaboration, and a commitment to sustainable tourism practices, we can ensure that tourism contributes to the well-being of local communities, preserves cultural and environmental heritage, and promotes a more peaceful and prosperous world.

TOURISM AND HERITAGE DESTINATIONS

Mr. K. Selvakumar
Assistant Professor
Department of Hotel Management and Catering Technology
Dr. M.G.R. Educational and Research Institute

Introduction

Heritage tourism represents a vital intersection between cultural preservation and economic development, drawing travellers to destinations of historical and cultural significance This chapter examines this multifaceted and multidimensional nature of tourism and heritage destinations, addressing the historical background, theoretical approaches, typologies and their socio-economic implications. Emerging technological innovations and potential policy frameworks are analysed in conjunction with key challenges including over tourism, preservation dilemmas and poor infrastructure. This research bears out these sustainable strategies, for the balancing of tourism growth and heritage conservation, through a review of best practice and case study analysis. These insights are expected to guide stakeholders in the balancing act of adapting modern innovation and policies to ensure heritage sites can sustain an active life. It also maps potential future paths towards using sustainable tourism initiatives to promote and enrich cultural heritage locations at a broader level.

Overview and Definition

Tourism and heritage destinations are locations of historical, cultural, or environmental significance that draw travellers from all over the world. Such sites give us physical links to the past, providing understanding of the history, customs and traditions of the peoples who came before us. Museums help retain cultural identity, timelessness, and history by creating an awareness of visitor perception and gratitude for different heritages. Heritage places refer to a broad range of attractions, from ancient ruins to centuries-old cities, from cultural landmarks to national parks and even UNESCO World Heritage Sites.

In addition to contributing towards cultural diversification, these destinations also benefit local economies by providing tourism capital, labour and regional development. Embracing both tangible heritage (monuments and artefacts) and intangible heritage (festivals, rituals, traditional crafts), they offer an all-round experience for the traveller.

Tourism and heritage destinations serve as mechanisms for cross-cultural exchange, facilitating a deeper global understanding, and appreciation for common histories and cultural diversity through the integration of education, recreation, and conservation. The importance of such sites are amplified and their preservation continues to be a pressing priority as sustainable tourism practices become central to ensuring that these treasures are accessible to future generations but also continue to benefit local communities and the global tourism market.

Historical Context and Development

The concept of heritage tourism has undergone significant evolution, transforming from an activity reserved for elite travellers into a global phenomenon embraced by diverse audiences. In its earliest form, heritage tourism was associated with the Grand Tour, a cultural journey undertaken by wealthy European elites in the 17th and 18th centuries to visit classical sites in Italy, Greece, and other cultural hubs. These journeys were motivated by education, leisure, and the acquisition of cultural knowledge, focusing predominantly on art, architecture, and antiquities.

Nineteenth-Century Industrial Revolution: The beginning of the Industrial Revolution heralded a new era in the history of tourism —inheritance tourism. With the new railways and steamships, the middle class could now travel. Organized tours became popular during this period, and many famous heritage sites were established as sites with great popularity such as ancient ruins, castles, and medieval towns. As a result, heritage tourism grew from broader social and economic groups seeking to experience cultural history and national identities.

By the late 20th century, increasing global reflection had led to more widespread understanding of the need to preserve cultural and natural heritage. This was recognized by the establishment of UNESCO's World Heritage Convention in 1972, highlighting the need to protect sites of "outstanding universal value." The era saw the emergence of sustainable tourism principles, combining and including cultural preservation with economic development.

Today, it continues to evolve with the times, utilising technological progressions and grappling with issues like tourism and climate change. This crucial activity enhances cultural exchange, conserves heritage sites, and fosters sustainable global development in community settings, which underscores the fluid interaction of cultural patrimony, global travel, and the capacity and evolution of nations' societal feelings.

Key Concepts and Theories

Theoretical Foundations of Tourism and Heritage Destinations The study of tourism and heritage destinations is grounded in several key theoretical frameworks that help to illuminate their cultural, economic, and environmental dimensions. These frameworks are used to comprehend the characteristics of heritage tourism, implications, and approaches towards sustainable management.

1. Cultural Capital Theory

According to this theory, heritage destinations serve as banks of cultural value, embodying the traditions, knowledge and artistic achievements of a society. Heritage sites are seen as valuable contributors to cultural identity and collective memory. Cultural capital can be material—monuments, artifacts—or immaterial—folklore, rituals. The theory further comments on how visitors consume and appreciate these assets, affecting their educational and aesthetic experience. It underscores the importance of heritage tourism in preserving cultural heritage and providing economic benefits to local communities.

2. Authenticity

The 'authenticity' phenomenon in heritage is also very much relevant because this gives tourists an ideal to seek after, the original and the unspoiled. This framework allows us to highlight the perspectives of authenticity and its impact on the representation of heritage sites." While some tourists are looking for bare-bones cultural experiences, other tourists could gravitate toward curated or reconstructed environments. The concept also explores "staged authenticity," in which cultural elements are selectively showcased to meet the expectations of tourists. Ensuring an authentic experience while maintaining the integrity of places that add cultural value and meaning to our lives is the challenge presented to all of us by the new forms of tourism.

3. Carrying Capacity

This theory determines the limited capacity of tourists a heritage site can receive without resulting in physical damage to the site, environmental impacts, and deterioration of the quality of experience of those who visit. There are multiple aspects of carrying capacity that include physical, social, and ecological limits. Overcrowding at heritage sites, for example, may result in wear and tear, hinder the local ecosystems, and reduce the quality of the experience for visitors. These three principles are fundamental to the design of a sustainable tourism policy, including visitor quotas, timed entry systems, and updating infrastructure to manage tourist flows.

4. Sense of Place

This article uses the concept of heritage by exploring the emotional and symbolic relationships people have with heritage sites. It shows how these destinations inspire a sense of identity, belonging, and pride in both locals and visitors. Sense of place is a concept that emphasizes the importance of maintaining the unique characteristics of a site as part of its culture and history.

5. Stakeholder Theory

Stakeholder theory recognizes the need for collaboration between different groups, including local communities, government, tourists, and private sectors, in managing and developing heritage tourism. Making decisions only for the minority may seem to be more efficient, a thought that gets lost in the global economy.

6. Sustainable frameworks

They incorporate environmental, social, and economic aspects into the planning and management of heritage tourism. They prioritize minimizing harm and maximizing benefits over the long term; which includes conservation, community well-being, and cultural continuity.

7. Postmodernism in Tourism

This theory examines how heritage tourism reflects changing societal values and consumption patterns in the postmodern era. It addresses the blending of high culture and popular culture in heritage representation. Together, these key concepts and theories provide a comprehensive understanding of the complexities of heritage tourism. They serve as essential tools for researchers, practitioners, and policymakers aiming to create meaningful, sustainable, and impactful heritage tourism experiences.

Heritage Tourism: Types and Forms

Heritage tourism can take on many forms and covers a variety of destinations and experiences, as people connect in different ways with history, culture, and nature. They help make sense of the multiple dimensions of heritage tourism also and therefore the different types of visitors and motivations behind their journeys.

4.1 Cultural Heritage Tourism

Cultural heritage tourism emphasizes the tangible manifestations of human imagination and history, such as museums, art galleries, cultural repositories, historical monuments, and architectural attractions. They include such famous buildings as the Taj Mahal, the Colosseum, and the Pyramids of Giza. Typically focusing on ancient civilizations and art, as well as architectural wonders; providing visitors with educational and aesthetic experiences. Cultural tourism helps in the conservation of historical artifacts as well as the fostering of cultural pride within local communities.

Fig:1 ---- Taj Mahal

Fig:2 ---- Colosseum

4.2 Natural Heritage Tourism

Natural heritage tourism focuses on the use of natural wonders, based on national parks, places with biological diversity and geological spots. Places like Yellowstone National Park, the Great Barrier Reef and the Amazon Rainforest embody the beauty and the diversity of nature on Earth. This tourism model is centred upon conservation, and both environmental awareness and protection. Seeking these new experiences, visitors also tend to engage in the activities of wildlife observation, hiking and ecosystems, which encourage connection to nature and its protection.

Fig:3 ---- Great Barrier Reef in Australia

4.3 Industrial Heritage Tourism

Industrial heritage tourism highlights sites reflecting the history of industry and labour, including old factories, mills, mines, and railways. Often these places offer a window into the technological progress and economic change of days gone by. Other industrial heritage sites include Ironbridge Gorge in England, a UNESCO World Heritage Site, and the Ruhr Valley industrial heritage trail in Germany. Such tours help to keep the legacy of industrial prosperity alive and, by doing so, they can also play a part in the regeneration of areas left behind by economic changes.

Fig:4 ---- Iron bridge Gorge in England

4.4 Intangible Heritage Tourism

Intangible heritage tourism focuses more on practices, representations, expressions, knowledge, and skills that communities recognize as part of their cultural heritage, e.g. festivals, rituals, music, dance, food, and crafts. That can include Japan's tea ceremony, India's Pushkar Camel Fair, or flamenco in

Spain. Intangible heritage tourism encourages cultural exchange and also supports the preservation of traditions that would otherwise be threatened by modernising forces.

Fig:5 ---- Pushkar Camel Fair **Fig:6 ---- Japan's tea ceremony**

4.5 Archaeological Heritage Tourism

Archaeological tourism can be defined as visiting archaeological emblem and remain of ancient civilization. Places like Machu Picchu in Peru, Angkor Wat in Cambodia and the 2,000-year-old city of Pompeii in Italy draw visitors who want to explore history. Archaeological tourism blends education and discovery, offering great insight into past civilizations.

4.6 Religious or Spiritual Heritage Tourism

Religious Heritage Tourism is basically for Pilgrimages visited to various sacred sites including temples, churches, mosques, and monasteries. Places like Mecca, the Vatican City, and Varanasi are of great spiritual and cultural importance. It is a type of tourism that both engages individuals in their own faith and educates them about global religious traditions.

Fig:7 ---- Vatican City

Fig:8 ---- Mecca

4.7 Maritime Heritage Tourism

Maritime heritage tourism focuses on sites and activities associated with maritime history including historic ports, shipwrecks, lighthouses, and naval museums. Examples include the Titanic.\

Fig:8. Titanic Belfast Museum **Fig:9National Maritime Museum**

4.8 Urban Heritage Tourism

Heritage — Exploring together with other interest communities' Urban heritage tourism tourists (Mason, & Avrami, 2007) Cities such as Prague, Kyoto and Istanbul demonstrate how urban landscapes merge history, art and modernity. This type of tourism will showcase a city's character, preserving sustainable urban development.

Fig:10 ---- Kyoto Japan

4.9 Culinary Heritage Tourism

Culinary heritage tourism focuses on historical foods and food experiences, frequently rooted in cultural heritage. Some examples are wine tourism in France's Bordeaux region, spice tours in Zanzibar or street food experiences in Bangkok. These forms of tourism promote preservation of traditional food practices and sensory exploration.

Fig:11 ---- Wine tourism in France

4.10 Rural and Indigenous Heritage Tourism

Rural and indigenous heritage tourism explores the traditions, lifestyles, and natural surroundings of rural and indigenous communities. Examples include visiting Maasai villages in Kenya or exploring the Amish culture in the United States. This form of tourism promotes cultural preservation and supports community-based tourism initiatives.

Fig:12 Maasai villages in Kenya

By engaging with different types and forms of heritage tourism, individuals have the opportunity to experience cultural diversity, learn from history, and contribute to sustainable tourism practices that preserve cultural heritage for future generations.

Benefits And Impacts of Tourism and Heritage Destinations

This includes the role of heritage tourism in economic development, cultural preservation, and environmental conservation. On the other hand, it brings along hurdles that demand prudent handling to ensure benefits outweigh the disadvantages.

Benefits

Economic Benefits

- Revenue generation: A vast majority of revenue is generated through heritage tourism, significantly contributing to local and national economies. From the tourist's point of view, spending money on accommodation, food, transport and souvenirs directly benefits the economic well-being of their local communities.
- Job Creation: Generates employment for many, like hotel, transportation, tour and heritage site operation. Traditional crafts gain, as demand for traditional products rises and local artisans and craftsmen benefit.
- Infrastructure Development: As the heavy flow of tourists demands better basic amenities, infrastructure development focuses on improvements in roads, public transport including buses and taxis, utilities, etc that benefit tourists as well as local residents.

Cultural Benefits

- Cultural Preservation: The funds generated from tourism go toward the conservation and restoration of valuable heritage sites, allowing them to remain for future generations.

- Cultural Appreciation: By visiting heritage sites, visitors learn to appreciate diversity, understand and respect each other through mutual admiration.
- Cultural Rejuvenation: Communities often feel an empowered sense of pride in their unique heritage, upholding cultural identity and solidarity.

Environmental Benefits

- **Conservation Efforts**; Heritage tourism creates incentives to conserve important natural and cultural sites, as the value of those sites to the tourism industry encourages protection and restoration efforts.
- Sustainable Practices: With a greater understanding of the impact of tourism on the environment, this also leads to eco-friendly practices and responsible travel behavior.

Impacts

Positive Impacts

- **Community Development**: Tourism has the ability to promote better-quality lives in a community through economic opportunities and community initiatives.
- **Global Recognition**; Heritage destinations become internationally recognized which improves their cultural and historical significance on a wider scale. Often this draws international funding for preservation and development.
- Cross-Cultural Exchange: Tourism has provided people from different cultures the opportunity to interact as visitors and locals.

Negative Impacts

- **Over tourism**: High numbers of visitors can result in overcrowding, which in turn can strain local infrastructure and diminish the quality of experiences for visitors.

- **Commercialism**: Efforts to meet tourist demands can also lead to the commercialization of culture, where practices are modified or performed, eliminating their traditional meaning.
- **Cultural Dilution**: Exposure to external cultures can also dilute the traditional value or the practice leading to homogenization of culture.
- **Environmental Degradation**: High tourist traffic can contribute to pollution, habitat destruction, and resource depletion at heritage sites. Foot traffic, for example, can physically wear down historic monuments.

Challenges and Constraints

This management must consider multiple, complex challenges to ensure long-term sustainability over time. The many constraints on tourism development come from the need to preserve cultural and natural assets. Environmental and social aspects, as well as economic drivers add to these challenges and require an integrated approach.

Preservation vs. Development and Conserving versus Tourism:

The Challenge of Heritage Sites One aspect is the cementing of infrastructure to support tourism that results in physical and aesthetic changes that threaten the integrity of such sites. The reason behind it is Commercial Pressure and it has a high impact on conservation goals as Tourism Revenue becomes more important than over all things there, so tourism gets irreplaceable and its importance gets removed.

Case Studies from India:

Hampi, Karnataka:

Developed a sustainable tourism model to control crowds and protect ancient ruins, allowing visitors to experience the ruins while safeguarding the archaeological site.

Taj Mahal, Uttar Pradesh:

Designed green initiatives such as waste management and water conservation and visitor education programs to preserve the integrity of the site.

Khajuraho Temples, located in Madhya Pradesh:

Visitor limits and educational programs were implemented to minimize the effect on the temple's historic architecture and to increase awareness of the sculptures' importance.

Fatehpur Sikri, Uttar Pradesh:

Implemented a sustainable tourism management strategy with a strong local involvement in guiding, maintenance and monitoring of a site. These examples highlight India's unique approaches to managing tourism and preservation through community engagement, sustainable management, and educational initiatives. 8. Technology and Innovation

Technology and Innovation

Technological tools (e.g. virtual reality (VR), geographic information systems (GIS) and digital storytelling) enhance visitor engagement and site management. Advanced mobile applications and smart ticketing systems enhance operations and enable immersive experiences.

Policy and Regulatory Framework of protection of heritage sites:

World Heritage Convention (UNESCO):

- Established in 1972, this convention creates a universal framework to protect the cultural and natural heritage of outstanding universal value. It establishes standards and guidelines for conservation, restoration and sustainable tourism at heritage sites.

National Policies:

- In India, the Archaeological Survey of India (ASI) plays a key role in protecting archaeological sites. Policies such as the Ancient Monuments and Archaeological Sites and Remains Act (1958) regulate the protection and maintenance of heritage sites.

State-Specific Legislation:

- For instance, states such as Rajasthan have enacted laws such as the Rajasthan Ancient and Historical Monuments and Archaeological Sites and Remains Act (1961) that protect heritage sites via-site specific regulations and conservation measures.

Leading Local Governance and Sustainable Tourism:

- These guidelines shall encourage sustainable tourism by issuing region specific restrictions, which is done by local authorities like municipal corporations or heritage departments. This includes controlling the number of visitors, the effect of tourism on heritage buildings and sustainable practices.

International Collaboration and Partnerships:

- Some agencies such as UNESCO work along with local and global authorities to develop standards for safeguarding heritage locations. This means putting cultural integrity above tourism, while also encouraging it responsibly.

Research and Innovation:

- Modern technologies such as GIS and digital documentation are encouraged through the frameworks to enable better monitoring and management of heritage sites.

Capacity Building and Community Involvement

- Sustainable practices are often written in these policies as there is a strong focus on training local communities, artisans, and stakeholders in heritage preservation, which costs would over time.

These frameworks strike a balance between preservation and economic development through sustainable tourism and community involvement.

Future Directions and Prospects

- Sustainable Models of Tourism: Focus on Green Practices
- Community Involvement: Guarantees that local people benefit and participate.
- Digital Transformation: Increases access, improves conservation.

Additional Considerations for Heritage Tourism Management:

Integration of Cross-Disciplinary Approaches

A holistic approach to heritage tourism management draws on a number of different areas, including:

- Sociology: To study social structures, meanings, and the influence of tourism on host societies.
- Environmental Science: To evaluate ecological impact, conservation of natural resources, and sustainable practices.
- Economics: To assess the economic benefits of heritage tourism, create balance in the tourism industry and mitigate economic development at the expense of preservation.

Stakeholder Collaboration:

The management of heritage sites is generally undertaken in cooperation with different groups of interest:

- Residents: Involving residents to secure their stake in decisions and preservation.
- Governments: Enabling sustainable site management at a policy level and through funding
- NGOs: They support conservation, education, and advocacy for heritage protection.
- Private Sector – Facilitating sustainable tourism development by promoting corporate social responsibility and investment in heritage-based businesses.

Public-Private Partnerships (PPP):

Publicly and privately led collaborations can support alternative approaches to managing heritage sites ranging from infrastructure investment to marketing or enhancing the visitor experience.

Community-Based Tourism:

Utilization of community-based tourism models where communities benefit directly through tourism for employment, income generation, and skill building can help integrate sustainable and inclusionary practices into heritage management.

Sustainable Source Management:

Integrating environmental sustainability practices (including waste management, water conservation, and energy-efficient infrastructure) while balancing the needs of tourism against the conservation of heritage sites.

Continuous Feedback:

On-going training and capacity development for local communities, tourism professionals, and stakeholders are crucial for the sustained preservation of cultural and ecological integrity at heritage sites.

Monitoring and Evaluation:

Establishing frameworks for continual monitoring and adaptive management, using visitor impact assessments, cultural mapping, and sustainability indicators to protect heritage sites for future generations.

Engaging multiple stakeholders and encouraging cross-disciplinary cooperation can lead to sustainable and responsible heritage tourism development that benefits the authentic fabric of the history and environment.

Conclusion

The intricate relationship between tourism and heritage destinations is multifaceted and far-reaching, encompassing cultural, economic, and environmental dimensions. Through the lens of various theoretical frameworks, this chapter has explored the complexities of heritage tourism, highlighting its significance in preserving cultural heritage, promoting cross-cultural exchange, and fostering sustainable development. As the tourism industry continues to evolve, it is imperative that stakeholders adopt a nuanced approach, balancing the needs of conservation, community engagement, and economic growth. By embracing sustainable tourism practices and prioritizing the preservation of cultural and natural heritage, we can ensure that these precious resources remain vibrant and accessible for future generations, while promoting a deeper understanding and appreciation of our shared cultural heritage.

TOURISM AND MUSEOLOGY

Author
Ms. Sharon. K
PhD Research Scholar,
Department of History,
PSGR Krishnammal College,
Coimbatore

Co-Author
Dr. Hemalatha
Assistant Professor
Department of History
PSGR Krishnammal
College, Coimbatore

Introduction

Tourism is the activity of spending time away from the usual space for relaxation by utilizing the commercial supply of services. Everyone travels; it is no longer a specialized and occasional experience but a normal part of life. In terms of relative sophistication, tourism is a larger factor that encompasses a wide range of academic streams, including history, archaeology, museology, etc. The performance of each of its components is ultimately what determines how successful tourism is. Additionally, tourists' expectations for the excursion have also increased.

All places can never be considered as a tourist attraction. Only locations with certain qualities that magnetize potential tourists can be called tourist destinations. The most sought-after man-made tourist attraction is a museum. According to a survey, one of the top five reasons people travel is, to engage in art and cultural pursuits. There is no question that the tourism industry and museums directly contribute to each other's advantageous economic effects. The objectives and disciplinary requirements of these two sectors are similar in some ways as seen by their overlap and shared basic interests. The disciplinary link between tourism and museums exists in a parallel way. The idea of 'sustainable development' might be viewed as the tangent where the fundamental ideology of both domains converges.

Tourism and Museum - A Cultural Entity

According to UNWTO, "Tourism is a social, cultural and economic phenomenon which entails the movement of people to countries or places outside their usual environment for personal or business/professional purposes". The International Council of Museums (ICOM) gives the definition of 'Museum' as "a non-profit making, permanent institution in the service of society and of its development, and open to the public, which acquires, conserves, researches, communicates and exhibits for the purposes of study, education, and employment, material evidence of man and his environment".

A museum is a building that preserves an assemblage of artefacts and items of historical, artistic, or numerous specific significances and creates them accessible to the general public through either temporary or permanent exhibits. Museums serve a variety of purposes, from the general public to scholars and experts. Museum is a form of culture and tourism is the process of experiencing the culture. A broad audience with specific cultural and educational norms emerged as a result of this fact. Cultural tourism offers a wide range of perks for places of interest and culture itself. A Museum plays an indispensable role in society and is connected to the people in social, economic, traditional, and ethnic aspects. Museums of India, which are naturally bound to heritage, keep their framework and elements in a secure manner.

Evolution of Tourism and Museum

The Latin term "*tourmus*," which implies circular movement, is where the word "tourism" originates. The French word "*tour*" can occasionally be interpreted as a journey that ends with a return trip to the starting point. Beginning in the early 1800s, tourism has a long history. The first establishment of systematic tourism from England to France was in 1815. The first railway excursion was planned in 1843 by Thomas Cook, an English missionary who is credited with founding tourism. Ibn Battuta, an Arab traveller, began his voyage in the East and made his way on foot through nearly every country in East and North Africa.

The word 'museum' is inferred from the Greek word "*Mousein*" with the synonym as the abode of the angel of knowledge. The Renaissance saw the emergence of museums as we know them today, and the European Age of Enlightenment saw their expansion. There have been four stages of museum growth thus far:

i) It began to store items of artistic and scientific value in the 14th century and continued to do so until the 17th century.

ii) The next stage occurred in the 18th and 19th centuries when the state took control of numerous museums and transformed them into public establishments. Projecting the prestige of rapidly industrializing regions and growing imperial powers was the goal.

iii) The Museum took on an instructional role in the 20th century through the exhibitions.

iv) The orientation of museums has changed once again since the 1970s, when mass tourism first emerged. Its instructional function has diminished in favour of making more money from tourism and entertainment. The trend has shifted more and more in favour of equality. The public now has a significant effect, and museums work hard to serve the interests of the general public.

Since the beginning of time, museums and similar establishments have been a component of human society. The museum's concept, which originated in European countries and has some similarities to India as well, is essentially a collecting and exhibition site for antiquities. The analysis of the museums' evolution is divided into two sections, with a focus on Europe and India for the Western world.

In the 3rd century B.C., the first museum was founded in Alexandria. Before being demolished during the civil unrest, it operated for around six centuries. There was no museum development for many years after this. There was a resurgence of interest in museums throughout the 14th century. Early museums were private collections of uncommon natural artefacts owned by rich households. These were frequently on exhibit in so-called "wonder rooms". Leonard Wooley, an archaeologist, uncovered the first museum. In 1683, the first public museum was established.

There were art galleries (chitravithis) and painting galleries (chitrashalas) in ancient India. The royal class and nobles had their own lavish private collections during the Middle Ages. The first modern museum in India dates back to 1796. The Asiatic Society of Bengal made the decision in 1784 to properly house a number of antiques that it had accumulated over the years in Calcutta. The proposal, however, failed, and the group went on to create a legitimate museum in 1814. India had twelve different kinds of museums by 1857. Established in 1875, the Indian Museum in Calcutta was the first significant museum.

Discovering The Roots - Heritage Tourism in Museum

A significant part of cultural tourism that depends on the integrity and legacy of the past is heritage tourism. The aspects of our inherited past that we adore are referred to as heritage. A form of tourism that has flourished around heritage is referred to as heritage tourism. The United Nations Conference on Trade and Development (UNCTAD) generally grouped the creative industries into four categories,

1) Heritage
2) Arts
3) Media
4) Functional Creations

It is divided into three distinct groups,

1)Natural group
2)Cultural group
3)Built group

From the above classification, Museums come under the category of 'Heritage' and the group of 'Built' which resembles a cultural expression and man-made site. Museums are classified in various ways based on numerous bases notably

- Art Museum
- Architectural Museum
- Archaeological Museum
- Anthropology Museum
- Automobile Museum
- Aerospace Museum
- Biography Museum
- Ethnology Museum
- Design Museum
- Fine Arts Museum
- History Museum
- Maritime Museum
- Medical Museum
- Memorial Museum
- Military Museum
- Mobile Museum
- Natural History Museum
- Science Museum
- Specialized Museum
- Virtual Museum

Expanding Horizons - Intellectual Tourism in Museum

The primary findings for diverse themes pertaining to an understanding of hominids and the environment can be found in museums. 'Edutainment' refers to the combination of educational and entertaining experiences that a visit to a museum can provide.

In addition to satisfying educational goals, this gives the museum some competitiveness in the leisure sector. A museum serves as a community information hub and a great proponent of "Intellectual Tourism". Some activities for the tourists in the museums are:

Exhibitions

Aside from collection and preservation, museums are also set up to display artefacts. Museums display artefacts by setting up exhibitions periodically or permanent showcases. It sends artefacts for display at a museum located in another city or nation as travelling exhibitions. Museums occasionally send their artefacts on a mobile exhibition via their Museo-vehicles to unreached places.

Theatrical Screenings

In addition to its static exhibits, museums host daily shows on pertinent topics that educate tourists about the various fields of subjects. It also hosts film screenings, creatives, and theatrical performances that complement its collection which throws out so much scope into the tourism needs.

Research and Education

Edu-tourism is developing mainly with museums. Museums host lectures, seminars, and workshops where they invite distinguished professionals to give their perspectives on heritage and culture or a particular topic. Museums open out for researchers both abroad and locally, which attracts foreign tourists and students.

Publications

The tourism department and museum department publish a variety of popular materials, such as tourism statistics, magazines, guidebooks, posters, pamphlets, and collaterals. Students can benefit from the catalogues that museums publish on particular collections and monographs, etc. Additionally, the museum publishes annual reports, policy notes, newsletters, journals, and bulletins.

Awareness Campaigns and Community Development

Museums with tourism lines prioritize community development by serving many awareness campaigns, stakeholders awareness workshops, etc., for the tourists through their outreach programs in a variety of creative ways.

Progression Of Museo-Tourism Paradigm

Museum practices altered after World War II, even though up to the 20th century the museum catered to the public with specialized knowledge about the items on display. Later it shifted to a larger society. This shift was brought about by the 'globalization' of educational access, and museums made an effort to adapt to the difficulties these social changes imposed. The late 20th century saw the emergence of new museological practices, which highlighted the importance of museums to the tourism industry. A multidisciplinary understanding of museology that fostered the development of technical museums, eco-museums, and other museological phenomena unacknowledged before emerged.

As a result, a new paradigm for museums emerges that differs from the conventional museum. The new paradigm has a 'de-centralized' organization that understands a community-owned domain. These museological practices which "broke with the conventional museological routine," presented museums with fresh scope and attracted tourists. Nonetheless, the relationship between museums and tourism is not always in tune; in fact, it may even be enticing. Museums and tourism have distinct perspectives regarding cultural heritage. On a deeper level, however, museums and tourism share a common basis: travel. This is because both the tourists and artefacts travel from and location to another. It is clear that museums and tourism are typically regarded as two distinct and functionally distinct domains. Tourism is linked to the leisure and holiday industries, while museums are motivated by the preservation and display of art for educational purposes. One calls for commitment, while the other calls for relaxation. The asset is valued for its innate appeal to business when viewed through the lens of tourism. While museums are concerned about the asset's well-being and conservation. Both create an intriguing opportunity at different ends of the spectrum.

Government Initiatives from Time to Time

There are several key worldwide tourism bodies that play significant roles in steering global tourism such as the United Nations World Tourism Organization (UNWTO) which encourages the execution of 'Global Code of Ethics for Tourism' and the World Travel and Tourism Council (WTTC), a private sector organization focuses on business aspects of tourism. Focusing on India, the Government has taken many initiatives with respect to tourism and museums.

The Ministry of Tourism and the Ministry of Culture as a united domain regulate the actions together. Some initiatives holding significance strongly are individuated below. Both ministries handle all policy matters including growth strategies, promotion, investment, marketing, and manpower development. It coordinates regular interaction between various departments and stakeholders. It scrutinizes and recognizes diverse service providers. It provides proper financial assistance and regulates infrastructure enhancement. Following all the implementation measures, proper monitoring and evaluation have been done by the Government. A Think Tank "National Tourism Advisory Council" was also constituted.

A special tourism task force on Tourism Sectoral Plan is constituted by merging tourism ministries with various ministries. In all the recent initiatives or innovations of tourism, museums hold an indispensable presence. Some initiatives for the upgradation of Museo-Tourism by the Government such as Museum Grants Scheme, 'Incredible India' Programme, 'Swadesh Darshan' Scheme, '*Dekhoapnadesh*' programme, Adopt a Heritage '*Apni Dharohar, Apni Pehchaan*' programme, 'PRASHAD ('Pilgrimage Rejuvenation, Spiritual, Heritage Augmentation Drive)' Scheme. Few significant legislations dealing with Museo-Tourism such as

- The Treasure Trove Act, 1878
- The Ancient Monument Preservation Act, 1904

- The Antiquities and Art Treasures Act, 1972 with its subordinate legislation-
- The Antiquities and Art Treasures Rules, 1973
- The Ancient Monuments and Archaeological Sites and Remains Act, 1958 with its amendment-
- The Ancient Monuments and Archaeological Sites and Remains [Amendment and Validation] Act, 2010 along with sub-ordinate legislations:
- The Ancient Monuments and Archaeological Sites and Remains Act, 1959
- The Ancient Monuments and Archaeological Sites and Remains [Framing of Heritage Bye-laws and other functions of the competent authority] rules, 2011
- The National Monument Authority [Condition of Service of Chairman and Members of the Authority and Conduct of Business] Rules, 2011.

According to the Travel and Tourism Development Index (2024) released by the World Economic Forum, India ranks close to the top for cultural, recreational, and natural resources and has one of the biggest tourism economies in the world.

Unveiling The Future Trends

Museums are the cultural watersheds that delineate the prominence of the past. The principal purpose of every institution is to elevate its success margin without squandering resources. So, it streamlines the activities to be performed in an efficient way accordingly. Irrespective of the size of the institutions an organizational order is necessary. In simple words, Organisational structure enforces a systematic approach to the workflow. Analysis of past and current tourist outflow trends is necessary. Following analysis, proper examination of the projected demand for tourist infrastructure. Execution of the recommended interventions after analysis is essential.

The vision developed by the Government should be inclusive of the growth that is balanced with a rise in both foreign and domestic tourist footfall to the monument sites and heritage sites. The project's vision must be precisely stated down to the granular aspect. The objectives to be attained in the near future are: An upsurge in the tourist outfall. Enhancement of the perception of the tourism industry as a whole. Advancement in the generation of employment. Enhancement of developing abilities, and building capacity to deliver value-added services to heritage tourism.

Museums ought to have a significant influence on the tourism industry. Additionally, tourism and museums are directly related, and the development of tourism requires an unquestionable partnership with museums. Through tourism, the Tourism and Museum departments operate with multi-pronged programmes including workshops, seminars, and exhibitions. Heritage Activists observed that improper management can frequently result in the ruin of heritage assets due to over-crowding and ill-suited behaviors of tourists. By implementing a comprehensive management plan, museums can ensure the preservation of their collections and enhance the visitor experience. There is more emphasis on vacations to be time-efficient as well as cost-effective. As tourists are finding it harder to satisfy these demands by themselves, tourism operators also report an increase in preference for indulgence. Governments may offer direct strategic support to tourism operators to improve and enhance service quality. The students can possibly be in the immense clientele bracket as the museums offer entertainment and education. It provides tourists from other countries with comprehensive information on the nation they are visiting. Thus, both are linked along with the administration and management of each other entities.

There are certain mechanisms that support the relationship between museums and tourism, and it is inextricably linked to the evolution of society. Since tourism today has different features than it did in the past, the museum of today distances itself from the museum of the 18th century. As a tourist spot, museums face a number of challenges due to the growing significance of cultural tourism and the growing interest of tourists in museums. The museum must be appealing and offer visitors a distinctive and enriching experience in order to draw tourists. The museum should make investments in heritage interpretation for this reason. The promotion of tourism has been a concreted feat of museums.

Conclusion

The Museums are the standing source of instilling the wisdom of art and literature in the minds of the people. With a view to salvaging the rare and valuable artefacts, the Museums were established. Renowned museums for instance, Louvre Museum, British Museum, Salar Jung Museum, and Calico Museum are now a feast for the eyes and minds of people in many parts of the world.

Museums are the apex of aesthetic progress and of the civilization itself. The current situation of Indian Museums is partially business-focused and it caters to the Tourism department with a good amount of revenue. The goal of the current study is to highlight the fundamental ideas that underpin how heritage is interpreted through tourism and museums and the potential value of this interpretation in attracting tourists, particularly those who visit museums. Tourism and Museums should invest in heritage interpretation because it stimulates the senses and the critical spirit.

TOURISM AND TECHNOLOGY

Dr. S. Meenakshi
Assistant Professor
Department of History (SOHTS)
Tamilnadu Open University

Introduction

Tourism technology is revolutionizing the travel and tourism industry by integrating advanced digital tools to enhance customer experiences, streamline operations, and promote sustainable growth. With the rapid development of technologies such as Artificial Intelligence (AI), Virtual Reality (VR), Augmented Reality (AR), the Internet of Things (IoT), and Big Data Analytics, the tourism sector has transformed into a more efficient, accessible, and personalized service-driven industry. Online booking systems, AI-powered chatbots, virtual tours, and smart tourism infrastructure have simplified travel planning and improved visitor satisfaction. Additionally, data analytics provides valuable insights into consumer behavior and market trends, enabling businesses to offer tailored experiences and optimize resources.

As tourism technology continues to evolve, it fosters innovation, supports eco-friendly initiatives, and addresses the challenges of modern tourism. This paper explores the role, applications, and impact of technology in tourism, highlighting its potential to reshape the future of travel and hospitality.

In today's digital era, tourism technology has become a cornerstone for the growth and transformation of the travel and hospitality industry. The rapid advancement of technologies such as **Artificial Intelligence (AI)**, **Virtual Reality (VR)**, **Augmented Reality (AR)**, **Big Data Analytics**, **Internet of Things (IoT)**, and **Cloud Computing** has redefined how people plan, experience, and share their travel journeys. These innovations have enabled a seamless and more personalized travel experience, addressing the needs of modern-day tourists who seek convenience, efficiency, and unique experiences.

Online platforms for booking flights, accommodations, and activities have replaced traditional travel agencies, offering real-time information and user-friendly interfaces. AI-driven tools such as chatbots and virtual assistants provide instant support, while VR and AR allow travellers to explore destinations virtually before making decisions. Smart tourism, powered by IoT, enhances visitor experiences through connected devices, digital kiosks, and mobile applications. Additionally, Big Data Analytics helps businesses understand traveler preferences, optimize services, and forecast trends.

Tourism technology not only enhances user satisfaction but also drives sustainability by promoting digital solutions that reduce operational costs and environmental impacts. In a post-pandemic world, contactless services, digital payments, and virtual experiences have become integral, ensuring safety, convenience, and accessibility. Today's tourism technology reflects a future-driven approach, fostering innovation to meet the dynamic demands of travellers and reshape the global tourism landscape.

Need of Information Technology in E-Tourism Development

The integration of information technology in e-tourism development is essential in today's digital era, transforming how travel services are planned, delivered, and experienced. IT enhances accessibility by enabling real-time booking systems, mobile applications, and global connectivity, making it easier for travellers to plan and manage their trips. It supports the personalization of services by analyzing customer data and preferences to offer tailored recommendations and AI-driven experiences. IT optimizes resource management through tools that manage inventory, implement dynamic pricing models, and reduce operational inefficiencies.

Additionally, it plays a vital role in marketing and promotion, enabling businesses to reach targeted audiences through digital campaigns and social media platforms. With real-time information sharing, travellers receive instant updates on travel conditions, while navigation tools and interactive maps enhance their experiences. IT also fosters innovation in virtual and augmented reality, allowing users to explore destinations virtually or gain enriched on-site experiences. By leveraging big data analytics, businesses gain valuable insights for decision-making and predictive planning.

Furthermore, IT ensures secure online transactions, integrating advanced technologies like blockchain for transparency and trust. It promotes sustainable tourism development by facilitating eco-friendly practices and resource efficiency. Overall, IT is indispensable for expanding the reach, efficiency, and customer satisfaction in e-tourism, empowering the industry to thrive in a competitive global market.

Role of Technology in Tourism

Technology plays a transformative role in the tourism industry, revolutionizing how businesses operate and travellers experience their journeys. The integration of advanced tools and platforms has made travel planning more accessible and convenient. Online booking systems, mobile applications, and interactive websites enable customers to search, compare, and book flights, accommodations, and tours with ease. Additionally, technology fosters global connectivity, breaking geographical barriers and allowing businesses to reach a broader audience. For travellers, this means instant access to diverse options and the ability to customize their experiences from anywhere in the world.

Another significant impact of technology is the personalization of services. By leveraging big data, artificial intelligence (AI), and machine learning (ML), businesses can analyze customer preferences and behavior to deliver tailored recommendations and offers. AI-powered chatbots provide real-time assistance, while predictive analytics help forecast demand, ensuring businesses stay ahead of market trends. Dynamic pricing models, supported by technology, adjust rates based on demand and availability, maximizing revenue while maintaining customer satisfaction.

Technology also enhances the on-ground travel experience. Augmented reality (AR) and virtual reality (VR) offer immersive ways to explore destinations, from virtual tours before booking to enriched site visits with AR guides. Smart cities and IoT-enabled infrastructure provide seamless navigation, smart transportation options, and automated services such as biometric check-ins. Real-time updates on travel conditions, weather, and itinerary changes further improve the journey, ensuring travellers are well-informed and better prepared.

Finally, technology contributes to sustainability and operational efficiency in tourism. Smart resource management systems optimize energy and water use in accommodations, while digital tools encourage eco-friendly practices like paperless ticketing and carbon footprint monitoring. Additionally, blockchain and secure payment gateways ensure transparency and trust in transactions, reducing fraud and enhancing the overall reliability of the industry. By integrating these technological advancements, tourism businesses not only meet evolving customer expectations but also set the stage for a more sustainable and innovative future.

Evolution of technology in tourism

The evolution of technology in tourism has drastically transformed how people plan, experience, and share their travels. From pre-internet days to the current digital age, each phase has introduced innovations that have enhanced convenience, accessibility, and personalization for travellers.

Pre-Internet Era (Before 1990s)

Before the internet revolutionized the tourism industry, travellers primarily relied on traditional travel agencies to make bookings for flights, hotels, and car rentals. Printed materials such as brochures, maps, and guidebooks were essential for planning trips, with travellers relying heavily on physical resources to decide on destinations. Communication with hotels or airlines often occurred through telephone calls or faxes, making the process slower and more manual.

The Internet Revolution (1990s - Early 2000s)

The introduction of the internet in the 1990s marked a significant shift in tourism. The rise of online travel agencies (OTAs) like Expedia, Priceline, and Booking.com enabled users to book flights, hotels, and car rentals from the comfort of their homes. The availability of travel information expanded dramatically, with websites like TripAdvisor providing user reviews and tips. Email became the standard communication tool for confirming reservations and staying in touch with service providers. Search engines like Google made it easy to find information and plan trips online, reducing the reliance on physical travel agents.

Smartphones and Mobile Apps (Mid-2000s - Present)

With the advent of smartphones in the mid-2000s, the tourism industry experienced another major transformation. The development of mobile apps for booking services like Airbnb, Skyscanner, and Uber allowed travellers to plan and book their trips on the go. Navigation tools like Google Maps and Waze provided real-time, GPS-based directions, making it easier to navigate unfamiliar locations. Social media platforms such as Instagram and Facebook also began to play a key role, with travellers using them to share experiences, discover new destinations, and follow travel influencers, which in turn influenced tourism trends. Additionally, apps enabled real-time updates for flight status, hotel availability, and instant check-ins, improving the convenience and flexibility for travellers.

Artificial Intelligence and Big Data (2010s - Present)

In the 2010s, the rise of artificial intelligence (AI) and big data further personalized the travel experience. AI-powered algorithms analyze user behavior and preferences to offer tailored travel recommendations. Companies began using big data to predict travel trends, optimize pricing strategies, and enhance customer experiences. Chatbots and virtual assistants have become common in customer service, offering instant support for bookings, inquiries, and troubleshooting. These technologies not only improve efficiency but also help travellers make informed decisions by providing personalized suggestions based on past trips and behaviors.

Emerging Technologies (2020s)

The most recent phase of technological evolution in tourism includes the integration of cutting-edge innovations like augmented reality (AR), virtual reality (VR), blockchain, and sustainability technologies. AR is now used in apps for virtual tours and enhanced navigation, allowing tourists to explore destinations in new and interactive ways, such as through virtual museum tours or historical site explorations. VR is enabling immersive travel experiences, where potential tourists can virtually visit locations before making travel decisions. Blockchain technology is also making waves by providing secure, transparent payment systems and facilitating the adoption of cryptocurrencies for travel-related transactions. Moreover, sustainability technologies are becoming increasingly important in the tourism industry, with eco-friendly innovations in transportation and accommodation aimed at reducing the carbon footprint of travel.

The evolution of technology in tourism has shifted the industry from traditional methods of booking and planning to highly interactive, personalized, and digitally driven experiences. Each phase of technological advancement has made travel more efficient, accessible, and enjoyable, while also offering innovative ways to engage with destinations and plan trips. As emerging technologies continue to evolve, the future of tourism promises even greater opportunities for enhancing the traveler's experience.

Emerging Technologies Transforming Tourism

Impact of Artificial Intelligence (AI) in Revolutionizing Tourists' Experience

Artificial Intelligence (AI) has emerged as a game-changer in the tourism industry, revolutionizing the way tourists plan, experience, and share their travels. By automating processes, analyzing vast amounts of data, and delivering personalized services, AI has significantly enhanced efficiency and satisfaction in tourism.

1. Personalized Travel Recommendations

AI algorithms analyze user preferences, behavior, and past travel history to offer tailored suggestions for destinations, accommodations, and activities. Platforms like **TripAdvisor**, **Booking.com**, and **Google Travel** use AI to provide customized itineraries, ensuring travellers have experiences that match their interests.

2. AI-Powered Virtual Assistants and Chatbots

AI-driven virtual assistants and chatbots offer real-time, 24/7 support to tourists, handling inquiries about bookings, cancellations, travel guides, and more. Tools like **Alexa**, **Siri**, and hotel chatbots provide quick, efficient responses, reducing human workload and improving customer satisfaction.

3. Seamless Booking Processes

AI optimizes online booking systems by predicting flight prices, hotel availability, and offering discounts through dynamic pricing algorithms. Platforms like **Skyscanner** and **Kayak** leverage AI to assist tourists in finding the best travel deals.

4. Smart Airports and Contactless Travel

AI enhances the airport experience through **facial recognition**, **biometric check-ins**, and **automated security systems**, reducing wait times and ensuring seamless passenger flow. AI-driven contactless services have also become essential post-pandemic, offering safer and faster travel processes.

5. Enhanced Customer Service

Hotels and airlines use AI to predict customer needs, personalize services, and deliver exceptional experiences. AI tools analyze guest preferences to automate room settings, such as temperature and lighting, while voice-activated devices like **Amazon Echo** improve in-room convenience.

6. AI in Language Translation

Real-time AI translation tools like **Google Translate** bridge communication barriers, enabling tourists to interact effortlessly in foreign countries. These tools translate conversations, signs, and menus, making travel more accessible and enjoyable.

7. AI-Enhanced Navigation and Smart Travel Apps

AI-powered navigation tools and smart travel apps provide real-time route optimization, weather forecasts, and traffic updates. Apps like **Google Maps** and **Waze** help tourists navigate destinations smoothly and explore efficiently.

8. Predictive Analysis for Future Travel Trends

AI analyzes traveler data to predict emerging tourism trends and behaviors. Businesses use these insights to create targeted marketing campaigns, optimize resources, and develop personalized offers that cater to future demands.

9. Immersive Experiences Through AI Integration

AI combined with technologies like **Augmented Reality (AR)** and **Virtual Reality (VR)** allows tourists to explore destinations virtually before traveling. AI-powered virtual tours help travellers make informed decisions while enhancing engagement and excitement.

Artificial Intelligence has redefined tourists' experiences by offering smarter, more personalized, and seamless solutions. From enhancing customer service through chatbots to enabling contactless travel and predictive analytics, AI streamlines every stage of the travel journey. By improving efficiency, reducing costs, and enhancing satisfaction, AI is not just a technological advancement but a critical driver of innovation in the tourism industry. As AI continues to evolve, its integration will play a pivotal role in creating more immersive, sustainable, and memorable travel experiences for tourists worldwide.

Embracing Big Data: Shaping the Future of the Travel Industry

In the tourism industry, as in many other business sectors, big data plays a pivotal role in enabling accurate decision-making. It is commonly applied in areas such as forecasting customer demand, personalizing services, optimizing travel marketing efforts, and refining pricing strategies. Big data is frequently combined with artificial intelligence (AI) and machine learning (ML), empowering analytics teams to automatically identify patterns within vast amounts of unstructured information. For instance, this synergy allows businesses to pinpoint specific hotel features that influence user satisfaction or predict, based on past travel history, which destinations a customer is most likely to choose.

Typically, big data is not utilized as a standalone technology; it requires supplementary tools for storage, structuring, and analysis. However, this very integration enables tourism businesses to gain deeper insights into their customers, anticipate their preferences, and deliver more tailored experiences. While big data analytics can be a game-changer for the travel industry, it also presents challenges, particularly regarding data privacy and security.

Big data analytics in tourism can be broadly categorized into three types, each serving distinct purposes and offering unique insights:

Type	*Focus*	*Purpose*	*Example Usage*
Descriptive	Past and present	Understand trends and patterns	Visitor numbers analysis over time
Predictive	Future	Forecast and prepare for future scenarios	Anticipating demand for holiday destinations
Prescriptive	Actionable advice	Optimize decision-making and strategies	Adjusting hotel prices during peak periods

These analytics types work together to empower the tourism industry with data-driven strategies, ensuring efficiency and enhanced customer experiences.

Transaction Data (by operations)

This source includes web search data, web page visit data, online booking data etc. Typically, advanced web services such as google analytics are used to obtain this data.

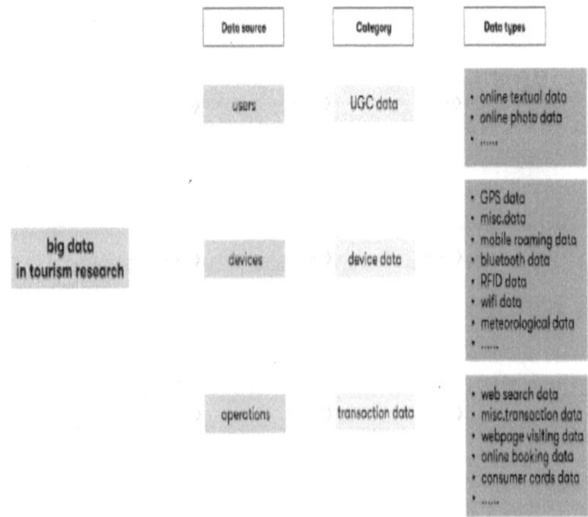

Virtual Reality (VR) & Augmented Reality (AR) in Tourism

Virtual Reality (VR) and Augmented Reality (AR) are reshaping the tourism industry by offering innovative and immersive experiences. VR allows travellers to virtually explore destinations, hotels, or attractions before making bookings, providing a "try-before-you-buy" experience. This technology is particularly beneficial for promoting lesser-known destinations, giving users a chance to experience them from the comfort of their homes. Tourism boards and businesses utilize VR to create 360-degree videos of landmarks, museums, and cultural sites, enticing potential visitors and enhancing marketing strategies.

On the other hand, AR enriches the on-site travel experience by overlaying digital information on real-world environments. Tourists can use AR-enabled mobile apps or wearable devices to receive real-time information about historical landmarks, attractions, or local restaurants. For example, pointing a smartphone at a historical monument can display its history, architectural details, and related multimedia content. AR also improves navigation in unfamiliar places, offering directions and recommendations tailored to the traveler's preferences.

The combination of VR and AR not only enhances the customer experience but also boosts operational efficiency for tourism businesses. Hotels, for instance, use VR to offer virtual tours of rooms and facilities, helping customers make informed decisions. Similarly, travel agencies leverage these technologies to simulate adventure experiences like scuba diving or hiking, providing a glimpse of what travellers can expect. AR applications streamline logistics by integrating language translation tools, currency converters, and cultural etiquette tips, ensuring seamless travel experiences. The integration of VR and AR in tourism is paving the way for a more interactive and personalized industry. These technologies cater to modern travellers' desire for unique and convenient experiences, while also helping businesses stand out in a competitive market. By providing immersive previews and enriching real-world interactions, VR and AR not only enhance satisfaction but also encourage sustainable tourism practices by reducing the need for physical resources during the planning and exploration phases.

Comparison Table: VR vs. AR in Tourism

Aspect	*Virtual Reality (VR)*	*Augmented Reality (AR)*
Definition	Simulates entire environments digitally.	Overlays digital information on the real world.
Key Use Case	Virtual tours of destinations, hotels, and attractions.	Enriching on-site experiences with real-time information.
Devices Required	VR headsets (e.g., Oculus Rift, HTC Vive).	Smartphones, tablets, or AR glasses.
Customer Benefit	"Try-before-you-buy" experiences for decision-making.	Enhanced navigation and contextual information.
Business Benefit	Boosts marketing and decision-making for travellers.	Streamlines logistics and enriches customer interaction.
Example	Virtual museum walkthroughs.	AR-guided tours of historical landmarks.

Internet of Things (IoT) in Tourism

The Internet of Things (IoT) is revolutionizing the tourism industry by creating interconnected ecosystems that enhance the traveler experience and improve operational efficiency. IoT refers to a network of smart devices that communicate with each other through the internet to collect, share, and analyze data. In tourism, this technology enables seamless services, personalized experiences, and real-time updates that cater to the modern traveler's expectations for convenience and efficiency.

One major application of IoT in tourism is in smart accommodations. Hotels increasingly deploy IoT-enabled devices such as smart thermostats, lighting, and voice assistants, allowing guests to control room settings through their smartphones or voice commands. Keyless entry systems using mobile apps improve security and reduce check-in times. These innovations not only enhance the guest experience but also contribute to energy efficiency and cost savings for hotel operators.

IoT also plays a pivotal role in transportation within the tourism sector. Smart airports utilize IoT technologies for real-time baggage tracking, automated check-ins, and personalized flight updates. Similarly, connected rental cars and public transportation systems provide travellers with navigation assistance, traffic updates, and vehicle diagnostics, ensuring a smoother journey. IoT-enabled wearables, like smartwatches, further enhance travel convenience by offering features such as boarding pass integration, language translation, and health monitoring.

The adoption of IoT in tourism is paving the way for a more personalized and sustainable industry. Destination management organizations (DMOs) use IoT sensors to monitor tourist footfall and environmental impact, enabling better crowd management and resource allocation. For instance, sensors in popular attractions can notify tourists of peak hours and suggest alternative times to visit, reducing overcrowding. IoT not only elevates the overall travel experience but also ensures that tourism evolves in a more efficient, eco-friendly direction.

Table of Benefits and Applications of IoT in Tourism

Aspect	*IoT Applications*	*Benefits*
Smart Accommodations	IoT-enabled rooms with smart devices for lighting, climate, and entertainment.	Enhanced guest convenience and energy efficiency.
Transportation	Real-time baggage tracking, automated check-ins, and connected vehicles.	Seamless and stress-free travel experiences.
Wearable Technology	Smartwatches and fitness trackers for boarding passes and language translation.	Increased traveler convenience and personalized services.
Sustainable Tourism	IoT sensors for monitoring tourist flow and environmental impact.	Improved crowd management and eco-friendly practices.
Customer Engagement	IoT apps for location-based notifications and travel suggestions.	Personalized recommendations and enhanced satisfaction.

IoT is redefining tourism by making experiences more efficient, personalized, and sustainable, ensuring the industry remains competitive in a technology-driven world.

Benefits of Technology in Tourism

Technology has significantly enhanced accessibility in tourism, making travel planning more seamless and convenient. Online booking platforms, mobile applications, and interactive websites have simplified the process of searching, comparing, and reserving services like flights, accommodations, and tours. This accessibility has not only empowered travellers to make informed decisions but also allowed businesses to connect with a global audience, thereby expanding their reach.

Personalized experiences are another major benefit brought by technology. Advanced tools like artificial intelligence (AI) and big data analytics allow tourism businesses to tailor services to individual preferences. From customized travel packages to real-time recommendations via mobile apps, technology ensures that every traveler's journey feels unique. Personalization has become a key driver of customer satisfaction and loyalty, giving businesses a competitive edge in the crowded tourism market.

Operational efficiency has also improved with the integration of technology. Automation in processes like check-ins, inventory management, and customer support reduces manual effort and errors. Smart systems in hotels and transportation hubs ensure smooth operations, such as optimized energy use in accommodations and real-time updates on flights and traffic. These advancements save time and resources for both businesses and customers, creating a win-win scenario.

Lastly, technology supports sustainability in tourism. IoT-enabled devices monitor environmental impact, helping businesses implement eco-friendly practices. Digital solutions like paperless ticketing and virtual tours reduce waste and carbon footprints. By promoting sustainable practices, technology not only addresses environmental concerns but also meets the growing demand for responsible travel options among eco-conscious tourists.

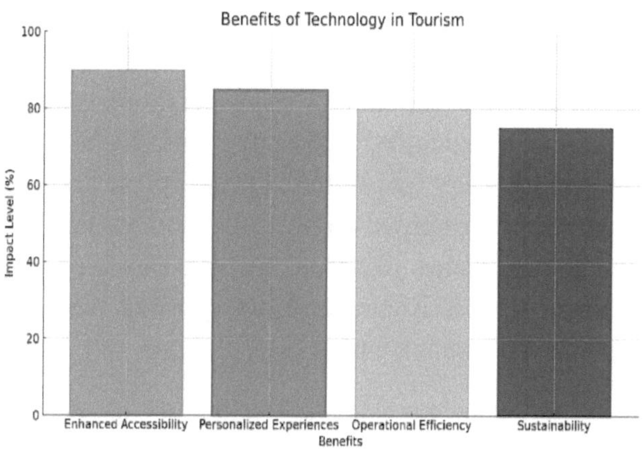

The bar graph above illustrates the relative impact of these benefits, highlighting their importance in shaping a more accessible, personalized, efficient, and sustainable tourism industry.

Technology in the Post-Pandemic Era in tourism

In the post-pandemic era, technology has significantly reshaped the tourism industry, enhancing both customer experiences and operational efficiencies. One of the most prominent technological trends in tourism is the rise of contactless travel. Airlines, hotels, and airports have implemented touchless check-ins, mobile boarding passes, and digital room keys to minimize physical contact and ensure safety. For example, Delta Airlines introduced the use of facial recognition technology at some U.S. airports, allowing passengers to board flights using their face rather than a boarding pass.

Virtual reality (VR) and augmented reality (AR) have also become game-changers in the tourism industry. Many destinations and travel companies now offer virtual tours to engage potential visitors. The Louvre in Paris, for instance, provides virtual museum tours, allowing people worldwide to explore its art collections from the safety of their homes. AR apps like Google Lens enable tourists to interact with their surroundings in real time, providing instant translations, historical context, and recommendations just by scanning landmarks or menus.

The use of AI-powered chatbots has seen widespread adoption in customer service, offering personalized travel advice and bookings. For example, Skyscanner's AI chatbot, "Skyscanner Assistant," helps users find flights, hotels, and car rentals quickly, providing suggestions based on previous searches and preferences. Additionally, companies like Booking.com and Expedia use AI to predict travel trends, recommend personalized destinations, and offer real-time customer support.

E-commerce platforms and digital payment solutions have streamlined travel bookings. With the rise of apps like Airbnb, travellers now have the ability to book unique accommodations directly from their smartphones. Additionally, digital payment methods such as Apple Pay and Google Wallet have become common, reducing the need for physical cash, making payments seamless and secure, especially when traveling internationally.

Drones and 360-degree cameras have revolutionized the way destinations market themselves. Tourist spots like Bali and the Maldives have incorporated drone footage into their marketing campaigns, offering stunning aerial views of beaches and resorts that entice potential visitors. These visual technologies give tourists a preview of their experiences, influencing decision-making in the planning process.

Lastly, the use of data analytics has helped the tourism industry recover and thrive post-pandemic. Airlines, travel agencies, and destination marketers now rely on real-time data to monitor travel patterns, adjust services, and manage crowd control. For instance, Amsterdam's Schiphol Airport uses predictive analytics to optimize passenger flow and manage airport operations efficiently, reducing congestion and enhancing customer satisfaction.

In summary, technology has played a pivotal role in transforming the tourism industry post-pandemic, enhancing safety, convenience, and personalization, while also helping businesses adapt to new consumer expectations.

Challenges of Technology in Tourism

While technology has revolutionized the tourism industry, it also presents several challenges that businesses and travellers must navigate. One of the primary challenges is **digital divide**—the disparity in access to technology across different regions and demographics. In many developing countries, tourists may face difficulties accessing digital services due to limited internet connectivity, outdated infrastructure, or low technological literacy. For example, rural areas in countries like India or parts of Africa may not have reliable internet, making online bookings and access to digital guides challenging for travellers in those regions.

Another challenge is **data privacy and security**. With the increasing use of digital platforms and applications for bookings, payments, and personal information sharing, the risk of data breaches has escalated. In 2020, a cyberattack on the hotel chain MGM Resorts exposed the personal data of more than 10.6 million guests. Tourists are becoming more cautious about sharing their personal information online, which has prompted businesses to invest in stronger cybersecurity measures.

Over-reliance on technology also poses challenges, particularly for businesses that may become too dependent on automated systems and AI. While automation and AI-powered chatbots can streamline processes, they may also lead to a lack of human touch in customer service. For instance, travellers may encounter frustrations when interacting with a chatbot that doesn't fully understand their needs or provide nuanced responses, leading to dissatisfaction. Additionally, if technology malfunctions, businesses may be ill-equipped to handle situations, which can negatively affect customer experiences.

The **complexity and cost of implementing new technologies** can be overwhelming for smaller businesses in the tourism sector. For instance, integrating AR experiences or advanced booking systems can be expensive and technically complex for small hotels or local tour operators. While major players like Marriott or Expedia can afford large-scale investments in technology, smaller businesses may struggle to keep up, which can hinder their ability to compete.

Environmental concerns are another challenge with tourism technology. The use of drones for marketing, or for services like aerial tours, while popular, can lead to environmental damage. In some cases, drone usage has disrupted wildlife in nature reserves and protected areas. For example, in certain U.S. national parks, drones have been banned to protect wildlife and preserve the natural landscape, highlighting the need for responsible use of technology in tourism.

Lastly, there are issues with **AI bias and algorithmic discrimination**. Algorithms that personalize travel recommendations or pricing may unintentionally favor certain groups over others. For example, some AI-based hotel booking systems have been found to price rooms higher based on the user's search history or demographic data. This can lead to unequal pricing and accessibility issues for certain groups of travellers, reinforcing inequalities.

While technology brings significant benefits to the tourism industry, these challenges ranging from accessibility issues and data security to over-dependence on automation require careful consideration. Balancing technological advancements with ethical practices and inclusivity is essential for sustainable growth in the sector.

Future of Tourism and Technology

The future of tourism will continue to be heavily influenced by advancements in technology, creating more personalized, seamless, and immersive experiences for travellers. One of the most prominent trends will be **personalized travel experiences** driven by artificial intelligence (AI) and machine learning. AI will analyze data from past travel behavior, preferences, and social media activity to curate tailor-made itineraries for travellers. For example, companies like **Trip.com** are already utilizing AI to recommend destinations, activities, and even restaurants based on individual traveler profiles. In the future, these recommendations will become even more accurate, offering an experience that feels uniquely designed for each traveler.

Virtual and augmented reality (VR/AR) will further transform how people plan and experience travel. Virtual tours will allow users to explore destinations before booking, providing a clear picture of what to expect. For instance, tourists could virtually "visit" a hotel or a sightseeing spot in VR before committing to a booking. This will significantly reduce uncertainty and enhance confidence in travel decisions. Moreover, AR will play a role in on-site experiences, where travellers can point their smartphones at landmarks to instantly access historical facts, reviews, or nearby attractions. The use of AR in guiding visitors at popular tourist spots like museums and heritage sites is already being experimented with, and its application will expand in the future.

Sustainability will also be at the forefront of tourism technology. Digital platforms will help reduce the environmental footprint of tourism by promoting eco-friendly travel options, managing tourism flows, and reducing over-tourism. For example, platforms like **Skyscanner** already provide users with options to book flights with the lowest carbon emissions, and similar tools will be integrated into more services. The future will likely see more widespread use of electric transportation, drone-based deliveries, and smart city infrastructure to ensure that tourism grows without negatively impacting the environment.

Blockchain and **cryptocurrency** could also revolutionize transactions within the tourism industry. Blockchain's decentralized nature will provide a more secure and transparent way of handling payments, contracts, and even travel insurance, reducing fraud and administrative costs. Cryptocurrency adoption is also expected to grow, allowing international travellers to make payments across borders without the need for currency conversions or high transaction fees. Travel agencies like **Travala** are already accepting cryptocurrencies for bookings, and this trend is likely to gain more momentum in the coming years.

Below is a table showing potential growth areas in tourism technology over the next decade:

Technology Area	*Growth Expectation*
Personalized Travel (AI)	40%
Virtual and Augmented Reality	35%
Sustainability	25%
Block chain & Cryptocurrency	20%

As shown in the chart, **personalized travel** and **virtual/augmented reality** are expected to experience the highest growth, reflecting the increasing demand for tailored and immersive experiences. **Sustainability** is also gaining significant attention, indicating a shift toward responsible travel. Meanwhile, **blockchain and cryptocurrency** adoption, while growing, is expected to see more gradual integration into mainstream tourism services.

The future of tourism and technology is bound to bring more convenience, sustainability, and immersive experiences to travellers. The technologies discussed here are likely to reshape the industry, making travel more accessible, personalized, and environmentally responsible.

Conclusion

Tourism technology has significantly transformed the travel and hospitality industry, offering innovative solutions to meet the evolving demands of modern travellers. By integrating advanced tools such as **Artificial Intelligence (AI)**, **Virtual Reality (VR)**, **Internet of Things (IoT)**, and **Big Data Analytics**, the sector has achieved greater efficiency, personalization, and accessibility. These technologies have enhanced travel planning, improved customer experiences, and fostered sustainable practices, ensuring a positive impact on both businesses and tourists.

The advent of digital technologies has profoundly transformed the tourism landscape, revolutionizing the way we travel, interact, and experience destinations. As the industry continues to navigate the complexities of a rapidly changing world, tourism technology has emerged as a vital catalyst for growth, innovation, and sustainability.

Embracing emerging technologies such as artificial intelligence, blockchain, Internet of Things (IoT), and virtual/augmented reality will be crucial for addressing pressing challenges, meeting evolving customer expectations, and driving business success. These technologies have the potential to enhance operational efficiency, personalize traveler experiences, and foster a more connected and resilient global tourism ecosystem. For instance, AI-powered chatbots and virtual assistants can provide 24/7 customer support, helping travellers plan and book their trips more efficiently. Blockchain technology can ensure secure and transparent transactions, protecting sensitive customer data and preventing fraud. IoT sensors can monitor and manage energy consumption, waste reduction, and environmental sustainability in tourism facilities and destinations.

Moreover, virtual and augmented reality experiences can enable travellers to explore destinations remotely, reducing the need for physical travel and promoting more sustainable tourism practices. These technologies can also enhance cultural heritage preservation, education, and interpretation, allowing visitors to engage more deeply and meaningfully with local histories and traditions. Ultimately, the strategic adoption of tourism technology will be instrumental in creating a more connected, sustainable, and resilient global tourism ecosystem. By harnessing the power of digital innovation, the tourism industry can mitigate its environmental footprint, promote cross-cultural understanding, and foster economic growth and development that benefits local communities and destinations.

REFERENCES

1. Achaya K T, ***A Historical Dictionary of Indian Food***, Oxford Publishers, 2001
2. Achaya K T, ***Indian Food***, Oxford Publishers, 1998
3. Agarwal, S, ***Tourism Development in India: A Socio-Economic Perspective,*** Annals of Tourism Research. 2002.
4. Alisha Ali, ***Managing Tourism and Hospitality Sectors for Sustainable Global Development***, Routeledge, 2013
5. Anand.M.M. ***Tourism and Hotel Industry in India - A Study in Management***, Prentice – Hall of India, 1976
6. Andres Artal-Tur, Metin Kozak, ***Culture and Cultures in Tourism - Exploring New Trends***, Routledge, UK, 2019
7. Andrew Holden, ***Environment and Tourism***, Routledge Publishers, London, 2008
8. Angela Hawke and Alison Raphael, ***The Global Study Report on Sexual Exploitation of Children in Travel and Tourism***, ECPAT International, Thailand, 2016
9. Annamalai Murugan, ***Tourism and Hospitality Management***, New Delhi Publishers
10. ***Annual plan (Draft) Tamil Nadu 2005-2006***, State planning commission, (2004-2005).
11. Arora RK, ***Sports Tourism***, Mohit Publications, New Delhi, 2009
12. Ashworth G., Hartmann R, ***Horror and Human Tragedy Revisited: The Management of Sites of Atrocities for Tourism,*** Cognizant Communication Corporation; Elmsford, NY, USA: 2005
13. Ashworth, G. J., & Larkham, P. J., ***Building a New Heritage: Tourism, Culture and Identity in the New Europe***, Routledge, 2002
14. Attfield, R, ***Environmental Ethics***, Cambridge, UK, 2003
15. Baker, M., Moore, K. ***Tourism, Development and Poverty in Emerging Economies: A Case Study,*** Tourism Geographies. 2016.

16. Baker, S., Kousis, M., Richardson, D. and Young, S. (eds), ***The Politics of Sustainable Development: Theory, Policy and Practice within the European Union***, Routledge, London, 1997
17. Bali, Parvinder S, ***International Cuisine and Food Production Management,*** Oxford University Press, 2012.
18. Bartelmus, P, ***Environment, Growth and Development: The Concepts and Strategies of Sustainability***, Routledge, London, 1994
19. Becken, S, ***Tourism and Climate Change: Risks and Opportunities for Small Island Destinations,*** Tourism Management. 2007.
20. Beverly, T., ***Heritage Management in Africa: Politics, Development, and Historic Sites***, Routledge, 2017
21. Bhatia A.K, ***Tourism Management***, New Delhi, 2003.
22. Bhatia A.K., ***International Tourism Fundamentals and Practices***, Sterling Publication Private Limited, 2002.
23. Bhatia AK, ***The Business of Travel and Tourism***, New Delhi, 2011.
24. Bhatnagar, S.K., ***Front Office Management***, Frank Bros & Co, 2005.
25. Boulud, Daniel. Braise, ***A Journey Through International Cuisine,*** Harper Collins, 2013.
26. Bramwell, B., Lane, B. ***Tourism and Sustainability: New Tourism in the 21st Century***, Routledge. 2008.
27. Brian W King, ***The Geography of Travel and Tourism***, London, 2015.
28. Bryman, Alan, ***Social Research Methods***, United Kingdom, 2001
29. Buhalis, D., & Jun, S. H, ***E-tourism***, Encyclopedia of Tourism. Springer. 2011
30. Chair Dennis Stevenson, ***Information and Communications Technology in UK Schools, an independent inquiry***, The Independent ICT in Schools Commission, London. UK. 1997

31. Chawla, Romila, ***Heritage Tourism and Development***, New Delhi, 2004
32. Chhabra, Deepak, ***Sustainable Marketing of Transformative Heritage Tourism***, New York, 2024
33. Chitkara, M.G, ***Tourism Development***, APH Publishing Corporation, New Delhi, 2012
34. Choudhary PNK, ***Tourism Marketing***, Mumbai, 2012.
35. Chris Cooper, ***Indian Tourism*** **Centre for Tourism Research, 2004**
36. Christoff, Peter, **Ecological modernisation, ecological modernities, *Environmental Politics*,** 1996
37. Cohen, E. ***Tourism and Development in the Third World***, Routledge. 2012.
38. Cooke, J. & Dickson, H, ***The Best in Travel 2007***, Lonely Planet Publications, *Australia* 2006
39. David Weaver, ***Sustainable Tourism*: *Theory and Practice***, London, 2011.
40. De Jong, Anna, *Gender,* ***Tourism Entrepreneurship and Social Policy***, New York, 2024
41. Desai S.S, ***Tourism and Hospitality: An Integrated Introduction***, Mumbai, 2014.
42. Dileep M.R, ***Tourism: Concepts, Theory and Practice***, New Delhi, 2020
43. Dixit, Manoj and Yadav, Charu Sheela, ***Tourism Products of India***, Royal Publishers, Lucknow,2006
44. Dodd, John & Sharma, Veena, ***Leisure and Tourism cultural Paradigms***, New Delhi,2012
45. Dr. Chakravarti, B.K, ***Concepts of Front Office Management***, APH Publishing Corporation, 2008.
46. Equations, ***A Situational Analysis of Child Sex Tourism in India (Kerala and Goa)***, ECPAT, December 2003
47. Erica Lorraine Williams, ***Moral Panic: Sex Tourism, Trafficking, and the Limits of Transnational Mobility in Bahia***, NYU Press, 2011

48. Evans, Nigel, ***Strategic Management for Tourism, Hospitality and Events***, United Kingdom, 2020
49. Farrer, James. ***The Globalisation of Asian Cuisines: Transnational Networks and Culinary Contact Zones***. Palgrave Macmillan, 2015.
50. Fennell A David, ***Sustainable Tourism: Theory and Practice***, London, 2014
51. Fennell, D.A, ***Ecotourism: An Introduction***, Routledge, London, 1999
52. Fennell, D.A. ***Ecotourism: An Introduction***, Routledge. 2008.
53. Foley, Malcolm, Lennon, John & Maxwell, Gillian, ***Hospitality, Tourism and Leisure Management***, Wellington, 1997
54. Frances Riemer, ***Front and Back Stage of Tourism Performance Imaginaries and Bucket List Venues***, Routledge, London, 2020
55. Freeman, E., ***Strategic Management: a stakeholder approach,*** Pitman Publishers: Boston, 1984.
56. Fyall, A., Garrod, B., & Leask, A., ***Managing Heritage Tourism***, Channel View Publications, 2003
57. G. Ravecndran. ***Tourism and Information Technology,*** Department of Tourism. Transport Bhawan. New Delhi.
58. George, Richard, ***Marketing Tourism and Hospitality: Concepts and Cases***, London, 2021
59. Getz, D. ***Festivals, Special Events, and Tourism***, Van Nostrand Reinhold, New York, 1991.
60. ***Global Report on Trafficking in Persons***, United Nations, 2024
61. Goeldner, R Charles, ***Tourism: Principles, Practices, Philosophies***, USA, 2012.
62. Goodall, B. and Stabler, M.J, ***Principles Influencing the Determination of Environmental Standards for Sustainable Tourism***, 1997

63. Gössling, S., Hall, C.M. ***Tourism and Global Environmental Change: Ecological, Social, Economic and Political Interrelationships***, Routledge. 2006.

64. Gössling, S., Scott, D., Hall, C. M., Ceron, J.-P., & Dubois, G. ***Challenges and opportunities for tourism in a green economy***. UNEP Green Economy Report. UNEP. 2010.

65. Gretzel, U., Sigala, M., & Xiang, Z. ***Smart tourism: Foundations and developments. Electronic Markets***, *25*(3), 2015.

66. Gunn. C, ***Tourism Planning: Basic, Concepts, Issues***, Taylor & Francis, London, 1994

67. Gupta SK, ***Travel and Tourism Management***, Agra, 2009.

68. Hall, C. Michael, ***The Geography of Tourism and Recreation***, London, 2014

69. Hall, C.M. ***Tourism and Political Economy: Global Frameworks of Analysis***, Routledge. (2013).

70. Hall, C.M., Williams, A.M. ***Tourism and Migration: New Relationships Between Production and Consumption***, Springer. 2008.

71. Hall, Colin Michael, ***Tourism and politics -Policy, Power and Place***, New York, 1994

72. Hardin, G, ***The tragedy of the commons.*** New York, 1968

73. Hariharan, ***Tourism Development in India***, Vista International publishing House, New Delhi,1995

74. Harrison, R., ***Understanding the Politics of Heritage***, Manchester University Press, 2013

75. Hein, G, ***Learning in the Museum***, London, 1998

76. Heyman, Patricia A. ***International Cooking: A Culinary Journey***. Pearson, 2016.

77. Holloway G William, ***The Transportation Experience: Policy, Planning, and Deployment***, USA 2003.

78. Honey, M. ***Ecotourism and Sustainable Development: Who Owns Paradise***? Island Press. 2008.

79. Iatrou Kostas, ***The History of Air Transport***, Canada, 2020

80. Isaac, Rami K., ***Tourism Safety, Security and Resilience***, New York, 2024

81. Jacob, Robinet and Joseph, Sindhu and Philip, Anoop, ***Indian Tourism Products***, Abijeet Publications, Delhi, 2007
82. Jain S,K, Sinha R.K, ***Tourism and Travel Management***, New Delhi, 2007
83. James Higham & Tom Hinch, ***Sport and Tourism: Globalization, Mobility and Identity***, Routledge Publishers, UK, 2009
84. James Higham & Tom Hinch, ***Sport Tourism Development***, Channel View Publications, UK,2018
85. Jha, S.M, ***Tourism Marketing***, Bangalore, 2013
86. Jiang, Y., & Li, M, ***The role of mobile technology in tourism***, Tourism Management, 2017.
87. Jokela, S. & Minoia P.. Parker Krieg & R. Toivanen (eds.), ***Situating Sustainability: A Handbook of Contexts and Concepts***, Helsinki, Helsinki University Press. 2021.
88. Julinc E. Mills. Rob Law, ***Handbook of Consumer Behavior. Tourism, and the Internet***, Routledge, New York, 2013
89. Kevin Griffin, Nigel D. Morpeth, Razaq Raj (Ed), ***Cultural Tourism***, CABI Publishers, 2013
90. Kevin Hannam, Anya Diekmann, Kevin Hannam, Anya Diekmann, ***Tourism and India: A Critical Introduction***, Routledge, 2010
91. Khan, M. A., ***Introduction to Tourism***, Anmol Publication Pvt. Ltd, New Delhi, 2005
92. Killion, L., Mason, P. ***Tourism in the Developing World: Trends and Emerging Issues***, Annals of Tourism Research. 2019.
93. Kim, H., & Lee, C. K. ***Technological innovations and their impact on the tourism industry***, Tourism Management Perspectives, 2020.
94. Kim, Seongseop, Wang Dan, ***Future of Tourism Marketing***, United Kingdom, 2021
95. Kinnaird, Vivian & Hall, Derek, ***Tourism A gender Analysis***, New York, 1994

96. Koens, K., Thomas, R. ***Tourism in Emerging Destinations: Opportunities and Challenges***, Tourism Review International. 2020.

97. Kotler, Philip, et.al., ***Marketing for Hospitality and Tourism***, USA, 2014

98. Kumar swan, Sampad and Mohan Mishra, Jitendra, ***Tourism Principles and Practices***, Oxford University Press, New Delhi, 2012

99. Lai, M.Y,, Khoo-Lattimore, C. & Wang, Y., ***Food and Cuisine Image in destination branding: toward a conceptual model,*** Tourism and Hospitality Research, 2019.

100. Lajipathi Rai H, ***Development of Tourism in India***, Rupa Books Pvt,1993

101. Lalita Sharma**,** ***Tourism and Hospitality Management*****, Centrum Press, 2011**

102. Lew, A.A., Hall, C.M., Williams, A.M, ***A Companion to Tourism***, Wiley-Blackwell. 2004.

103. Lijin Joseph, ***Travel journalism: Possibilities and challenges of Infotainment***, Journalism concepts, 2018.

104. Louloudes, A., ***Managing Heritage: An Integrated Approach***, Routledge, 2016

105. Maneet, K., ***Tourism Today- An Indian Perspective***, Kanishka Publishing House, New Delhi. 1994

106. Manohar S, ***Introduction to Tourism and Hospitality***, New Delhi, 2007.

107. Mariani, Marcello, et. Al., ***Tourism Management, Marketing, and Development: Performance, Strategies, and Sustainability***, United Kingdom, 2016

108. Mason, P. ***Tourism Impacts, Planning, and Management***, Elsevier, 2016.

109. Mason, Peter, ***Geography of Tourism: Image, Impacts and Issues***, Goodfellow Publishers Ltd, 2023

110. Mathur, Anurag, ***Indian Tourism: Tourist Places of India***, New Delhi. 2016

111. Maximiliano E. Korstanje, ***Cultural Tourism: Perspectives, Opportunities and Challenges***, Nova Science Publishers,USA, 2024
112. McLaren. D, ***Rethinking Tourism and Ecotravel***, Kumarian Press, Connecticut, 1998
113. Mehta, S, ***Discover India: Festivals of India***, Penguin Random House India Pvt. Limited, 2019.
114. Middleton, V.T.C., and Clarke, J.R., ***Marketing in Travel and Tourism***, USA, 2001
115. Miklos Banhidi & Farhad Moghimehfar (Ed), ***International Perspectives in Sport Tourism Management***, Routledge, London, 2024
116. Miller, M. L., Carter R. W. & Walsh S. J, ***A Conceptual Framework for Studying Global Change, Tourism, and the Sustainability of Iconic National Parks***, The George Wright Forum, 31(3), 2014.
117. Ministry of Tourism, ***Government of India - National Tourism Policy***, 2002
118. Mishra, Krishna Kumar, ***Tourism Product Development***, Notion Press Publication, Chennai, 2022.
119. Mishra, Shivangi, ***Celebration and Ritual: Food Practices in Contemporary Indian Festivals and Ceremonies***, 2004.
120. Misra, V.N., ***Prehistoric Culture Sequence of Bhimbetka, Prehistoric man and his art in Central India***, Deccan College, Sakal Press, Poona.1977.
121. Mohammed Zulfiker, ***Tourism and Hotel Industry***, Vikas Publishing House Pvt Limited, 1998.
122. Mohd Aris, Muhammad Muzhaffar, Ameleya Ghazali, Nur Azhari, and Azrin Binti Abdul Razak. ***Food Trail as a Contributor to Malaysia Food Tourism Mapping: A Conceptual Paper***. Terengganu International Business and Economics Conference, 2023
123. Morrison, A.M., ***Marketing and Managing Tourism Destinations***, USA, 2023

124. Mowforth, M., Munt. I, ***Tourism and Sustainability: A New Approach***, Routledge, 2016.
125. Mowforth, M., Munt. I, ***Tourism and Sustainability: Development, Globalization, and New Tourism in the Third World***. Routledge. 2003.
126. Neeraj Agarwal, ***Tourism and Cultural Heritage of India***, 2015
127. Negi, Jagmohan, ***International Tourism and Travel***, S. Chand & Company Ltd, New Delhi, 2004
128. Newman, P., Beatley, T., & Boyer, H. **Urban Resilience: Cities of Fear and Hope. In Resilient Cities: Responding to Peak Oil and Climate Change**, Routledge, 2009
129. Owen, Charles, ***Britons Abroad: A Report on the Package Tour***, New York, 2024
130. Page J. Stephen, ***Tourism Management***, London, 2014.
131. Page, Stephen J., ***Tourism and Recreation: Environment, Place and Space***, London, 2014
132. Page, Stephen, ***Tourism Management: An Introduction***, Netherlands, 2011
133. Parn Nath Seth and Sushma Seth Bat. ***An Introduction to Travel and Tourism***, Sterling Publishers. New Delhi, 1993
134. Peeters, P., & Schouten, F. ***Sustainable tourism strategies for reducing carbon emissions in the tourism sector***. UNEP Technical Series. 2006.
135. Pizam, A., Mansfeld. Y, ***Tourism, Crime, and International Security Issues***, Elsevier, 2006
136. Praveen Sethi, ***Heritage Tourism***, Anmol Publications, 1999.
137. ***Preventing Human Trafficking, An Action Framework for the Travel and Tourism Sector***, World Travel and Tourism Council, July 2021
138. Prideaux, B, ***The Role of the Tourism Industry in the Development of Small Island Destinations***, Tourism Management. 2000.

139. Rajat Gupta, Nishant Singh, Ishita Kirar, and Mahesh Kumar Bairwa, ***Hospitality & Tourism Management*, Vikash Publishing House, 2015**
140. Rajesh Kumar, ***Sports, Adventure & Recreational Tourism***, SBS Publishers,New Delhi, 2009
141. Ramesh C Sharma, ***Tourism: Concepts, Models and Strategies***, New Delhi, 2004.
142. Rao.P.R., ***Indian Heritage and Culture***, Sterling Publishers, New Delhi, 1988.
143. Ravee Chauhan, ***Heritage and Cultural Tourism***, Vistha International publishers, New Delhi, 2006
144. Richards, Greg, ***An Overview of Food and Tourism Trends and Policies***, 2012.
145. Richards. G, ***Creative Tourism: A Global Overview***, Channel View Publications. 2018.
146. Rodrigue Jean-Paul, Comtois Claude, and Slack Brian, ***The Geography of Transport Systems***, New York, 2020
147. Ruhanen, L., et al. ***The Impacts of Tourism on Local Communities in Developing Countries***, Springer. 2015.
148. Saarinen, J. ***Sustainable Tourism in the Arctic: The Significance of Tourism for Local Development,*** Tourism Geographies, 2006.
149. Sandeep Gupta, ***Tourism in India: Concepts, Products and Services***, New Delhi, 2012.
150. Sandeep Munjal, Sudhanshu Bhushan, ***The Indian Hospitality Industry***, Apple Academic press, Canada. 2017
151. Sankpal, Girish, ***Study on The Impacts of Culinary Tourism in India***, IJCRT, 2023.
152. SANLAAP, ***A Situational Analysis of Child Sex Tourism in India (Kerala and Goa)***, ECPAT, December 2003
153. Santos, Jose, Silva, Oscar, ***Digital Marketing Strategies for Tourism, Hospitality, and Airline Industries***, USA, 2019
154. Seaton, A.V and Bennett, M. M, ***The Marketing of Tourism Products: Concepts, Issues and Cases***, Cengage Learning EMEA, U.K. 1996
155. Seth, Prannath, ***Tourism Product***, New Delhi, 1998

156. Sharma R.K, ***Tourism in India***, New Delhi, 2010.
157. Sharma, K.K, ***Tourism and Sociocultural Development***, New Delhi, 2004
158. Sharpley R., Stone P (Ed), **Contemporary Tourism Experience Vol. 96**, Routledge, New York, 2012.
159. Shukla U, ***Emerging Dynamics of Indian Tourism and Hospitality***, Uttarpradesh, 2019
160. Sigala, M. ***Social media and customer engagement in the tourism industry.*** Tourism Management, 2018.
161. Singh T.V (Ed), ***New Horizons in Tourism: Strange Experiences and Stranger Practices,*** CABI Publishing; Wallingford, CT, USA: 2004.
162. Singh, J.K., ***Fundamentals of Tourism and Travel***, New Delhi. 2008
163. Smith, M. K., & Richards, G. (Eds.). ***Cultural Tourism: Exploring the Impact***, Routledge. 2013.
164. Smith, M. K., ***Tourism, Heritage and Sustainability***, Channel View Publications, 2009
165. Sneha.N & Rene Samuel, ***A Study on The Travel Journalism in The Digital Age***, (2020)
166. Sørensen, A., Jorgensen, A, ***Understanding Community-Based Tourism in Developing Regions: A Case Study from Kenya***, Tourism Geographies. 2020.
167. Stephen Page, ***Tourism: A Modern Synthesis***, London, 2003.
168. Stephen Wearing, Deborah Stevenson & Tamara Young, ***Tourist Cultures: Identity, Place and the Traveller***, SAGE Publications Ltd, USA, 2010
169. Stronza, A., Hamer, S.A, ***The Role of Ecotourism in Conservation: The Case of the Peruvian Amazon***, Society & Natural Resources. 2009.
170. Sudhir Andrews, ***Hotel Tourism and Hospitality Management***, Tata McGraw-Hill Education, 2000.
171. Supriya Chaudhuri, ***Indian Travel Writing***, 2019
172. Sury.M,Vibha Mathur, ***Five-year Plans of India***, 2013

173. Susan Carson & Mark Pennings (Ed), ***Performing Cultural Tourism: Communities, Tourists and Creative Practices***, Routledge, London, 2017

174. Susan Dewey and Patty Kelly (Ed.), ***Policing Pleasure - Sex Work, Policy, and the State in Global Perspective***, NYU Press, 2011

175. Talia A. Dunyak, ***Tourism and Human Trafficking: A Mapping of Sex Trafficking & Labor Trafficking in the Tourism Sector***, Human Trafficking Search, 2021

176. Tosun, C. ***Expected Impact of Tourism Development in the Developing World: The Case of Turkey***. Tourism Management, 2006.

177. Tsaih, R. H., & Hsu, C. C. ***Artificial intelligence in smart tourism: A conceptual framework.*** Proceedings of the International Conference on Electronic Business (ICEB), December, 2018.

178. Tussyadiah, I. P., & Miller, G. ***The role of technology in the transformation of tourism experiences,*** Tourism Management Perspectives, *24*, 2017.

179. UNESCO, ***Sustainable Tourism at World Heritage Sites***, 2003

180. UNWTO (United Nations World Tourism Organization). ***Tourism and COVID-19: Impacts and policy responses***, UNWTO Report. 2020

181. UNWTO. ***Tourism and the SDGs: Good Practices in the Tourism Sector,*** United Nations World Tourism Organization. 2018

182. Vallière, A., Perret, F, ***Managing Sustainable Tourism: Strategies for Developing Destinations***, Springer, 2018.

183. Venkataraman, Srividya. ***Food Trail: Discovering Food Culture of North-East India,*** 2012.

184. Vikas Khanna, ***The Spice Story of India***, Xlibris Publishers, 2006

185. Walia, Sandeep K., ***Nature-Based Tourism Development***, New York, 2024

186. Weaver, D.B. ***Sustainable Tourism: Theory and Practice***, Elsevier. 2006.

187. Weil S, ***A cabinet of Curiosities: Inquiries into Museums and their Prospects***, Washington, 1995

188. White, Chris, ***Museum and Heritage Tourism***, United Kingdom, 2023

189. Wilson, Julie, ***The Routledge Handbook of Tourism Geographies***, Routledge, UK, 2024

190. World Tourism Organization, ***Climate Change and Tourism***, Madrid, UNWTO, 2003

191. Xiang, Z., & Fesenmaier, D. R. ***Internet Research in Tourism,*** Annals of Tourism Research, *34*(3), 2007.

192. Yashwant Singh Rawal, ***Research in Tourism and Hospitality Management*****,** AJR Publishers 2022

193. Zarimbetova Juldiz, ***History of the Formation of Travel Journalism***, February, 2009

194. Zhenhua Liu, ***Internet Tourism Marketing: The Scottish Hotel School***. University of Strathclydc. UK

GOVERNMENT DOCUMENTS

1. Adopt a heritage: Project Guidelines with MoU, Ministry of Tourism, GOI, (India, 2017)
2. Annual Report of 2023-24, Ministry of Tourism, GOI, (India, 2024)
3. Atulya Bharat Magazine 2023, Ministry of Tourism, GOI, (India, 2024)
4. Monthly Tourism Statistics for October 2024, Ministry of Tourism, GOI, (India, 2024)
5. Monthly Tourism Statistics for August 2024, Ministry of Tourism, GOI, (India, 2024)
6. Monthly Summary of November 2024, Ministry of Tourism, GOI, (India, 2024)
7. Newsletter for July 2024, Ministry of Tourism, GOI, (India, 2024)
8. The Organization of Museum: Practical Advice, UNESCO, (Paris, 1960)
9. Travel and Tourism Development Index 2024, World Economic Forum, (Switzerland, 2024)
10. United Nations Conference on Trade and Development (UNCTAD), Creative Industries and Development Agenda, 11th session, (Geneva, 2004).

ARTICLES

1. Alamineh, G. A., Hussein, J. W., Mulu, Y. E., & Taddesse, B, ***The negative cultural impact of tourism and its implication on sustainable development in Amhara Regional State,*** Cogent Arts & Humanities, 10(1), 2023
2. Ardabili, Farzad Sattari, Es-hagh Rasouli, Shahram Mirzaie Daryani, Manouchehr Molaie, and Bahman Sharegi. ***The Role of Food and Culinary Condition in Tourism Industry***, Middle-East Journal of Scientific Research, vol. 9, no. 6, 2011.
3. Ashton, C, ***Peking Duck as a museum spectacle: staging local heritage for Olympic tourism,*** Journal of Tourism and Cultural Change, *10*(2), 2012
4. Baker, D.A. and Crompton. J.L, ***Quality, Satisfaction and Behavioral Intentions***, Annals of Tourism Research. 27(3). 2000.
5. Balakrishnan, G., & Raghavan, R. ***Role of Food Festivals in Promoting Culinary Tourism: A Case Study of Kerala***, Indian Journal of Applied Research, 2017.
6. Bowes, G. '***Tourism Hangs in the Balance***', Observer, June 19, 2005.
7. Brian Deeney, ***Bringing Technology and Tourism Together***, Journal of Information Technology and Tourism published by Cognizant
8. Buhalis, D., & Law, R. ***Progress in information technology and tourism management: 20 years on and 10 years after the Internet—The state of E-Tourism research***. Tourism Management, 29(4), 2008.
9. Chamboko-Mpotaringa, Mavis, and Tembi M. Tichaawa, ***Tourism digital marketing tools and views on future trends: A systematic review of literature***, African Journal of Hospitality, Tourism and Leisure, Vol. 10, No. 2, 2021
10. Chen, J.S., Kerstetter, D.L. ***International Students' Image of Rural Pennsylvania as a Tourist Destination,*** Journal of Travel Research, 37(4), 1999.

11. Echtner, C.M., Ritchie, J.R.B. ***The Meaning and Measurement of Destination Image***, Journal of Tourism Studies. 2003.
12. Eijgelaar, E., Peeters, P., & Piket, P. ***Estimating CO2 Emissions for Cruise Tourism***, Journal of Sustainable Tourism, 18(3), 2010.
13. Font, X., and McCabe, S., ***Sustainability and Marketing In Tourism: Its Contexts, Paradoxes, Approaches, Challenges And Potential***, Journal of Sustainable Tourism, Vol. 25, No. 7, 2017
14. Furqan, A., Som A. P. M. & Hussin R, ***Promoting green tourism for future sustainability***, Theoretical and Empirical Researches in Urban Management, 5(8), 2010.
15. Greg Richards, ***Cultural tourism: A review of recent research and trends***, Journal of Hospitality and Tourism Management,Volume 36, September 2018, Pages 12-21
16. Herreman, Yani, ***Museums and tourism: culture and consumption***, Museum International, UNESCO, Paris,1998
17. Hjalager, A.-M., & Johansen, P.H., ***Food tourism in protected areas – sustainability for producers, the environment and tourism?,*** Journal of Sustainable Tourism, 2013.
18. Kumar, Alok. ***Cultural and heritage tourism: A tool for sustainable development***, Global Journal of Commerce & Management Perspective, 2017
19. Li, X. (Robert), & Wang, Y, ***Tourism and technology: The impact of new technologies on the tourism industry,*** Journal of Travel Research, 55(3), 2016
20. Lorenzo Angelini & Et.Al, ***Cultural tourism development and the impact on local communities: a case study from the South of Italy*** , CERN Idea Square Journal of Experimental Innovation, 4(2), pp.19-24, 2020
21. Mackay, A. '***Eco Tourists Take Over***', The Times, February 17, 1994.
22. Montgomery Heather, ***Buying Innocence: Child- Sex Tourists in Thailand***, Third World Quaterly, 2008, Vol. 29, No. 5, Tourism and Development in the Global South, 2008

23. Munar, A. M., & Jacobsen, J. K. S. Tourists' online information search: Perceived value and E-satisfaction. Tourism Management, 43, 2014
24. Polat, Eray, and Sami Ozdemir. ***Food and Beverage Experience in Tourism in the Context of Experience Economy***, Journal of Gastronomy Hospitality and Travel (JOGHAT), vol. 4, 2021
25. Qu, C., Timothy, D. J., & Zhang, C, ***Does tourism erode or prosper culture? Evidence from the Tibetan ethnic area of Sichuan Province, China***. Journal of Tourism and Cultural Change, 17(4), 2019
26. Rao, K, ***Technology in tourism: The rise of artificial intelligence and blockchain***, Tourism Review International, *23*(3), 2019
27. Roshan, Rai and Priyadarshinee, S. ***'Whose trash is it anyway? Six years of demanding extended producer responsibility in the Himalaya'***, Down to Earth, September 20, 2024.
28. Ryan Bishop and Lillian S. Robinson, ***In the Night Market: Tourism, Sex, and Commerce in Contemporary Thailand***, Women's Studies Quarterly, Spring - Summer, 1999, Vol. 27, No. 1/2, 1999
29. Sadiku, Matthew, Sarhan Musa, and Tolulope Joshua Ashaolu. ***Food Industry: An Introduction***, International Journal of Trend in Scientific Research and Development, vol. 3, 2019.
30. Sharpley, R. ***Tourism Development and the Environmental Impacts in Emerging Destinations***, International Journal of Tourism Research. 2014.
31. Sigala. M, ***Social Media and Customer Engagement in the Tourism Industry: Emerging Trends***, Journal of Tourism Management, 2016.
32. Sorupia Eden, ***Rethinking the Role of Transportation in Tourism***, Proceedings of the Eastern Asia Society for Transportation Studies, Vol. 5, Australia 2005
33. Soteriades, Marios, ***Tourism Destination Marketing: Approaches Improving Effectiveness and***

Efficiency, Journal of Hospitality and Tourism Technology, Vol. 3 No. 2, 2012

34. The Hindu, ***India's travel & tourism market likely to grow to $34.1 billion by 2029,*** 30 August 2024
35. The Hindu, ***Tourism marketing campaign to give thrust to Wayanad,* says Minister**, 04 September 2024
36. Topczewska, Jadwiga, Lechowska, Jadwiga, Kaszuba, Joanna, and Krupa, Wanda. ***Culinary Trails in Popularizing Ethnic Cuisines***, Journal of Ethnic Foods, Vol. 9, 2022
37. Tussyadiah, I. P., and Sigala, M., ***Shareable tourism: tourism marketing in the sharing economy***, Journal of Travel & Tourism Marketing, Vol. *35*, No.1, 2017
38. Upadhyay, Yogesh & Sharma, Dhiraj, ***Culinary preferences of foreign tourists in India***, Journal of Vacation Marketing, 2014
39. Vijayakumar, R., & Kumar, A. R. ***Impact of Food Festivals on Tourism Development: A Study on Kerala Food Festivals***, Journal of Culinary Science & Technology, 2018.
40. Vlachova, Marie, ***Trafficking in Humans: The Slavery of Our Age,*** Connections, Vol. 4, No. 4,2005
41. Zografos, C. and Allcroft, D, '***The Enviromental Values of Potential Ecotourists: A Segmentation Study***', Journal of Sustainable Tourism,15 (1): 44–65, 2007

WEB SOURCES

1. http://www.unwto.org/
2. https://anywhere.epam.com
3. https://ash.naf.org/public/learning/course/geography-for-tourism
4. https://dde.pondiuni.edu.in
5. https://doi.org
6. https://ecpat.org
7. https://eparlib.nic.in
8. https://epgp.inflibnet.ac.in
9. https://geographicbook.com/
10. https://guidersacademy.com
11. https://hospitality.economictimes.indiatimes.com
12. https://humantraffickingsearch.org
13. https://icom.museum/en/
14. https://intrans.iastate.edu/news/trains-a-history/
15. https://itdc.co.in/
16. https://medium.com
17. https://mize.tech/blog/6-examples-of-how-ai-is-used-in-the-travel-industry/
18. https://nmi.gov.in/
19. https://pib.gov.in/
20. https://rezdy.com/blog/use-cases-of-ai-in-travel-tourism/
21. https://schooloftraveljournalism.com
22. https://scroll.in/article/
23. https://sdgs.un.org
24. https://services.india.gov.in/
25. https://theimasonline.org/
26. https://tourism.gov.in/
27. https://tourismandhumanrights.com/
28. https://tourismteacher.com/history-of-water-transport/
29. https://transportgeography.org
30. https://unesdoc.unesco.org
31. https://whc.unesco.org
32. https://wttc.org/
33. https://www.academia.edu/
34. https://www.britannica.com
35. https://www.csu.edu
36. https://www.e-unwto.org
37. https://www.iccrom.org/
38. https://www.icomos.org

39. https://www.incredibleindia.org
40. https://www.indeed.com
41. https://www.india.gov.in/
42. https://www.indiaculture.gov.in/
43. https://www.internationalstudent.com
44. https://www.itaerea.com/air-transport
45. https://www.jstor.org/stable/43598382
46. https://www.linkedin.com
47. https://www.migrationdataportal.org
48. https://www.museumsofindia.org/
49. https://www.myscheme.gov.in/
50. https://www.nios.ac.in
51. https://www.nps.gov
52. https://www.overstaytonight.com/
53. https://www.researchgate.net/
54. https://www.revfine.com
55. https://www.sciencedirect.com
56. https://www.shiksha.com
57. https://www.slideshare.net/
58. https://www.solimarinternational.com
59. https://www.state.gov/reports/2024
60. https://www.tandfonline.com/journals
61. https://www.tomorrow.io/blog
62. https://www.ukessays.com
63. https://www.unep.org
64. https://www.unesco.org/en
65. https://www.unodc.org
66. https://www.unwto.org
67. https://www.wttc.org
68. https://youthtourismsummit.com
69. www.amritsar.nic.in
70. www.unwto.org
71. www.worldhistory.org

www.ingramcontent.com/pod-product-compliance
Lightning Source LLC
LaVergne TN
LVHW091141150826
845672LV00005B/1005

* 9 7 9 8 8 9 7 2 4 7 4 8 6 *